MANAGING COMPENSATION (AND UNDERSTANDING IT TOO)

A Handbook for the Perplexed

Donald L. Caruth
Gail D. Handlogten

Q

QUORUM BOOKS
Westport, Connecticut • London

Library of Congress Cataloging-in-Publication Data

Caruth, Donald L.
   Managing compensation (and understanding it too) : a handbook for the perplexed /
Donald L. Caruth, Gail D. Handlogten.
   p.   cm.
   Includes bibliographical references and index.
   ISBN 1–56720–380–9 (alk. paper)
   1. Compensation management.   I. Handlogten, Gail D., 1954–   II. Title.
HF5549.5.C67 C374   2001
658.3′22—dc21   00–062530

British Library Cataloguing in Publication Data is available.

Library of Congress Catalog Card Number: 00–062530
ISBN: 1–56720–380–9

First published in 2001

Quorum Books, 88 Post Road West, Westport, CT 06881
An imprint of Greenwood Publishing Group, Inc.
www.quorumbooks.com

Printed in the United States of America

The paper used in this book complies with the
Permanent Paper Standard issued by the National
Information Standards Organization (Z39.48–1984).

10 9 8 7 6 5 4 3 2 1

*For all those managers everywhere who have struggled to implement,
manage, or just understand compensation programs . . .
we dedicate this book to you.*

CONTENTS

FIGURES AND TABLES

FIGURES

TABLES

1

AN OVERVIEW
OF COMPENSATION
MANAGEMENT

What is compensation? Defined in its broadest sense, compensation is any reward or payment given to a person for services performed. It includes, but is not limited to, direct or indirect financial rewards. Operationally, the definition tends to narrow in scope according to the definer's perspective. Managers typically define compensation as the package of financial rewards—wages, salaries, commissions, and bonuses, plus insurance and other types of indirect monetary benefits—provided to employees in exchange for their services. Employees generally define compensation even more narrowly, as the wage or salary received from an organization for the work they perform. However, to understand compensation and to comprehend its crucial role in contemporary organizations, it is necessary to conceive of compensation in its broadest sense. Consequently, for our purposes, compensation is defined as the *total* reward package offered by an organization to its employees. Compensation encompasses *all* of the rewards or payments—tangible and intangible, monetary and nonmonetary, physical and psychological—that an organization provides its employees in exchange for the work they perform.[1]

What is the purpose of a formalized compensation program? Any organizational compensation program has three purposes: (1) to *attract* a sufficient number of qualified workers to fill positions the organization has, (2) to *retain* employees or keep them with the organization so that turnover is held to acceptable levels, and (3) to *motivate* employees to perform to the fullest extent of their capabilities.[2]

PURPOSES OF THIS BOOK

The general purpose of this book can be stated very simply: to provide a framework for understanding the implementation and operation of compensation systems in organizations. This book is not a theoretical or highly technical treatise on compensation. Its focus is on understanding the various aspects of compensation. More specifically, this book seeks to

• Illustrate the steps involved in installing compensation systems in organizations.
• Provide a how-to understanding of the inner workings of compensation systems.
• Remove the mystique surrounding compensation programs.
• Indicate the issues and problems that must be addressed in developing and managing compensation systems.
• Demonstrate the logic and rationale underlying compensation practices.

The intended audience for this book encompasses several groups:

• Operating managers who deal with established compensation systems and need a basic knowledge of how such systems work.
• Managers of organizations that are contemplating development and installation of a compensation program.
• Human resource managers desiring a quick overview of compensation principles.
• Consultants in need of a general perspective on compensation.
• Educators and students seeking practical guidance on compensation systems.

Hopefully, the information presented in this book will satisfy the needs of these groups as well as others who need an understanding of how pay and benefit programs work.

COMPENSATION COMPONENTS

Any organization's total compensation or reward package is comprised of three major components: direct monetary rewards, indirect monetary payments, and psychological satisfactions.[3] In designing an effective compensation package, all three elements must be carefully considered.

Direct Monetary Rewards

Direct monetary rewards are the most obvious compensation component. Sometimes referred to as cash compensation, these rewards encompass all those items involving the payment of dollars to employees for work accomplished or effort expanded (e.g., a wage, a salary, a commission). Whether paid by the hour, by the month, or by another method, direct compensation is discretionary income to the employee. He or she is able to spend it in whatever way desired for the purchase of goods and services.

Indirect Monetary Payments

Indirect monetary payments include those items of financial value the organization provides to employees that do not result directly in employees' receiving spendable dollars. This compensation component is usually referred to as benefits. Included in this category are various forms of protection (health insurance, life insurance, disability insurance) and services (financial counseling, employer subsidized cafeterias, uniforms, free parking).

Psychological Satisfactions

The third compensation component consists of the psychological satisfactions—sometimes called psychic income—which a worker derives from the work he or she performs and the environment in which it is performed. This form of compensation includes opportunities to perform meaningful work, social interactions with others in the workplace, job training, advancement possibilities, recognition, and a host of similar factors.

An effective compensation system must carefully address all three compensation components: direct, indirect, and psychological. The three components are inextricably interrelated. Direct compensation influences an employee's perceptions of psychological satisfactions. Psychological rewards contribute to an employee's interpretation of direct and indirect compensation as adequate or inadequate. Feelings about indirect monetary rewards affect feelings about direct compensation and psychological satisfactions.

In other words, design of the total compensation package must consider all elements comprising the package and not simply focus on any one piece of the total system to the exclusion of the other two. An effective total compensation package must achieve proper balance between all three components. Although this book looks most closely at direct and indirect compensation because these are the most obvious and costly elements of the compensation system, this is not to imply that the psychological aspects of compensation are unimportant. They are, in fact, vital to the success of any compensation program because they permeate all facets of the system. This book will illustrate how the direct and indirect components can and should be carefully constructed to set the stage for and support further efforts in the psychological area.

BENEFITS OF A FORMAL COMPENSATION PROGRAM

Every organization has a compensation program. Whether that program is well thought out, written, and formalized, or whether it is arbitrary, unwritten, and informal, is another matter. Compensation issues are far too important and complex to be left to chance or caprice. Every organization—even those with only a handful of employees—should have a carefully formulated plan for compensating its workers fairly and accomplishing the tasks of attracting, retaining, and motivating employees.

Facilitate Recruitment

One of the primary benefits of a formalized compensation program is that it enables an organization to attract the right quantity and quality of employees needed to perform the work of organization. In the absence of a carefully thought-out and objective compensation program, organizations typically experience difficulty in attracting sufficient quantities of qualified workers.

Where compensation has not been formally considered and structured, it is often out of touch with what the labor market is paying; consequently, it is difficult for an organization to attract the workers it needs. An inequitable compensation program may, therefore, make constant recruiting necessary just to secure needed workers. On the other hand, keeping compensation rates in line with market rates makes attracting employees less difficult.

Enhance Retention

Organizations with inadequate compensation systems may succeed in recruiting sufficient employees, but may not be able to retain them for long because employees will typically leave for better paying jobs as soon as opportunities arise. Equitable pay, a sound benefits program, and a psychologically supportive organizational climate enable a firm to reduce employee turnover. In today's highly competitive environment, indirect monetary compensation plays a significant role in worker retention by creating "golden handcuffs" that tie an employee to a firm. Employees often stay with organizations because they know that other organizations cannot match the level of benefits the employees are currently receiving. Likewise, retention will be higher when the institution's rates are in accord with the labor market. Because turnover may cost an organization 1.5 to 2.5 times the annual salary of the person leaving the organization, retention of employees increases profitability.[4]

Increase Motivation

Motivation, too, is difficult to accomplish in the absence of a formal compensation program. Where there is no rhyme or reason to an organization's pay system, employees tend to perceive the system as inequitable and respond accordingly as far as performance and productivity are concerned. A compensation system that rewards employees fairly according to efforts expended and results produced creates a motivating work environment. A formalized pay program also establishes lines of progression and promotion opportunities, thereby increasing the possibility of having a sufficiently motivated workforce to perform the work of the organization.

Control Costs

A formal compensation program enables an organization to establish and maintain control over the largest segment of its controllable costs: salaries and benefits. Informal approaches to compensation can lead to spending too much or too little money on compensation. A formal program sets pay ranges for each job and institutes a cost-control mechanism. Without an effective compensation system, salary and benefit costs may be too high or too low.

Salary budgets can also be prepared more easily and realistically when a formal program exists. Merit-increase amounts can be budgeted; staff replacement costs can be ascertained; the dollar impact of adding new positions can be determined. Formalization, in short, provides a basis for effective control of compensation expenditures. Without it there is little or no basis for systematic control of salaries and benefits.

Prevent Pay Discrimination

Without a formal compensation program an organization has no assurance that jobs requiring equal skill and effort are being compensated at equal rates of pay. In other words, an organization may be in violation of the Equal Pay Act of 1963 and Title VII of the Civil Rights Act of 1964 without even knowing it. Thus, a company using an informal approach to compensation matters may find itself open to charges of pay discrimination, a serious and potentially expensive situation. The risk of pay discrimination is minimized considerably with a formalized program because jobs that are essentially equal are compensated within the same range of pay. This one benefit alone may well be worth the effort and expense of installing a compensation system in many organizations.

Assure Equity

Equity consists of three separate issues. First, there is matter of the internal equity of the organization's pay structure itself. Internal equity simply means that jobs requiring greater amounts of skill, effort, and responsibility are compensated at higher rates of pay than jobs requiring lesser amounts of skills, effort, and responsibility. In other words, internal equity—fairness in rewarding jobs based on the degree of difficulty entailed in performing those jobs— is based on a hierarchical arrangement of jobs and compensation rates that recognizes as fairly as possible the differences inherent in jobs, and pays them accordingly. Without formalization and the concomitant analysis of jobs, an internally equitable ordering of jobs from the least difficult and responsible (the lowest paying) to the most difficult and responsible (the highest paying) is practically impossible to achieve. Under an informal approach to compensation, some jobs will always be compensated more and some jobs will always be compensated less than they should be when compared to other jobs in the organization. A formal compensation program recognizes the differences in jobs and structures a pay system that accurately reflects these differences—it establishes internal equity.

Second, there is the matter of external equity—the fairness of the organization's pay as compared to similar organizations in the labor market. External equity is said to exist when the pay rates of the organization are equal to or closely approximate market rates.

Finally, there is the matter of perceived equity—the apparent fairness of the pay system, either internally or externally, as seen through the eyes of employees. Because perception is the only reality that matters to many employees, perceived equity is an extremely important concept in compensation. When a compensation program is perceived as being fair, there are likely to be fewer complaints and problems related to pay. When a program is perceived as unfair, there are likely to be numerous complaints and problems. An informal program is rarely ever perceived as fair. Rather, it is usually seen as biased, arbitrary, or capricious because employees may feel that there is no logic or system attached to it. A formal compensation program, relying as it does on job analysis, systems, and logic, is more readily perceived by employees as fair or equitable. Formalization of compensation programs increases the likelihood of perceived equity on the part of employees.

Reward Performance

A formalized compensation program creates a mechanism whereby employees can be rewarded on the basis of how well they perform their jobs. These rewards, typically in the form of merit pay increases or performance bonuses, are based on actual accomplishments as determined through a periodic evaluation of results produced. A formalized program recognizes degrees of accomplishment and structures merit increases along the lines of job performance, thereby assuring that higher performers receive larger rewards than lower performers. Informal approaches to compensation do not usually define or take into consideration degrees of employee performance; periodic pay increases are apt to be based on factors unrelated to how well the job is carried out. Informal approaches often lead to demotivation because employees sense—and rightly so—that accomplishment in the job bears little or no relationship to the size of the reward given. A formal program corrects this problem and reinforces motivation to do a good job by relating the amount of pay increase to actual performance. A formalized compensation system thereby allows a firm to pay fairly for the job, and also reward the individual for his or her performance in that job.

Establish Hierarchy of Jobs

The development and establishment of lines of progression—a job hierarchy—along which employees advance from lower-level jobs to higher-level jobs is a further benefit arising from a carefully constructed compensation program. Job sequences are defined so that promotional sequences, sometimes called career paths or career ladders, are developed and can be communicated to employees, thereby allowing employees to recognize and prepare themselves for jobs of greater responsibility and higher pay. Informal programs usually have no clearly identified job sequences or career paths; at best only a hazy concept of career progression may exist. What is regarded in management's eyes as a promotion often turns out to be nothing more than a transfer in the eyes of the employee. The reverse may also be true.

Lines of progression contribute positively to employee motivation and morale. Employees are able to recognize promotional paths that are open to them and can take positive strides to move themselves forward along those paths.

Improve Morale

Morale refers to the general level of satisfaction that employees, either individually or as a group, have about their employer. A number of factors affect and shape morale: The work itself, quality of supervision, personnel policies, opportunities for advancement, coworkers, and pay are a few of the most prominent. Morale is based on perception; that is, how something appears to be when viewed through the mind's eye rather than how it is in reality. Pay plays a major role in shaping morale. When compensation in all its facets appears to be fair and equitable, other morale factors tend to take on the appearance of being satisfactory. Dissatisfaction with pay typically results in dissatisfaction with other aspects of the job and employment situation.

Inasmuch as a formal compensation program utilizes a logical, systematic approach to set pay rates and determine the appropriate configuration of benefits, its impact on morale is positive. A rational approach to setting compensation enhances an employee's perception of fairness relative to pay matters. Perceived fairness in this area tends to suggest fairness in other areas, thereby increasing the employee's general level of satisfaction with the work situation. Informal compensation determination carries with it the stigma of whim, capriciousness, or arbitrariness—unfairness, if you will—and colors an employee's view of other morale factors accordingly.

Establish a Basis for Answering Compensation Questions

"Why am I getting only a five-percent raise this year?" "Why doesn't the company pay for all of my health insurance?" "If I do a good job, to which position can I expect to be promoted?" "Why do administrative assistants make more than accounting clerks?" These questions probably sound familiar. Employees normally have a great many questions about their direct and indirect compensation and are increasingly willing to voice these concerns to their managers, supervisors, and human resource representatives. Without a formalized compensation system there is no basis for dealing with these questions objectively and factually. Answers in such cases must rely on subjectivity. A formalized program eliminates this problem by establishing a factual foundation for all compensation decisions and, consequently, provides an objective basis for explaining to employees why pay is what it is, why benefits are what they are, and so forth. Granted, formalization does not guarantee that employees will accept the answers, but it does go a long way toward increasing an understanding of the compensation area.

The benefits to be derived from a soundly constructed compensation program are real. Compensation is an important tool that helps an organization achieve its objectives of profitability, productivity, growth, and survival. In today's highly competitive labor markets, a formalized compensation system is not a luxury for organizations. It is a necessity.

COMPENSATION DETERMINANTS

Why do organizations pay what they pay? Nine major forces influence the general level of compensation that an organization must pay if it is to be successful in acquiring and retaining the kinds of skilled and motivated employees it must have to operate effectively and profitably. These factors are the labor market, ability to pay, cost of living, productivity, bargaining power, job requirements, worker competencies, managerial attitudes, and legislation.

The Labor Market

One of the primary determinants of compensation is the supply of workers with particular skills and the need that employing organizations within a particular labor market have for hiring workers with those skills. Where there is an abundance of available workers in the labor market, employers will have no difficulty in obtaining sufficient employees. Consequently, the level of compensation will tend to be lower because employers do not have to pay higher salaries and benefits to attract employees. On the other hand, where there is a shortage of skilled workers and the demands of hiring institutions for the particular skills possessed by those workers is great, compensation levels will tend to escalate as employers bid against each other to secure the talent they need. In either instance, the economics of the marketplace are operating to establish or at least significantly influence the level of compensation.

For several years now we have observed the forces of supply and demand at work in many industries and have witnessed their impact on compensation. The supply of workers with technical skills has trailed the demand for workers with these skills. As a result, compensation in technical occupations has significantly increased as firms vigorously compete against each other for the talent they need. Likewise, the demand for workers in services industries has outstripped the supply of workers for positions in these industries. In a tight labor market compensation rates have been forced upward. In other industries the demand for workers has fallen and compensation rates have been lowered.

Ability to Pay

Organizational profitability is another factor that affects compensation levels. Put quite simply, the higher the profitability of an organization, the more it can afford to pay; the lower the profitability, the less an organization can afford to offer in compensation. Profit margins allow some employers to pay more while they compel others to keep compensation as low as possible. Certainly no firm wants to pay more than is necessary to attract the quantity and quality of workers needed, but some firms do have a greater degree of latitude than others, based on profit margins, in establishing specific levels of compensation.

Cost of Living

Cost of living refers to the amount of direct monetary compensation required by workers to maintain an adequate standard of living for themselves and their families. Although colored by individual perceptions of what is an adequate standard of living, the concept of cost of living establishes a *floor* for compensation levels. Workers will not normally accept a job at a rate less than the one they consider to be the floor, assuming of course that all other conditions are equal. Compensation rates for employers, consequently, are controlled on the low side by the perceived cost of living.

Employers who conduct business at geographically dispersed locations can attest to the impact that cost of living has on compensation levels. Living costs are not uniform throughout the United States, and neither are compensation rates. In New York City—a high-cost area—one can expect to find higher pay levels than in El Paso, Texas—a low-cost-of-living area.

Productivity

A fourth determinant of compensation is productivity, the ratio of output to personnel hours of input. While productivity is often a vague, elusive, and hard-to-measure concept, it does influence compensation. Generally speaking, the more a worker can produce, the higher his or her compensation will be. Productive workers produce more goods at a lower cost, allowing the company to make a greater profit on the sale of these goods. This basic generalization is the foundation for paying various types of incentive compensation—pay based directly on output. At the level of the individual job, worker performance may be measured and rewards given for increased productivity due to individual worker efforts. At the office or facility level, compensation may be increased for exceeding stipulated measures of performance. In either case, compensation is affected by the productivity of employees.

Even where productivity cannot be directly linked to measurable output, it still exerts an influence on compensation rates. The notion that those individuals, those positions, or those groups that produce more than others should be compensated at higher rates is a strong one.

Bargaining Power

Bargaining power refers to the ability of groups of workers to exert pressure on an employer and thereby increase compensation levels. This power is typically gained by banding together in unions. Unions have been able to raise rates of pay in specific companies and in the economy in general. Both direct and indirect compensation levels have been pushed to higher and higher levels because of the power or threat of collective bargaining.

Compared to an employer, an individual employee normally has little or no bargaining power—certainly not enough to affect general compensation rates. But collectively through unions, employees can, by threatening to withhold the supply of labor if necessary, influence compensation amounts and practices. Although the influence of unions has waned as the percentage of union members in the total American workforce has declined (only 14.6 percent of the total U.S. workforce was represented by unions in 1996), unions still exert pressure on compensation rates.

Even those institutions that are not confronted by unions feel the impact on pay rates brought about by bargaining power. As collective bargaining increases compensation rates in specific companies and industries, other companies and industries periodically have to adjust compensation levels to stay competitive in attracting and retaining the workers they need. Thus, bargaining power affects, directly or indirectly, all labor market organizations.

Job Requirements

Another determinant of compensation rates is the requirements of performing a particular job. Where long training periods are required to learn the skills necessary for successful job performance, compensation rates tend to be higher than they are for jobs where the training period is short or nonexistent. Higher rates attract more people to the field, thereby assuring employers of an adequate pool of talent from which to select employees.

Where jobs involve dangerous, difficult, or unpleasant work, pay rates typically include a financial inducement to attract workers to those jobs. For example, second- or third-shift employees are usually paid more than their counterparts on the first shift in order to offset the inconvenience—even danger in some urban areas—imposed by the requirement of working unusual hours. Job requirements, as these examples point out, directly affect compensation rates for certain groups of positions.

Worker Competencies

Organizational downsizing and the rampant development of technology have created a new compensation determinant: worker competencies. In a world of scaled-down organizations or small companies that thrive on rapid shifts in products or technologies, workers may be called upon to perform a number of jobs. In these companies employees are compensated not on the basis of the job they are currently performing, but on the basis of the number of different jobs they can perform. Workers are paid for the knowledge and skills they have acquired, regardless of whether these skills are actually being used.

Managerial Attitudes

Pay structures vary widely across company lines because of managerial attitudes concerning pay. Management's feelings about compensation lead to an organization's adopting one of three possible wage and salary positions: (1) compensate workers at rates that are comparable to the rates being paid by other firms in the labor market, (2) compensate employees at rates below those paid by other labor market organizations, or (3) compensate workers at rates that are above those currently being paid in the labor market. Each of these positions reflects management attitudes and philosophies about pay. Paying market rates suggests that management is concerned with maintaining external equity in order to assure a sufficient supply of workers and to hold employee turnover to an acceptable level. Paying below market rates suggests that management views compensation largely as a cost. Paying above market rates suggests that management is interested in attracting and retaining the best workers possible and is willing to spend money to do so.

Legislation

Since the 1930s federal legislation has had a significant impact on compensation levels. The Fair Labor Standards Act of 1938 established a minimum wage and specified requirements for the payment of overtime. The minimum wage set forth by this act, as of 1997, $5.15 per hour, creates a base compensation rate that covers most U.S. workers. Moreover, the base rate stipulated by the act functions as an index that leads to wage increases for many other workers who are well past the minimum compensation level. As the minimum wage is increased, other wages also tend to rise. The specified minimum wage has been raised a number of times since 1938, and will continue to be adjusted periodically in the future.

The Equal Pay Act of 1963, an amendment to the Fair Labor Standards Act, requires equal pay for equal work for men and women performing the same work. Equal work is defined as work that requires the same skill, effort, and responsibility and is performed under similar working conditions. The result of this piece of legislation has been to raise the general level of compensation for female employees. Both the Fair Labor Standards Act and the Equal Pay Act have significantly affected overall compensation levels.

These nine factors tend to work in concert with each other rather than independently to affect compensation levels. A knowledge of and appreciation for the influence they exert are important for understanding that compensation levels are products of forces existing outside as well as inside a specific organization. The determinants of compensation, in effect, reduce the degree of latitude that an organization has in setting compensation rates.

THE COMPENSATION PROGRAM FRAMEWORK

The thrust of this book, as previously indicated, is to familiarize managers with compensation systems and how they are developed and managed. Throughout the text, it will be emphasized that designing, implementing, and managing a compensation system is essentially an exercise in logic. It entails following a series of sequential steps to arrive at a desired conclusion. Crucial to performing any exercise in logic is an understanding of the background concepts and constraints that impinge upon the steps or sequences of actions to be taken.

As far as direct, indirect, and psychological compensation programs are concerned, the background concepts and constraints are legislation and motivation. The series of sequential steps are job analysis, job evaluation, compensation surveys, job pricing, indirect monetary payments, nonmonetary rewards, incentives and team-based pay, rewards for special groups, performance appraisal, and program administration. Figure 1.1 shows this overall framework for a total compensation system. Each element of this framework is briefly described in order to provide a general understanding or overview of what is involved in designing, developing, implementing, and managing an effective compensation program for an organization.

Legislation

Legislation establishes the externally imposed rules and regulations to which an organization's compensation program must conform; it defines the legal constraints. Understanding the legally mandated aspects of compensation is crucial to assuring that the program meets the minimum specifications defined by law. Failure to comprehend these requirements can cause unnecessary problems or complications for a compensation program. Compensation legislation is the topic of Chapter 2.

Motivation

Motivation is the psychological underpinning and conceptual basis of compensation. A clear understanding of motivation, the factors that enhance it, the factors that detract from it, and its relationship to compensation is necessary to put compensation in its proper context and keep it in correct perspective. Unless compensation is built upon knowledge of motivation theory and concepts, it is likely to be ineffective and may, in the extreme, produce completely undesired results. Creating a motivating work environment is essential to the success of any compensation program. It is not, however, the responsibility of the compensation specialist to create it. A motivating work environment—where employees are willing to exert effort to accomplish results because they experience a sense of job satisfaction—is created by top management. Top management is the architect of corporate culture and the creator of policies and practices that provide opportunities for achievement, recognition, empowerment, autonomy, and growth. Unless management creates the proper psychological climate, efforts to develop a technically sound compensation system may falter. Chapter 3 examines basic principles of motivation as well as the crucial role of psychological compensation.

Job Analysis

The actual first step in the development of a compensation system is job analysis, the process of collecting, studying, and reporting information on job content and identifying the skills, efforts, and responsibilities needed to perform a job successfully. Although all steps in the design and implementation of a compensation program are important, job analysis is critical because it establishes the base upon which direct compensation will be built. Mistakes in job analysis will result in errors or deficiencies in other program steps and activities. Necessary job information must be carefully gathered, thoroughly analyzed, and accurately synthesized to assure that other program steps will produce the desired results.

The end products of job analysis are job descriptions and job specifications. A job description is a written statement of the duties, responsibilities, and working conditions of a job. It identifies, defines, and characterizes a job as it is actually being carried out; it describes the job, not the individual who performs it. A job specification, on the other hand, is a written enumeration of the minimum acceptable qualifications that a person should possess to perform a job. It identifies the necessary education, experience, specific skills, and physical abilities required. In short, a job description tells what is done in a job and a job specification tells what is needed to be able to perform that job.[5]

Figure 1.1
Framework for Developing a Compensation Program

Concepts and Constraints

Motivation (The Basis for Behavior)	Legislation (Legal Requirements)	Job Analysis (Identify Duties and Skills)	Job Evaluation (Establish Internal Equity)	Compensation Survey (Determine Market Rates and Practices)

Job descriptions are used as the basis for evaluating an organization's jobs; they are also used in recruiting, selecting, and placing employees. The importance of these uses should suggest the criticality of developing accurate job descriptions and job specifications. Job analysis is described in detail in Chapter 4.

Job Evaluation

Job evaluation is the process of determining the value or worth of a particular job within an organization relative to all other jobs in the organization. Its primary purpose is to establish internal equity; that is, to develop a structure of all the jobs in an organization that recognizes their similarities, differences, and contributions to achieving the work of the organization. The end product of job evaluation is a hierarchy of jobs that identifies the relative worth of each job to the organization.[6] Job evaluation enables an institution to differentiate between jobs on some objective, predetermined basis and to establish a rationale for different compensation rates between jobs.

Job descriptions are crucial to job evaluation because they provide the basic data on jobs. Accurate descriptions permit accurate differentiation between jobs. Accurate differentiation between jobs produces an internally equitable structure of job relationships. An internally equitable structure of jobs enables an organization to develop a pay structure that is fair and objective because it is based on what the organization considers to be important in carrying out the work of the organization. Job evaluation is covered in Chapters 5 and 6.

Compensation Surveys

Once the internal job hierarchy has been established through job evaluation, the next step in the process of developing a compensation system is to

Figure 1.1 (*continued*)

The Steps   **The Goal**

Job Pricing (Develop Pay Structure)	Benefits (Design Protection and Services Package)	Incentives (Pay for Direct Results)	Performance Appraisal (Reward Job Performance)	Management (Assure Ongoing Operation)	**Effective Compensation Program**

determine what is happening in the labor market.[7] This is the function of the compensation survey. A compensation survey can be defined as a systematic procedure for collecting information on wages, salaries, benefits, payment methods, compensation policies, and related matters from other organizations in the labor market. In essence, it is an attempt to find out what competing organizations are paying to attract, hold, and motivate skilled people. The purpose of a compensation survey, in other words, is to determine the going rate of pay.

An organization cannot remain out of touch with its marketplace for very long and continue to be successful. A firm must know what products and services its competitors are offering. Likewise, it also must know what competing labor market institutions—those organizations vying for people with similar skills and abilities—are doing in the compensation area. A compensation survey satisfies the need for this kind of competitive intelligence on pay, benefits, and compensation practices.

Because the survey provides information that forms the basis for assigning pay rates as well as making other compensation program decisions, it is important that the survey be a representative sample of the labor market and accurately reflect current conditions and practices. Therefore, the survey must be carefully designed and carried out. Compensation surveys are the subject of Chapter 7.

Job Pricing

The focus of job analysis and job evaluation is internal to the organization. The focus of the compensation survey is external. These two focuses come together in job pricing.[8] Job pricing can be defined as the process of assigning dollar values to the relative worth of each job within an organization. Job evaluation determines the relative value of each job; job pricing attaches the monetary worth to each job to assure that all jobs are compensated fairly relative to each other. Job evaluation produces the job structure or job hierarchy; job pricing sets the rates of pay for all jobs in the hierarchy. Normally, jobs that are similar to each other are grouped together in job classes for convenience; it is much easier to price twelve job classes, for example, than it is to price ninety-six separate jobs.

Job pricing is the most challenging and complex part of developing a compensation plan. There is, unfortunately, no precise formula that automatically produces an equitable price structure; there are a number of decisions that have to be made. Among the issues that must be addressed and resolved are the number of job classes to be established, the minimum and maximum rates of pay for each class of jobs, the amount of overlap in monetary amounts between classes, making adjustments to the pay structure based on information from the compensation survey, determining the basis for granting merit increases within job classes, what competitive position the organization should take vis-à-vis other labor market institutions, and how to handle those employees whose current rates of pay are outside the established minimum and maximum rates of compensation for job classes.[9]

Motivational and organization policy considerations are of utmost importance in job pricing. The range of compensation within a pay class, the amount of monetary overlap between classes, or the amounts of merit increases may directly affect employee motivation. A firm's policy establishes the extent to which compensation rates will meet those of the labor market; that is, whether compensation will match, exceed, or lag behind the rates paid by other organizations.

Job pricing is an activity that requires the exercise of astute professional judgment as well as a complete understanding of a firm's compensation philosophies and objectives. Job pricing is discussed in Chapter 8.

Indirect Monetary Compensation

Indirect monetary compensation packages—benefits—are designed, at least in theory, after decisions about basic direct compensation—the pay structure—have been made. The benefits provided by an organization should complement and reinforce both direct and psychological compensation components.[10] Consequently, logic suggests that indirect rewards, if they are to fulfill their bolstering function effectively, can only be determined after the pay structure has been put into place. In practice, however, almost all organizations already have, even in the absence of a formalized compensation plan, an existing program of benefits. To develop and implement an effective compensation program it is often necessary to reevaluate and revise the existing configuration of protections and services an organization provides to its employees. The basis for much of this reevaluation and revision comes from information collected by the compensation survey.

In addition to supporting other compensation elements, indirect rewards should be competitive, adequate, and cost effective. If the package is not competitive with what other labor market organizations are providing, an employer may find its efforts to attract, hold, and motivate employees impeded. The need to maintain a competitive position in the human resource arena underscores the importance of collecting data on benefits during the compensation survey. The matter of adequacy in indirect rewards, although greatly influenced by what labor market competitors are doing, is an organizational policy issue. Management is the final arbiter as to what constitutes adequacy. Cost effectiveness refers to getting the greatest result possible from the dollars that have been allocated to expenditures for indirect rewards. This is also a management policy area.

At this stage of compensation program development, an organization must consider all aspects of benefits and develop what it considers to be an effective package. As with all other aspects of compensation, decisions on indirect monetary rewards require careful attention and should not be passed over lightly. Indirect monetary rewards are discussed in Chapter 9.

Incentives: Pay for Performance

Incentives are direct financial rewards given to an employee or group of employees for meeting specific quantity or quality goals; they are direct rewards for specific quantified results.[11] Inasmuch as incentives are normally financial inducements over and above base wages and salaries, their consideration in compensation program development and implementation should occur after the basic pay structure and package of indirect monetary rewards has been determined. Because of the difficulty of precisely quantifying output, incentives cannot be applied to all jobs in an organization. Consequently, attention is logically directed to their use only after other fundamental compensation decisions have been made.

Of all the areas in compensation, the issue of incentives stirs up more negative emotional reactions than any other. Because incentives have been misused in the past, the mere mention of them often brings to mind images of sweatshops and visions of unscrupulous employers driving employees to higher and higher levels of output. Yet, the intent of incentives—directly linking pay to results in order to increase productivity and lower unit costs—is a good one. To ignore the possible use of pay-for-performance plans is surely a mistake. Whether they are eventually used or not, they should be considered whenever an organization is developing a compensation program.

During this stage of program development an organization examines its jobs to see if some of them lend themselves to incentives, investigates the potential benefits to be derived from their use, and determines if their use is consistent with the institution's underlying philosophy on compensation. If conditions are favorable, some type of pay-for-performance plan is developed.

While some forms of incentives are team based and would therefore fall under the umbrella of team-based compensation, there are other aspects involved in rewarding groups rather than individuals. The American workplace is changing. One of the more significant changes is the way work is organized and performed. Increasingly work is performed by teams rather than by individuals, a departure from the long accepted concept of specialization of labor.[12] When people work together on teams they must ultimately be paid as members of a team or they will not continue to work as a team. To assure that people work effectively as a team, pay must be based on some aspect of team performance. Incentive plans and team-based compensation are examined in Chapter 10.

Performance Appraisal Systems

Performance appraisal is the periodic assessment of how well an individual—or a team, for that matter—is carrying out the duties and responsibilities of a job.[13] Its primary purpose as far as compensation management is concerned is to recognize and reward the individual for accomplishments in the job: The higher the level of accomplishment, the greater the amount of financial reward given. Ideally, any compensation system should adhere to the principle "pay the job and reward the individual." Job pricing accomplishes the former and performance appraisal accomplishes the latter.

Performance appraisal, if properly developed, has many organizational uses other than simply awarding pay increases. For example, it can be used to heighten communication between supervisor and employee, to enhance employee motivation through feedback on progress, to identify individuals with the potential for promotion to positions of greater responsibility, to uncover training needs, or to validate the process by which employees are selected. Its multifaceted nature suggests that the full range of possible uses for performance appraisal be carefully assessed during this step in developing a compensation program.

A number of issues must also be addressed in this phase of program development: the frequency with which performance is to be formally evaluated, the measures to be used in rating it, who will be responsible for evaluating it, and the relationship of various performance levels to merit increase amounts. Performance appraisal is considered in detail in Chapter 11.

Special Issues in Compensation

Special issues in compensation include the development of effective means of compensating sales personnel, managers, and executive officers of an organization. Separate pay plans must be developed for each of these groups.[14] Another special issue that many U.S. organizations face is the development of separate pay plans to be used to compensate employees and managers who work overseas. All these issues are considered in Chapter 12.

Compensation Administration

Managing the compensation program is both a development step and an ongoing process.[15] As a developmental activity management is that phase of program development concerned with formulating policies, constructing procedures, and establishing rules to guide the operation of the compensation system. Many of the necessary guidelines, obviously, are developed as the program is being implemented. In this final step of implementation the task is to assure that policies, procedures, rules, and other guidelines have been formulated for all aspects of the program, that they have been established in sufficient detail for successful ongoing operation of the program, and that they are consistent with each other as well as with the organization's philosophy on compensation. This is no simple task. It is one that requires careful attention to detail and an ability to anticipate situations that may arise in the future. It is, moreover, a very important task, in that policies, procedures, and rules must be perceived by employees as being fair in order to generate employee confidence in the compensation program.

The ongoing side of a compensation administration is concerned with the day-to-day operation and functioning of the compensation system. Its focus is twofold: (1) handling the myriad of details involved in overseeing the program, and (2) making periodic adjustments to maintain the viability of the program. A compensation system cannot manage itself; it must be fed and nurtured; it must be carefully monitored to assure that it runs smoothly; it has to be fine-tuned and changed as the need arises.[16] Chapter 13 addresses compensation administration.

This overview of what is involved in designing and installing an effective compensation program in an organization is intended as a big-picture sketch that identifies major concepts and activities and illustrates the various interrelationships among implementation steps. This overview will make it easier to see how specific activities described in the following chapters fit into the total system of compensation.

NOTES

1. Donald L. Caruth, *Compensation Management for Banks* (Boston: Bankers Publishing, 1986), 1.

2. Ibid., 7.

3. Ibid., 1.

4. Wayne F. Cascio, *Costing Human Resources: The Financial Impact of Behavior in Organizations*, 3rd ed. (Boston: PWS–Kent, 1991), 19.

5. Donald L. Caruth and Gail D. Handlogten, *Staffing the Contemporary Organization*, 2d ed. (Westport, Conn.: Quorum Books, 1997), 111–112.

6. Caruth, *Compensation Management*, 14.

7. George T. Milkovich and Jerry M. Newman, *Compensation*, 5th ed. (Chicago: Irwin, 1996), 246.

8. Caruth, *Compensation Management*, 15.
9. Ibid., 15–16.
10. Milkovich and Newman, *Compensation*, 422.
11. Caruth, *Compensation Management*, 17.
12. Steven E. Gross, *Compensation for Teams* (New York: AMACOM, 1995), 1–5.
13. Caruth and Handlogten, *Staffing*, 228.
14. Milkovich and Newman, *Compensation*, 582.
15. Caruth, *Compensation Management*, 18–19.
16. Ibid.

2

THE LEGAL FRAMEWORK
OF COMPENSATION

The legal framework surrounding compensation is a complex, comprehensive one that shows signs of becoming even more complicated in the future. This chapter reviews the major federal laws, as well as some of the minor ones, that directly or indirectly affect compensation, benefits, and terms and conditions of employment. In addition to the statues described, there are other federal laws, executive orders, state laws, and local laws that affect or impinge upon compensation. For example, the city of Tucson, Arizona, has a minimum wage of $8.00 per hour as opposed to the federally imposed one of $5.15 per hour.[1] The intent of this chapter is not to offer a complete compendium of legislation, but to illustrate for managers and others the nature of the legal environment with which compensation specialists must contend.

To help maintain a historical perspective on the evolution of the legal environment, laws are shown in chronological order. A thumbnail sketch of the major provisions and coverage of each statue is given.

DAVIS–BACON ACT OF 1931

The Davis–Bacon Act gives the secretary of labor the authority to establish minimum wages to be paid to employees of firms working on government construction contracts. These rates are the prevailing wage rates in the geographical area where construction is occurring. Under the Davis–Bacon Act, fringe benefits become a portion of all wages paid to an employee.[2]

COPELAND ACT OF 1934

The Copeland Act prohibits federal contractors from requiring their employees to pay a portion of their wages back to the employer in order to continue their employment. This act was passed after it was discovered that some contractors were circumventing the prevailing wage provisions of the Davis–Bacon Act by requiring employees to kick back a portion of the wages they were paid.[3]

SOCIAL SECURITY ACT OF 1935, AS AMENDED

This act created the Social Security Administration and established the existing system of old age, survivors, disability, and unemployment compensation insurance. Employees and employers share equally the cost of old age, survivors, and disability insurance, those items that are typically described as Social Security.[4] Employers pay the full cost of unemployment insurance. Funding is accomplished through a payroll tax and benefits are paid through agencies in each of the fifty states. The act also created a minimum period of twenty-six weeks of unemployment compensation. Both Social Security and unemployment compensation are discussed more fully in Chapter 9.

NATIONAL LABOR RELATIONS ACT OF 1935

Commonly known as the Wagner Act, this legislation gives employees the right to form unions and requires employers to recognize unions of employees and to bargain with them in good faith relative to wages, hours of work, and other terms and conditions of employment.[5] As specified in the act, "Employees shall have the right to self-organization, to form, join, or assist labor organizations, to bargain collectively through representatives of their own choosing, and to engage in other concerted activities, for the purpose of collective bargaining or other mutual aid or protection. . . . The rights given to employees are protected against interference by employers." Specifically, employers are prohibited from the following: (1) interfering with, restraining, or coercing employees in their exercise of the right to form unions; (2) dominating a union or interfering in the affairs of a union; (3) discriminating against employees in regard to hiring, job tenure, or any condition of employment for the purpose of encouraging or discouraging union membership; (4) discriminating against or terminating an employee who has filed an unfair labor charge or has given testimony under the act; and (5) refusing to bargain in good faith with the chosen representatives of employees.

The act created the National Labor Relations Board, which has the responsibility for conducting elections to determine if employees wish to be represented by a union, determining which of two competing unions will be certified as the bargaining agent for a group of employees, preventing unfair labor practices in unionization activities, and investigating reported claims of unfair labor practices.

WALSH–HEALY PUBLIC CONTRACTS ACT OF 1936

The Walsh–Healy Act extended the Davis–Bacon Act requirements to all federal contractors. Contractors must stipulate that all employees working on a government contract will be paid no less than the prevailing minimum wage as determined by the secretary of labor, without subsequent deduction or rebate of any kind.[6]

FAIR LABOR STANDARDS ACT (FLSA) OF 1938

Popularly known as the Wage and Hour Act, this statute established a minimum wage for the vast majority of workers in the private sector. The original minimum wage was set at 25 cents per hour in 1938. By September 1997 it had increased to $5.15 per hour.[7] It also established the standard workweek of forty hours. Workers covered by this statute are divided into two categories: exempt and nonexempt. Nonexempt workers must be compensated at a rate of one and one-half times their regular hourly rate of pay for hours worked in excess of forty during a given workweek. A workweek is defined as a recurring period of 168 hours or seven consecutive twenty-four-hour periods. The workweek does not have to conform to the calendar week, and it may begin at any hour of the day. Exempt employees—managers, administrators, and professionals, for example—are excluded from the overtime pay requirement. In addition, the act set the minimum working age for covered employment at sixteen; if the work is hazardous, the minimum working age is eighteen.[8] Some jobs that are considered hazardous are manufacturing of explosives, mining, meatpacking or processing, roofing, excavating, and driving a motor vehicle.[9]

EQUAL PAY ACT OF 1963

This act is an amendment to the Fair Labor Standards Act of 1938 and covers the same employers as the FLSA. The statute makes it illegal for an employer to discriminate in pay on the basis of sex where jobs require equal skill, effort, and responsibility and are performed under similar working conditions. Pay differentials between sexes are permitted when such differences are based on seniority systems, merit systems, production-related pay plans (wage incentives), or factors other than sex. Premium pay differences for working undesirable shifts are also allowed. In 1972 the act was amended to cover employees in executive, administrative, professional, and outside sales positions as well as employees in most state and local governments, hospitals, and schools. Over the years the act has become less significant because a violation of the Equal Pay Act is also a violation of Title VII of the Civil Rights Act of 1964, a broader and more powerful statute.[10]

TITLE VII, CIVIL RIGHTS ACT OF 1964, AS AMENDED

The one statute that has had the greatest impact on human resource management is Title VII of the Civil Rights Act of 1964, as amended by the Equal Employment Act of 1972.[11] Under Title VII it is illegal to discriminate in hiring, firing, promoting, compensating, or in terms, conditions, or privileges of employment on the basis of race, color, sex, religion, or national origin.

Title VII covers employers engaged in or affecting interstate commerce who have fifteen or more employees for each working day in each of twenty calendar weeks in the current or preceding calendar year. Also included in the definition of employers are state and local governments, schools, colleges, unions, and private employment agencies that procure employees for an employer having fifteen or more employees.

Three notable exceptions to discrimination as covered by Title VII are bona fide occupational qualifications (BFOQs), seniority and merit systems, and testing and educational requirements. According to the act it is not "an unlawful employment practice for an employer to hire and employ employees . . . on the basis of his religion, sex, or national origin in those certain instances where religion, sex, or national origin is a bona fide occupational qualification reasonably necessary to the normal operation of the particular business or enterprise." Thus, for example, religious institutions such as churches or synagogues may legally refuse to hire individuals whose religious persuasion is different from that of the hiring institution. Likewise, a maximum security correctional institution housing only male inmates may decline to hire females as security guards. The concept of bona fide occupational qualification was designed to be narrowly, not broadly, interpreted and has been so construed by the courts in a number of cases. The burden of proving the necessity for a BFOQ rests entirely on the employer.

The second exception to discrimination under Title VII is a bona fide seniority system, such as the type normally contained in a union contract. Differences in employment conditions among workers are permitted "provided that such differences are not the result of an intention to discriminate because of race, color, religion, sex, or national origin." Even if a bona fide seniority system has a discriminatory impact on those individuals protected by Title VII, the system can only be invalidated by evidence that the actual motives of the parties to the agreement were to discriminate.

In the matter of testing and educational requirements, Title VII states that it is not "an unlawful employment practice for an employer to give and to act upon the results of any professionally developed ability test provided that such test, its administration, or action upon the results is not designed, intended or used to discriminate because of race, color, religion, sex, or national origin." Employment testing and educational requirements must be job related, and the burden of proof is on the employer to show that a demonstrable relationship exists between actual job performance and the test or educational requirement.

The Civil Rights Act of 1964 also created the Equal Employment Opportunity Commission (EEOC) and assigned enforcement of Title VII to this agency. The Equal Employment Opportunity Commission consists of five members appointed by the president of the United States. The EEOC is empowered to investigate, conciliate, and litigate charges of discrimination arising under provisions of Title VII. In addition, the commission has the responsibility for issuing procedural regulations and interpretations of Title VII and the other statutes it enforces.

When a charge—such as alleged pay discrimination—is filed under Title VII, the EEOC investigates the evidence to determine if there is a possible violation of the statute. Where there is a state or local agency similar to the EEOC that meets EEOC standards, the complaint is first referred to that agency. The state or local agency (the deferral agency) then has at least sixty days of exclusive jurisdiction over the charge. After sixty days, or if the deferral agency has terminated its proceedings or waived jurisdiction, the EEOC assumes jurisdiction over the complaint. Title VII requires deferral to a state or local agency where one exists, and if the EEOC fails to defer, it may lose not only its jurisdiction but also its ability to conduct an investigation.

If after investigation the EEOC finds no probable cause, it ends its involvement and notifies the complainant that he or she has the right to pursue the case in federal court. If the EEOC's investigation finds that there is probable cause for a discrimination charge, the first attempt at settlement will be through conciliation, a negotiated arrangement between the complainant, the employer, and the EEOC that is satisfactory to all parties and adequately compensates the victim or victims of discrimination and meets the standards set by the EEOC.

Failing to achieve a settlement by conciliation, the EEOC next has the option to file suit in federal district court against the employer in question. Under Title VII charges may be filed by any of the EEOC commissioners, any aggrieved person, or anyone acting on behalf of an aggrieved person: for example, an attorney. The time limit for filing charges is 180 days after the occurrence of the alleged discriminatory act. If the complainant is first required to file the charge with a state or local agency, the time limit for filing with the EEOC is extended to 300 days.

The Civil Rights Act of 1964 also prohibits retaliation against employees who have opposed an allegedly illegal employment practice. Anyone who testifies, assists, or participates in discriminatory proceedings is also protected.

The importance of Title VII to compensation is that it establishes pay discrimination on the basis of race, color, sex, religion, or national origin as an illegal compensation practice.

AGE DISCRIMINATION IN EMPLOYMENT ACT (ADEA) OF 1967, AS AMENDED

This act protects individuals over the age of forty from discrimination by employers in matters of hiring, compensation, wage reduction, benefit plans, job retention, job privileges, and other terms and conditions of employment.[12] Covered under the Age Discrimination in Employment Act are employers with twenty or more employees for twenty or more calendar months (either in the current or preceding calendar year), unions with twenty-five or more members, employment agencies, and federal, state, or local governments.

A 1986 amendment to the ADEA prohibits mandatory retirement of most private-sector employees at age seventy; however, high-level executives may be retired at age sixty-five if they are entitled to immediate, nonforfeitable pensions or deferred compensation of at least $27,000 annually. A 1978 amendment had previously eliminated the maximum retirement age of seventy for federal employees.

An exception to the provisions of the act provides that age may be used as a bona fide occupational qualification in those instances where age is reasonably necessary for business operations or safety factors; for example, actors and actresses required for youthful roles, persons employed to advertise or promote the sale of products designed for youthful consumers, or intercity bus drivers. Age is also a bona fide occupational qualification where federal statutory or regulatory requirements impose a compulsory age limitation. For instance the Federal Aviation Agency sets a ceiling of age sixty for commercial airline pilots.

ADEA differs from Title VII in that it provides for trial by jury and there is a possible criminal aspect to an age discrimination charge. Trial by jury has significant implications for employers because jurors may have greater sympathy for older persons who have allegedly suffered discrimination. The punitive aspect of the ADEA means that an employee may receive more than lost wages if discrimination is proven. (Juries tend to perceive corporations, especially large ones, as "deep pockets" and may not hesitate to award large settlements to an aggrieved employee.)

REHABILITATION ACT OF 1973

This statute covers government contractors, subcontractors, or organizations receiving federal monies in excess of $2,500.[13] Individuals are considered handicapped or disabled if they have a physical or mental impairment that substantially limits one or more major life activities, have a record of such impairment, or are regarded as having such impairment. Only physical or mental impairments are covered by the act. Disadvantages arising from environmental, cultural, or economic factors are not covered. Clearly protected, however, are such diseases and conditions as epilepsy, cancer, cardiovascular disorders, blindness, deafness, mental retardation, emotional disorders, and dyslexia. Under certain circumstances, alcoholism and narcotics addiction are also protected.

While an employer is not required to hire a person with a disability who cannot perform the duties of the job, the employer is required to provide reasonable accommodation of the individual's disability in hiring as well as promotion. The prohibition against discrimination applies to all terms, conditions, and privileges of employment, including compensation and benefits.

The Rehabilitation Act is administered by the Office of Federal Contract Compliance Programs (OFCCP), which investigates and attempts to settle (normally through conciliation where possible, but through litigation if necessary) complaints of discrimination. There is no private right of action under the act; consequently, the complainant must file a complaint with the OFCCP within 180 days of the alleged discriminatory act, at which time the OFCCP assumes responsibility for all further action.

There are two primary levels of the act. All contractors or subcontractors exceeding the $2,500 monetary base are required to post notices that they agree to take affirmative action (that is, positive steps over and above normal employment practices) to recruit, employ, and promote qualified disabled individuals. If the contract or subcontract exceeds $50,000, or if the contractor has fifty or more employees, the employer must prepare a written affirmative action plan for review by the OFCCP.

HEALTH MAINTENANCE ORGANIZATION (HMO) ACT OF 1973

Employers with twenty-five or more employees offering health benefit plans to their employees are required to provide the option of membership in an HMO in lieu of medical insurance coverage if an HMO exists within a twenty-five-mile radius of the employment site.[14] If other health care benefits are paid through payroll deduction, the employer must also allow workers to pay their share of HMO costs through payroll deduction. The act covers employers engaged in interstate commerce who are covered by the Fair Labor Standards Act and provide health care coverage to their employees—if they have twenty-five or more employees.

EMPLOYEE RETIREMENT INCOME SECURITY ACT (ERISA) OF 1974

The ERISA is without doubt one of the most complex pieces of compensation legislation ever enacted. It is designed to provide uniform standards for all employee benefit plans, but particularly pension and retirement plans.[15]

The ERISA defines two types of pension or retirement plans: defined contribution plans and defined benefit plans. A defined contribution plan is one wherein the amount of employee contribution to the plan is defined but there is no stipulation as to the amount that will be received at retirement. A defined benefit plan is one wherein the amount to be received at retirement is specified in advance.

The statute regulates three important areas in retirement plans: eligibility and vesting requirements; fiduciary duties, reporting, and disclosure standards; and funding requirements for defined benefit plans. The ERISA requires that all employees who are twenty-one years old or older and have completed one year of employment with an organization must be covered by the employer's pension plan if there is one. Vesting refers to an employee's irrevocable right to his or her pension plan. There are three standards for vesting: (1) fully vested after five years of service (or ten years service in multiemployer plans); (2) 20 percent vested after two years of service and 20 percent for each year of service thereafter, so that the employee is fully vested at seven years of service; or (3) fully vested upon reaching the plan's specified retirement age, regardless of length of service.

Fiduciaries (those who manage pension and retirement plans) are required to manage plans with "the care, skill, prudence, and diligence under the circumstances then prevailing that a prudent [person] acting in like capacity and familiar with such matters would use in the conduct of an enterprise of a like character and with like aims." Fiduciaries also have a responsibility to keep plan participants informed of their rights under the benefit plan. Termination insurance must be provided to protect employees in the event that an employer defaults on its pension plan obligations.

PREGNANCY DISCRIMINATION ACT OF 1978

Passed as an amendment to Title VII of the Civil Rights Act of 1964, as amended, the Pregnancy Discrimination Act prohibits discrimination in employment (including compensation) based on pregnancy, childbirth, or related medical conditions such as an abortion. The basic premise of the act is that women affected by pregnancy or related conditions must be treated the same as other employees not so affected but similar in their ability or inability to work. A pregnant woman or one affected by a related condition is therefore protected from being refused a job, denied a promotion, or being fired merely because she is pregnant, has recently delivered, or has had an abortion. An employer generally cannot cause a woman to take a leave of absence as long as she, under the advice of her physician, is able to work. Likewise, the employer cannot require a woman who has delivered to remain off work for a set period of time after the delivery. If other employees on disability leave are entitled to return to their jobs when they are able to work again, the same right must be granted to women who have been unable to work because of pregnancy and subsequent delivery.

In the benefits area—health insurance, sick leave, and disability coverage—the same principle applies. A woman unable to work for pregnancy-related reasons is entitled to disability benefits or sick leave on the same basis as employees unable to work for other medical reasons. Any health insurance provided must cover expenses for pregnancy-related conditions on the same basis as expenses for other medical reasons. However, health insurance for expenses arising from abortion is not required except where the life of the mother would be endangered if the fetus were carried to term or when medical complications arise from an abortion.

The net effect of the pregnancy discrimination amendments to Title VII has been to raise the cost of employee benefit plans and possibly penalize employers who have vigorously pursued affirmative action plans to increase their numbers of female employees.[16]

CONSOLIDATED OMNIBUS BUDGET RECONCILITATION ACT (COBRA) OF 1985

Group health plans are required by COBRA to provide transitional coverage to employees and their dependents in the event of a change of employment or a change in job status, such as a reduction in hours that renders an employee ineligible to participate in the group health plan.[17] Death, divorce or legal separation, Medicare entitlement, change in dependent child status, or the employer's bankruptcy are also qualifying events that trigger COBRA's continuing coverage. Continuation coverage applies to the core benefits provided under any group health plan that offers medical care coverage to employees. Terminated or otherwise separated employees can choose to maintain the same health care coverage they previously had with their employers for a period of eighteen months. Employers, however, are not required to pay the premiums for this continuing coverage. Employees can be required to pay the premiums, but the premiums may not exceed 102 percent of the premium in effect when the individual was an employee. Spouses and other dependents of an employee also have the option to continue coverage. COBRA covers employers with twenty or more employees.

AMERICANS WITH DISABILITIES ACT (ADA) OF 1990

The Americans with Disabilities Act applies to employers with fifteen or more employees. The ADA prohibits disability discrimination with respect to all terms, conditions, and privileges of employment, including compensation and employee benefits.[18] If an employer provides insurance or other benefits to its employees, it must provide the same coverage to employees who have disabilities. It is estimated that 43 million Americans are protected by this act. The act defines the following as disabilities: (1) a physical or mental impairment that substantially limits one or more of the major life activities of an individual, such as walking, talking, seeing, hearing, or learning; (2) a record of such an impairment; or (3) an assumption by the employer that the individual has such a disability.

Various obligations are imposed on employers under this legislation: (1) Employers cannot deny an individual a job or a promotion to a higher level position if the individual is qualified and can perform the essential functions of the job, with or without reasonable accommodation; (2) the employer must make reasonable accommodation for a qualified individual to perform the job unless to do so would result in undue hardship for the employer; (3) employers are not required to lower performance standards to accommodate an individual if the standards are job related and uniformly applied to all employees; (4) selection criteria that screen out or tend to screen out applicants or candidates for promotion on the basis of disability must be job related and consistent with business necessity; (5) any tests or procedures used to evaluate qualifications must reflect the skills and abilities of those individuals rather than impairments in sensory, manual, or speaking skills, unless such skills are job-related skills that the tests or procedures are designed to assess; (6) preemployment physicals after a conditional offer of employment is extended are permissible only if all employees are subject to them; (7) medical information on employees must be kept separate from other personal information; and (8) employers cannot make inquiries about an applicant's past workers compensation claims or disabilities in general.

One of the big impacts of the ADA on compensation has been in job analysis and job descriptions. Employers must carefully analyze jobs to ascertain essential job functions and marginal job functions and clearly delineate these items on job descriptions. A job function may be considered essential if (1) the position exists to perform the function specified, (2) the number of employees available to perform the function is limited, (3) the function is highly specialized, (4) a significant amount of time is spent performing the function, (5) failure to perform the function has serious consequences, (6) the function is based on the terms of a labor agreement, and (7) the current and past experience of job incumbents indicates that the function is important. Any written job description prepared by the employer prior to advertising or interviewing candidates for the position is construed to be evidence that establishes the essential functions of a job.

OLDER WORKERS BENEFIT PROTECTION ACT OF 1990

This act is an amendment to the Age Discrimination in Employment Act of 1967. It codifies the so-called equal benefit or equal cost principle of employee benefits so that if the cost of providing a particular benefit to an older worker is greater than the cost of providing the same benefit to a younger worker the employer can elect to provide smaller benefits to older workers if the employer spends at least the same amount of money for all workers. However, reduced benefits for older workers must be based on employer-specific, age-related cost justifications and not on arbitrary age discrimination. The act covers all benefits an employer may offer.[19]

CIVIL RIGHTS ACT (CRA) OF 1991

The Civil Rights Act of 1991 has been described as "the most sweeping amendment to employment discrimination regulation since Title VII."[20] One of the primary purposes of the act is "to strengthen existing protections and remedies available under federal civil rights laws to provide more effective deterrence and adequate compensation for victims of discrimination." The act amended five statutes: (1) the Civil Rights Act of 1866; (2) Title VII of the Civil Rights Act of 1964, as amended; (3) the Age Discrimination in Employment Act of 1967, as amended; (4) the Rehabilitation Act of 1973; and (5) the Americans with Disabilities Act of 1990.

The CRA applies to all employers engaging in or affecting interstate commerce who have fifteen or more employees. The coverage is the same as Title VII. In addition, the CRA extended coverage to include employees of Congress and the White House.

The CRA prohibits discrimination based on race, color, religion, sex, or national origin in every aspect of the employment process, including compensation and benefits, except where religion, sex, or national origin is a bona fide occupational qualification or where differences in wages are based on a bona fide seniority, merit, quantity, or quality system.

Under the CRA spousal benefits, such as health insurance, must, if the employer provides such coverage, be made available to male and female employees. The CRA also requires that pregnancy and childbirth be treated the same as other disabilities covered under medical insurance plans.

Individuals who feel that they are victims of intentional discrimination predicated on race, gender (including sexual harassment), religion, or disability can seek compensatory damages for pain and suffering and punitive damages as well. These damages are available only from private-sector employers and are not applicable to adverse-impact cases. Alleged victims of intentional discrimination are provided the right to demand a jury trial. The amount of damages that can be awarded depend upon the size of the employer's workforce and range from $50,000 for employers having 15 to 100 employees to $300,000 for employers having 500 or more employees.

The Civil Rights Act of 1991 established a Glass Ceiling Commission and charged it with the responsibility of investigating the barriers to advancement of women and minorities in the workplace and making recommendations for the purpose of eliminating those barriers.

FAMILY AND MEDICAL LEAVE ACT (FMLA) OF 1993

The Family and Medical Leave Act guarantees up to twelve weeks of unpaid leave per year for birth or adoption of a child; caring for an ill child, spouse, or parents; or the employee's own serious health condition. Where practicable, employees must give the employer a thirty-day notice of intent to take leave. Employers must maintain health insurance benefits during the leave period. In addition, employees are guaranteed the right to return to their same or comparable jobs when their leaves are over. Employers can require workers to provide medical certification of serious injuries as well as a second medical opinion. A company may exempt from FMLA coverage the top 10 percent of its highest-paid employees.[21]

To be eligible for leave under the FMLA, an employee must have been on the job for at least one year and have worked a minimum of 1,250 hours during the preceding twelve-month period. Employers may require that covered employees use vacation and sick leave before the period of unpaid leave begins, provided that vacation and sick leave are compensated at the rates normally used by the company.

There are four methods of determining the twelve-month period constituting the period in which FMLA leave may be taken: (1) any calendar year; (2) any fixed-month leave year, such as a fiscal year; (3) the twelve-month period as measured by the employee's first FMLA leave; or (4) a rolling twelve-month period measured backward from the date an employee first uses any FMLA leave. The calculation method selected must be applied consistently and uniformly to all covered employees.

The FMLA applies to private-sector firms employing fifty or more workers, including part-time workers, within a seventy-five-mile radius; that is, not all fifty employees are required to work at any one particular job site for an employer to be covered. Public-sector employers subject to the provisions of the Fair Labor Standards Act of 1938 as well as the federal government are also covered.

It is estimated that while only 5 percent of U.S. employers are affected by the FMLA, approximately 40 percent of all employees are covered.[22]

HEALTH INSURANCE PORTABILITY
AND ACCOUNTABILITY ACT (HIPPA) OF 1996

The Health Insurance Portability and Accountability Act is an amendment to the Employee Retirement Income Security Act of 1974. The purpose of the HIPPA is to assure the portability and availability of health care coverage by limiting the extent to which preexisting conditions can be used to exclude individuals from health care coverage.[23] A group health plan may exclude preexisting conditions for only twelve months, or eighteen months for late enrollees. The waiting period may be reduced, however, by counting prior coverage toward the exclusion period. After this period, any condition is eligible for coverage. Consequently, employees with the required months of coverage may move from one employer to another without becoming subject to the preexisting condition exclusion of the new employer. Under the HIPPA pregnancy is not considered to be a preexisting condition under any circumstances.

MENTAL HEALTH PARITY ACT (MHPA) OF 1996

The Mental Health Parity Act of 1996 is aimed at establishing parity between mental health care coverage and traditional physical health care coverage.[24] The act applies to all employers with fifty or more employees. While the act does not mandate mental health care benefits, it does stipulate that where a health care plan includes mental health care benefits, employers are precluded from setting lower annual and aggregate lifetime reimbursement limits for mental health benefits than for medical or surgical benefits. The MHPA specifically excludes substance abuse as a mental health condition.

SUMMARY

This chapter has presented a brief overview of the major federal statutes affecting compensation and benefits. The intent has been to demonstrate the scope and complexity of the legislation surrounding compensation. Space does not permit an in-depth examination of the specifics of each statute or the nuances of interpretation of each law. Those desiring more information should obtain a copy of the particular statute in question or seek advice and counsel from an employment law attorney.

NOTES

1. "Tucson Becomes the 39th City to Join the Living Wage Movement," *The Wall Street Journal*, 12 October 1999, A1.

2. Patrick J. Cihon and James Ottavio Castagnera, *Employment and Labor Law*, 2d ed. (Cincinnatti: West Educational Publishing, 1999), 304.

3. Frederick S. Hills, Thomas J. Bergmann, and Vida G. Scarpello, *Compensation Decision Making*, 2d ed. (Fort Worth: Dryden Press, 1994), 119.

4. Donald L. Caruth and Gail D. Handlogten, *Staffing the Contemporary Organizations*, 2d ed. (Westport, Conn.: Quorum Books, 1997), 21–22.

5. Ibid.

6. Cihon and Castagnera, *Employment*, 304.

7. "The Federal Hourly Minimum Wage Since Its Inception," *HR-News*, December 1999, 34.

8. George T. Milkovich and Jerry M. Newman, *Compensation*, 6th ed. (Boston: Irwin–McGraw-Hill, 1999), 542–548.

9. "Job Out of Bounds," *HR Magazine*, October 1999, 59.

10. Caruth and Handlogten, *Staffing*, 21–22.

11. Ibid., 22–24.

12. Ibid., 24–25.

13. Ibid., 25.

14. Donald L. Caruth, *Compensation Management for Banks* (Boston: Bankers Publishing, 1986), 255.

15. Hills, Bergmann, and Scarpello, *Compensation*, 128–130.

16. Caruth and Handlogten, *Staffing*, 26–27.

17. Milkovich and Newman, *Compensation*, 408.

18. Caruth and Handlogten, *Staffing*, 30.

19. Dawn D. Bennett-Alexander and Laura B. Pincus, *Employment Law for Business*, 2d ed. (Boston: Irwin–McGraw-Hill, 1998), 339–343.

20. Caruth and Handlogten, *Staffing*, 30–32.

21. Cihon and Castagnera, *Employment*, 116–118.

22. Caruth and Handlogten, *Staffing*, 33.

23. "Group Health Plan Portability, Access, and Renewability Requirements," *Employment Coordinator*, vol. 3 (Stamford, Conn.: Clark Boardman Callaghan, a division of Thomson Information Services, 1997), B-14,569–B-14,575.

24. Milkovich and Newman, *Compensation*, 542.

3

MOTIVATION AND COMPENSATION

A basic knowledge of motivation theory is a prerequisite to understanding compensation's role in contemporary organizations. All major compensation components—direct, indirect, and psychological—are rooted in motivation theory. Without an awareness of what motivation is and how it relates to monetary and nonmonetary rewards, there is little possibility of designing a compensation program that simultaneously satisfies the needs of the employing institution and the needs of its workers. Knowledge of psychological compensation and the creation of a motivating work environment are also essential to developing compensation systems that are effective.[1]

In this chapter fundamental motivation concepts and theories are examined, the idea of perceived equity is considered, and the relationship between money and motivation is explored. Psychological compensation and its components as well as the motivating work environment and its elements are also considered.

BASIC MOTIVATION CONCEPTS

Motivation is defined as the willingness to exert effort toward the accomplishment of a task. While this definition is a simple one, it is far from simplistic. Implicit in this definition is the notion that all motivation is internal to the individual and is produced by inner needs, drives, ideas, emotions, or other factors that stimulate an individual to take action. The term "self-motivated" is often used to describe people who exhibit a great deal of drive and ambition. In reality, all motivation is self-motivation. Motivation is not something one person does to another person; it is something people do to themselves as they become willing, for whatever internal reasons, to exert effort in the undertaking or accomplishment of a task. The key to motivation in the workplace, consequently, is understanding the kinds of things that make people willing to exert the necessary effort to get work done and then endeavoring to provide these things.[2]

The study of human behavior has yielded three fundamental principles that are important to comprehending the process of behavior and motivation in the workplace.[3] First, all behavior is caused; that is, all behavior is motivated behavior. No matter how absurd the behavior may appear to others or even to the person exhibiting it, behavior is the result of inner needs, tensions, drives, urges, or emotions that move a person to act. In other words, there is something operating within a person (the stimulus or motive) that arouses him or her to action (the response or motivation).

Second, all behavior is self-centered behavior. Each of us acts with our individual self-interests uppermost in our minds. We do the things we do because we perceive that it is to our benefit to do these things. Whether we respond to a particular stimulus or not depends on how we interpret the self-interest value of responding. If action is perceived as likely to produce a benefit to self, we act; if action is perceived as unlikely to result in a benefit to self, we do not act.

Third, all behavior is goal-directed behavior. The response to the inner urge, tension, drive, or need is to seek out something that will satisfy that urge, tension, drive, or need. Behavior is directed toward seeking and then experiencing those things that appear to have the potential to provide satisfaction of a person's needs, urges, etc.

Each of these three principles reinforces the definition of motivation as an internal phenomenon. People motivate themselves as they put forth effort to gain the satisfactions they believe will produce a personal benefit. This means that managers cannot motivate employees. Managers can, however, create the conditions and circumstances under which employees will motivate themselves because the employees perceive that a personal benefit will be gained from exerting effort. To create this type of motivating environment managers must recognize the basic kinds of needs that employees have and the kinds of satisfactions that employees seek in the workplace.

MOTIVATION THEORIES

A good perspective on motivation in the workplace can be gained by examining three contemporary theories of motivation. These theories are (1) the hierarchy of needs concept postulated by Abraham H. Maslow, (2) the motivation–hygiene construct developed by Frederick Herzberg, and (3) the expectancy theory approach espoused by Victor H. Vroom. While there are other motivation theories, these three offer a good basic summary of contemporary thinking on the subject.

Hierarchy of Needs

Maslow first presented the hierarchy of needs theory of human motivation in 1943.[4] It is by far the best known of the various motivation theories and, while lacking in scientific proof, offers some sound insights into understanding human behavior. According to Maslow, all human beings have five broad categories of needs they endeavor to satisfy: physiological, safety, social, esteem, and self-actualization. These needs are arranged in an ascending hierarchical fashion from lowest (physiological) to highest (self-actualization). The needs vary in their degree of prepotency or urgency. The lower-level needs are the most prepotent because their satisfaction is essential to a person's survival. As the lower-level needs become reasonably well satisfied, the higher-order needs assume increasing importance as causal factors in human behavior.

Physiological needs are comprised of those things required to maintain and sustain life, such as food, air, water, sleep, shelter, and physical survival. These needs are basic because if they are not satisfied life cannot be sustained for very long. Moreover, some reasonable degree of satisfaction is also essential if the quality of a person's life is to be adequate enough to allow the person to pursue the satisfaction of other needs.

Safety needs are concerned with protection from danger, risk, uncertainty, or threats to one's person. Physical safety, situational stability, economic security, freedom from fear or anxiety, and the desire for order are examples of general safety needs. In the workplace safety needs would include job security, safe working conditions, and freedom from physical or mental harm.

At the third level in the hierarchy are the social needs such as love, affection, meaningful relationships with other people, and occupying an important place in a group. Off the job these needs are fulfilled through family, friends, neighbors, and belonging to social groups, such as bowling teams or service clubs. Social needs are reflective of the gregarious nature of human beings. Once the survival and protection needs of the first two levels in the hierarchy are reasonably well satisfied, social needs assume importance as a motivator of behavior.

At the fourth level are the esteem needs. These encompass the desire for status, self-respect, adequacy, confidence, independence, reputation, prestige, recognition, attention, and appreciation. Basically, these needs are concerned with feeling good about oneself and having others recognize one's worth as a person—the need for self-respect and the need for respect from others.

At the top of the hierarchy are the self-actualization needs. Maslow described these as the *being* needs because they are concerned with a person's being all that he or she can be. These needs include personal growth, creativity, realization of potential, autonomy, and intellectual vitality. These are the needs to fulfill one's highest potentialities, however the individual might define those potentialities.

The hierarchy of needs is a general framework for understanding human motivation that provides some important insights into a complex process. It illustrates, for example, that there is an underlying logical pattern of motivation, a progression from one level to another as a person seeks to satisfy different needs. Granted, specific individuals do not always follow the pattern in a step-by-step, mechanical fashion, but the majority of people tend to follow the pattern most of the time.

Inherent in the concept of a hierarchy of human needs, and central to its application in an organizational setting, is the premise that a satisfied need no longer motivates behavior. As one need becomes relatively well satisfied, another need becomes preeminent. For example, a person who is hungry will be motivated by the need for food, but once he or she has eaten, the offer of additional food will not move that person to action. According to Maslow, it is also important to note that a need does not have to be completely satisfied before the emergence of another need is felt. The need only has to be relatively well satisfied, as defined by the individual, before a person begins to seek satisfaction of other needs.

In the context of designing effective compensation programs, one should bear in mind that the lower-order needs—physiological and safety—are primarily satisfied by the direct and indirect components of compensation (i.e., wages, salaries, and benefits). It is the psychological component of compensation that addresses social, esteem, and self-actualization needs. Figure 3.1 shows Maslow's hierarchy of needs and its basic relationship to compensation.

Motivation–Hygiene

Another widely known theory of motivation is Frederick Herzberg's motivation–hygiene approach that developed out of research aimed at determining the factors that lead to satisfaction on the job. According to Herzberg, the factors that produce job satisfaction are different from the factors that produce job dissatisfaction. Thus, there are in reality two sets of factors that must be addressed in order to assure productive behavior in the workplace. The set of factors that leads to job satisfaction are called *motivators* and the set that leads to job dissatisfaction are labeled *hygiene*.

Years after his original research, Herzberg's theory is still controversial among behavioral scientists and practicing managers. Herzberg contends that there is not a single continuum that ranges from job satisfaction at one end of the continuum to job dissatisfaction at the other end of the continuum. Rather,

Figure 3.1
Maslow's Hierarchy of Needs

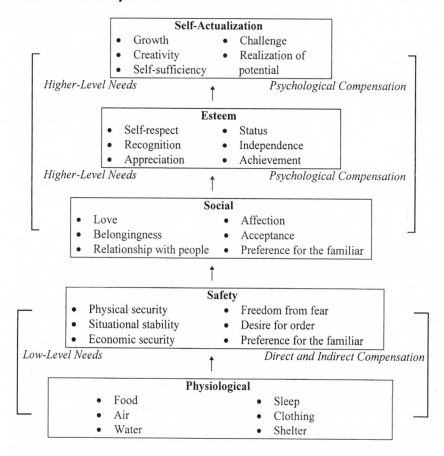

there are two separate continuums: one ranging from job satisfaction to no job satisfaction (motivation) and one ranging from dissatisfaction to no dissatisfaction (hygiene). Figure 3.2 shows the two continuums and the major items comprising both hygiene and motivation.

The role of hygiene factors in an organizational setting is to maintain an employee in a healthy state of mind relative to the institution. If these factors are not properly addressed and provided for to some reasonable degree, job dissatisfaction will result. However, properly addressing and providing for the satisfaction of these factors, even in superabundance, will not elicit positive motivation from employees; it will only eliminate the possibility of dissatisfaction with the organization or the setting in which work is performed.

The role of motivation factors is to stimulate employees to higher performance. When opportunities for achievement, recognition, advancement, and

Figure 3.2
Motivation–Hygiene Components

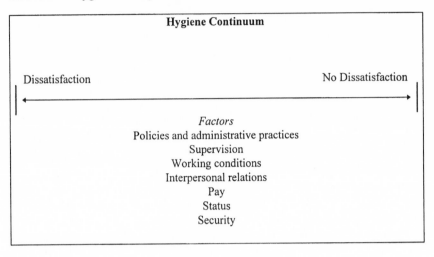

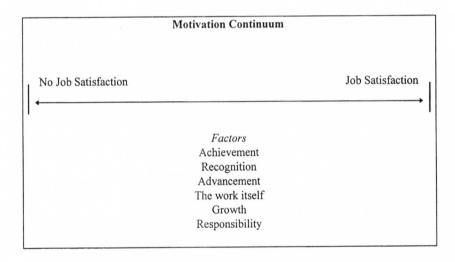

so forth are present in the work environment in sufficient amounts, job satisfaction, and concomitantly, higher levels of productivity, will ensue, according to Herzberg, because a motivating work environment has been created.
Conversely, failure to provide for adequate satisfaction of these factors will
result in employees who are not motivated to produce beyond some minimum level of performance.

There is a fairly close relationship between motivation–hygiene theory and the hierarchy of needs theory. In fact, the two approaches seem to suggest the same conclusion about motivation. Herzberg's hygiene factors correspond very closely to Maslow's physiological, safety, and social needs, while the motivation factors clearly mirror esteem and self-actualization needs. To prevent job dissatisfaction, wages, salaries, and indirect monetary rewards, as well as policies for their administration, must be carefully formulated to assure their sufficiency and reasonableness. But having good pay, good benefits, and sound compensation policies will not, according to motivation–hygiene theory, produce job satisfaction or cause employees to motivate themselves to work harder, produce more, or become more conscientious in the performance of their jobs. More productive work behavior can only be stimulated by assuring adequate satisfaction of the motivation factors—the psychological components of compensation. The hierarchy of needs suggests that a person's lower-order needs are satisfied by pay and benefits; motivation–hygiene theory suggests essentially the same thing. Moreover, both theories suggest that psychological satisfactions in the workplace are of paramount importance in eliciting employee motivation once direct pay and benefits have been provided.[4]

Expectancy Theory

The hierarchy of needs and motivation–hygiene theory are attempts to explain why people as a whole behave as they do. Expectancy theory, developed by Victor Vroom, is an attempt to explain why individuals, in light of their own goals and their expectations of reaching them, behave as they do.[5]

According to expectancy theory, motivation is determined by two factors: *expectancy* and *valence*. Expectancy is a person's perception of the likelihood that a particular outcome will result from particular behaviors. Valence is the value that an individual assigns to a particular outcome that may result from certain behaviors; it is an index of how much a person desires a specific outcome.

Expectancy is actually comprised of two separate components: effort to performance expectancy and performance to outcome expectancy. Effort to performance expectancy is a person's perception of the likelihood that increased effort will result in increased performance. Performance to outcome expectancy is a person's perception of the likelihood that increased performance will result in increased rewards.

Algebraically, the expectancy theory of motivation can be expressed as follows:

$$\text{Motivation} = \left[\left(\begin{array}{c} \text{Effort to} \\ \text{Performance} \\ \text{Expectancy} \end{array} \right) \left(\begin{array}{c} \text{Performance} \\ \text{to Outcome} \\ \text{Expectancy} \end{array} \right) \right] \left[\begin{array}{c} \text{Reward} \\ \text{Valence} \end{array} \right]$$

According to this model, if motivated behavior is to occur, three conditions must be fulfilled: (1) performance expectancy must be greater than zero, (2) outcome expectancy must be greater than zero, and (3) reward valence must be greater than zero. High expectancies or high valence alone will not produce motivation.[6]

Two examples will illustrate how this model works. First, consider the case of Bill Stone, a business development officer in a suburban branch office of a large metropolitan bank. From past experience Bill knows that he secures for his bank one new account for every seven personal calls he makes on prospective customers. Thus, he perceives a direct link between effort and performance: The more calls he makes, the more accounts he obtains. Bill knows that he could easily make another ten calls per week; consequently, his effort to performance expectancy is high. Bill also perceives that getting more accounts for his bank will almost certainly earn him a promotion to the bank's downtown office. His performance to outcome expectancy is high: Obtaining more accounts will result in a promotion. But Bill is fifty-six years old, lives only ten minutes from his suburban branch office, values security and stability in his job situation, and dislikes the thought of the hour-and-a-half commute each way to and from downtown that working in the central office would entail. Consequently, his reward valence is low. Under these circumstances Bill Stone will not be motivated to make more business development calls. His performance and outcome expectancies are both high, but his reward valence is zero or less (it is possible for any of the three factors to have a negative value). In this case Bill will keep on making the same number of calls that he has always made because the reward factor has a low value to him.

Consider a second example. Bobbie Gomez is a sewing machine operator in a garment manufacturing company who was compelled to take a job last year when her husband died suddenly of a heart attack. She is struggling to support two small children on a tight budget. Bobbie's company has just installed an incentive pay plan for sewing machine operators whereby they will be paid on a piece-rate basis for every item processed beyond a standard number of items per day. Bobbie is confident that through additional effort she can produce at least 100 more items per day than she is currently producing. As a result, her performance expectancy is high. She also knows that the more items she handles, the more she will earn. Thus, her outcome expectancy is high. Because of her current economic situation she places a high value on additional earnings. This means that reward valence in her case is also high. Under these circumstances Bobbie will be motivated to produce more items because greater effort will result in greater outcomes and greater outcomes will result in greater rewards that are highly valued by her.

As these two examples show, motivating employees to higher performance is not a simple matter. Specific needs of specific individuals must be considered, as well as the values that these individuals attach to fulfilling those needs.

[1] The expectancy theory of motivation has some important implications for compensation management: (1) A clear relationship between rewards and performance must be established, (2) the relationship between rewards and performance must be communicated to employees, (3) rewards must actually be given on the basis of performance, (4) rewards must meet specific employee needs to be effective in eliciting a high level of motivation, and (5) organizational obstacles to good performance must be removed to assure motivated behavior.

How does expectancy theory relate to the hierarchy of needs and motivation–hygiene theory? Clearly, expectancy theory is not an attempt to show the kinds of needs people have; rather, it is an attempt to explain why specific individuals behave as they do in their efforts to satisfy whatever needs may be important to them. However, expectancy theory does tend to support some underlying assumptions of the other two theories. First, expectancy theory reinforces the concept of motivation as an internal function. A person responds or acts in accordance with his or her inner feelings and drives. Second, expectancy theory adds another dimension to motivation by postulating that motivation is dependent upon a person's individual assessment of the likelihood of outcomes as well as the value of the reward associated with these outcomes. Third, it suggests that people will exert effort to satisfy various needs as long as there is a positive relationship in terms of a personal payoff between effort and reward. Fourth, expectancy theory implies that the intensity of needs is processed through the filters of a personal evaluation of a person's particular situation.

THE CONCEPT OF EQUITY

Of central importance to any compensation system is the concept of equity developed by J. Stacey Adams and others.[7] Equity is a person's belief or perception that he or she is being treated fairly relative to other people. It is a person's interpretation of the justice of his or her situation, arrived at by comparing that situation with the situations of others. Because equity is determined by an individual's perceptions, beliefs, and interpretations, the term *perceived equity* is often used when referring to this concept.

Equity theory suggests that the principle of distributive justice is extremely important to each of us. Distributive justice occurs when all parties involved in an exchange relationship—such as the exchange of effort by an employee for compensation from the organization—have equal outcome and input ratios. In an organizational setting, outcomes include such items as pay, recognition, promotion, social relationships, and various psychological rewards. Inputs include time, experience, effort, education, loyalty, skills, performance, responsibility, competence, and tolerance of unusual working conditions. As each person makes his or her inputs and receives his or her outcomes, the person compares the ratio of these items with that of others. Conceptually, this calculation is made as follows:

$$\frac{Outcomes \text{ (self)}}{Inputs \text{ (self)}} \quad compared\ to \quad \frac{Outcomes \text{ (others)}}{Inputs \text{ (others)}}$$

Equity exists when the two ratios are the same:

$$\frac{Outcomes \text{ (self)}}{Inputs \text{ (self)}} \quad = \quad \frac{Outcomes \text{ (others)}}{Inputs \text{ (others)}}$$

Inequity exists for a person whenever his or her ratio of inputs and outcomes is not equal to what he or she perceives the ratio of others to be. The person will feel underrewarded if

$$\frac{Outcomes \text{ (self)}}{Inputs \text{ (self)}} \quad < \quad \frac{Outcomes \text{ (others)}}{Inputs \text{ (others)}}$$

On the other hand, a person may feel overrewarded if

$$\frac{Outcomes \text{ (self)}}{Inputs \text{ (self)}} \quad > \quad \frac{Outcomes \text{ (others)}}{Inputs \text{ (others)}}$$

Where inequity is perceived to exist, a person will make efforts to correct the situation. If the inequity is one of overreward, an employee may conceivably respond by (1) exerting more effort to increase inputs, (2) changing his or her basis of comparison, or (3) rationalizing away the differences in the ratios. Realistically, overreward inequity does not present much of a problem to a person; there are many ways that an individual can justify such a situation.

If the inequity is one of underreward—the more common condition—the situation can be very serious. The employee will probably feel that he or she is not being treated fairly vis-à-vis other employees. In this case, the employee may attempt to rectify the situation by (1) decreasing inputs (exerting less effort) or making fewer positive contributions to the organization, (2) asking for more rewards in order to increase outcomes, (3) attempting to get others to decrease their inputs, or (4) leaving the organization for a more equitably perceived situation.

An important variable in equity theory is the referent; that is, the other individual(s) to whom a person compares himself or herself. The referent may be one or more individuals with similar jobs in the organization, friends, relatives, neighbors, or professional associates. In equity theory referents in this group are designated as *other*. It is important to note, however, that a person may also use the system as a referent; that is, organizational pay policies, procedures, and practices. Consequently, a person may be computing how well he or she fares against other people in determining equity or a person may be determining how well he or she fares against the compensation system in general.

Equity theory emphasizes that an individual is concerned not only with the absolute rewards for efforts contributed, but also, and perhaps more important, with the relationship of his or her rewards and efforts to the rewards and efforts of others. One of the critical roles of a formalized compensation program, then, is to foster employees' perceptions of equity or fairness in pay matters, particularly the relationships between efforts expended by the employee and rewards given by the organization.[8]

One crucial implication of equity theory for managers is that motivation will not flourish unless employees perceive rewards as fair and equitable. Where rewards are given haphazardly, where there is no direct relationship between pay and performance, where favoritism or bias characterize the reward system, demotivation will occur because of perceived inequity. Motivation can only occur in a climate of perceived equity.

Equally important for managers as well as compensation specialists to remember is that simply saying that a compensation program is fair does not automatically make it fair in the eyes of an organization's employees. The program must constantly be demonstrated to be fair. Policies, procedures, and practices—both written and unwritten—must be designed and administered equitably at all times for positive employee perceptions to develop.

IS MONEY A MOTIVATOR?

Equity theory is anything but precise. It does call attention, however, to an issue that must be addressed if compensation is to contribute to positive motivation in the workplace. Does money motivate people? Years of research findings support the conclusion that the answer to this question is yes and no.[9] Admittedly, this is not a very satisfactory answer for managers seeking hard and fast answers about the role of money in an organizational setting. It is obvious that people want money, people expect money, and people demand money. But does money alone stimulate people to put forth extra effort, to "turn themselves on" for their employing institutions? Thus far, research has not been able to reach a definitive conclusion about the role of money as a motivator.

Maslow's hierarchy of needs theory tends to suggest that money is important primarily for satisfying lower-level needs. Economic behavior provides the wherewithal for assuring adequate satisfaction of one's survival and safety requirements. But after these needs are met the hierarchy of needs suggests that items that cannot be satisfied through economic behavior alone become more urgent and important to a person. Without saying so directly, the hierarchy of needs intimates the necessity of a total compensation system: direct and indirect compensation to provide for physiological and safety needs, and psychological compensation to address the higher-level needs of employees. However, it does not totally answer the question of money's role as a stimulator of productive behavior in the workplace.

Motivation–hygiene theory boldly asserts that money is a source of job dissatisfaction rather than job satisfaction. It states that money does not motivate employees, but only serves to place them in a homeostatic condition that is a prerequisite for motivation. Of all the research findings and theories extant today, motivation–hygiene theory contends most definitely and most clearly that money does not stimulate employees to higher performance. As with Maslow's hierarchy of needs, it suggests that direct and indirect compensation must be adequate to address basic needs, but at the same time indicates that motivation can only be engendered through the psychological component of compensation.

Expectancy theory further clouds the issue of money as a motivator by indicating that money—or any other reward, for that matter—may motivate under some conditions, but under other conditions will not motivate. According to expectancy theory, the ability of money to motivate depends on several contingencies: the employee's ability to improve performance, the organization's likelihood of rewarding increased performance, and the value the employee attaches to monetary rewards. The conclusion is that when all three contingencies are met, money will motivate; otherwise, it will not.

The concept of equity creates additional confusion about the role of money. Equity theory suggests that it is not money as an absolute that motivates employee behavior; rather, it is money as relative to its proportions that creates dissatisfaction or demotivation.

Other research also tends to cast further doubt on money's usefulness as a good basic motivator. For example, in one series of surveys originated in 1946 and replicated several times since, employees have been asked to rank in order of their preference ten items—specific items supplied by the researchers—of importance in a working relationship. In the first survey, as well as all subsequent ones, employees have ranked "good wages" as fifth in importance. Appreciation for work done and feeling in on things have consistently been ranked at the top of the list. This series of surveys would tend to support the notion that psychological considerations, not monetary ones, have the greatest potential for stimulating employees to higher performance in an organizational setting.[10]

It is important to note that none of the research conducted and none of the theories presented here state that money is unimportant. On the contrary, money is very important to employees.[11] What the evidence seems to suggest is that money buys a minimum level of performance. Dangling an economic carrot at the end of an organizational stick probably cannot purchase performance beyond this minimum level.

It is probably reasonable, then, to postulate that money is a *threshold* motivator; that is, it is money that entices an individual to take a specific job with a particular organization, it is money that encourages an individual to stay with an institution, and it is money that elicits a minimal amount of effort from an individual, thereby enabling an organization to get its work accomplished. It is probably also reasonable to say that money is not the sole motivator in a work environment and may, in fact, function more as a behavioral irritant than as a behavioral stimulant.

It is easy to denigrate money as a motivator, but there are many individuals in the workforce who display a great deal of money motivation: salespeople on straight commission, workers on piece-rate incentives, executives and managers who strive to earn performance-based bonuses. For these people money is a motivator. For others it is not.

As the preceding discussion has illustrated, money is a confusing subject. The major difficulty in stating with any degree of certainty that money either motivates or does not is that money, in our society, is a symbol. As a symbol it can represent almost every other value or outcome that an individual is motivated to pursue: status, prestige, self-esteem, achievement, power, security, possessions, and so on. Money is a handy means of comparison with others; it is an individual's personal scorecard in the game of work or in the larger game of life.

Within the context of designing an effective compensation system for an organization, it is important to keep money in proper perspective. Such a perspective recognizes four things about money. One, money does motivate to some extent. It is the incentive that induces a person to take a job with a particular institution. It produces some minimum level of employee effort for the organization. It is highly desired by some employees who will work very hard to get it. Two, money does not motivate all people. The lure of additional economic gain does not elicit "turned-on, tuned-in" behavior from everyone because all people do not attach the same degree of importance to money. Three, money has a great potential for creating dissatisfaction and demotivation if handled inappropriately in the compensation system. Money actually becomes a "turn-off" when it is perceived to be distributed unfairly. It becomes a demotivator when it bears no clear-cut relationship to performance on the job. Four, the economic portions of the compensation package are extremely important if the organization is to attract and retain people to perform the work of the institution, but the psychological component is also extremely important in attracting, holding, and actually motivating employees. A compensation program, then, must recognize that salaries, wages, and indirect monetary rewards form the foundation for motivation, but cannot be construed as constituting the entire compensation package (attention will be directed to creating a motivating work environment in the following section).

From a motivational and human behavior point of view, an organization must create a compensation system that will be perceived as equitable. An equitable compensation system, as discussed in this chapter, is one that does the following:

- Provides sufficient economic rewards to satisfy the basic needs of employees.
- Assures external equity; that is, its direct and indirect compensation package favorably compares with what is offered by other institutions in the labor market.
- Creates internal equity by recognizing the differences between jobs and compensating them accordingly.
- Relates rewards—merit increases, bonuses, promotions, and so forth—to performance.
- Distributes rewards fairly on some recognized, objective basis.
- Takes into account individual differences; that is, it recognizes that people have different needs and may choose different paths to satisfy those needs.[12]

PSYCHOLOGICAL COMPENSATION

Compensation specialists do not devise psychological compensation. Managers and the policies and practices of the organization are the instruments that create the system of psychological compensation. This vital form of compensation is frequently overlooked as salary structures are devised and systems of indirect financial rewards are constructed. And yet the best-designed pay structures and benefits systems are likely to fail in the absence of a psychologically sound work environment. An important element in fulfilling the purposes of a compensation system—to attract, hold, and motivate employees—is the organizational climate of an institution.

Psychological compensation encompasses all possible nonmonetary rewards organizations provide their employees. These rewards can take many forms, from the simple company logo coffee cup to allowing employees autonomy, from length of service pins to involvement in problem solving. These and other elements suggest to employees that they are valuable to the organization, a key ingredient in developing a psychologically nurturing work environment.

The Motivating Work Environment

The *motivating work environment* is a concept widely discussed in management circles. However, many managers probably do not really understand what this environment is. They frequently do not know how to achieve improved performance and higher productivity through proper motivational techniques, including creation of a working environment that is conducive to high performance. To make matters worse, many managers seem uncertain how to reinforce desired behaviors on the part of employees. A misconception held by many managers is that if they were only a little nicer to their employees then employees would respond by performing at higher levels. Such misguided attempts at motivation may even produce the opposite effect: poor performance.

Some managers misunderstand the role of pay and benefits, mistaking them for the things employees desire most from their jobs. As indicated earlier, surveys have shown money to rank well below other psychological satisfactions that employees expect from a working relationship. Money is often, however, a major dissatisfer if not handled properly.[13] What are the components of a motivating work environment? Five elements in particular seem to be of importance in creating a stimulating work environment: achievement, recognition, empowerment, opportunities for growth, and corporate policies.

Achievement

When employees have a feeling of job and career achievement they generally feel more motivated. Moreover, employees who are committed to both their organizations and their careers report both higher job satisfaction and career satisfaction. Managers can foster feelings of achievement and commitment through ongoing training and continued educational efforts. Typically, employees who are confident about their abilities also become more committed to their employers.

Employees want to know they are making contributions to their organizations. For most employees making a contribution is a function of having respect from peers, having managers who give them feedback when they do a good job, and being involved and informed about what is going on in the organization.

Recognition

Studies tend to confirm that recognition for a good job is what many employees value greatly in a working relationship. In the survey mentioned earlier in this chapter, where employees were asked to rank the top things they desire from their organizations, recognition for good work ranked above pay and benefits. Praise and recognition are important elements of a motivating work environment.

Empowerment

When employees feel empowered to perform their jobs with some reasonable degree of autonomy, feelings of job satisfaction are enhanced. Ultimately, empowerment leads employees to contribute more to their organizations, thereby increasing overall organizational productivity and furthering the success of the company. It is important for managers to remember that employees at all organizational levels need to feel empowered if they are to contribute to the greatest extent possible.

Opportunities for Growth

According to a recent study, career development—an opportunity for growth—is very important to employees. Managers, consequently, need to provide clear career development plans. Employees tend to feel that the work environment is more interesting when there is something new to learn or an additional opportunity to pursue. Employees need to feel that their working environment provides them with room to grow. Where employers recognize the talents of their employees and provide opportunities to learn, grow, and develop on the job, employees will tend to be more committed to achieving results for the organization.

Employees who are stimulated by interesting work and the ability to grow on the job are more likely to be satisfied with their employer and less likely to leave the organization.[14] Employers can realize at least two benefits from such a situation: (1) turnover is reduced, and (2) employees are more likely to contribute ideas that help the organization remain more competitive. Consequently, it is becoming more and more critical for organizations to provide employees with opportunities to enhance job skills on a regular basis.

Corporate Policies

Focusing on creating and maintaining a motivating and satisfying working environment requires managers to develop policies that support such an environment, policies that are employee friendly and express the concern of the organization for the well-being of the employee. These policies must also communicate the vision and philosophy of the organization.

Managers must strive to capture the essence of the corporation and create a psychologically motivating and satisfying environment for all employees. Moreover, when managers practice the organization's vision their actions can have a snowballing effect on employees, who may also be inspired to live the vision in the workplace.

ORGANIZATIONAL CULTURE

Organizational culture can be defined as the system of shared values, beliefs, habits, and practices of an institution. Organizational culture embodies the values and standards that govern people's behavior in an organization. Any organization is a social institution, with its customs, taboos, status groups, and pecking orders.

Corporate cultures must consider four practices essential to employee motivation: (1) The culture must provide meaning and purpose in the workplace—employees need to visualize a reason for the organization's existence beyond year-end profits; (2) the culture must be work and life friendly and offer employees a range of opportunities or advantages; (3) the culture must equitably allocate rewards between organization and employees; and (4) the culture must open and share information in order to create trust between employees and managers.

JOB SATISFACTION

Many managers are beginning to accept the proposition that employee satisfaction is crucial to organizational success. More specifically, organizations are expending a great deal of money and time on employee satisfaction initiatives in the hope that by doing so turnover can be reduced, productivity improved, and customer satisfaction increased. These efforts usually begin with employee opinion or climate surveys. These questionnaires are designed to determine both satisfiers and dissatisfiers extant in the work environment.

Unfortunately, managers whose organizations experience high turnover may not understand exactly why employees leave. The employee may simply turn in his or her notice and go across the street, down the block, or around the corner to join another employer—or worse, a competitor. Why is it that some employers retain dedicated employees while other organizations suffer from constant turnover? While there may be several answers to this question, often it boils down to a simple proposition: how employees are treated on the job. Management theorists postulate that job satisfaction is as important, or perhaps more so, than salaries and benefits. When employees are viewed and treated in a positive light they tend to stay with an employer. When they are not, they tend to leave.

THE FAMILY-FRIENDLY ORGANIZATION

Today it is important that organizations remember that the traditional corporate culture, which once provided job security, no longer exists. Employees, who once assumed they had to modify their lives to meet the demands of their organizations, have changed. Contemporary employees expect more from their employers.

Organizations are now more cognizant than ever before of employees' needs outside of the workplace. Organizations are recognizing that employees have lives outside of the workplace. It is estimated that 87 percent of the American workforce has family responsibilities.[15] Therefore, balancing work and family responsibilities is a major priority for today's employees. As a result, employers must provide their employees with a work- and life-friendly environment that is motivating, satisfying, and friendly for employees.

Organizations are now beginning to offer employees a wide range of satisfaction-oriented benefits, such as compressed workweeks, telecommuting, job sharing, and on-site childcare.[16] Employers are becoming more sensitive to the off-job needs of employees in order to create a family-friendly organizational environment that enhances job satisfaction. Many contemporary organizations do not simply help employees manage their lives outside the workplace; they allow them to bring their lives into their workplace. Employers that provide employees with a work- and life-friendly environment increase loyalty and stability in the workplace.

This chapter has examined a wide variety of concepts related to the psychology of compensation. Hopefully the point has been made that pay and benefit systems cannot be designed without considering the larger psychological aspects of compensation. Perfect compensation systems will ultimately fail unless they are based on a sound understanding of the psychological needs of employees.

NOTES

1. Donald L. Caruth, *Compensation Management for Banks* (Boston: Bankers Publishing, 1986), 20.

2. Ibid.

3. Ibid., 21.

4. Abraham H. Maslow, "A Theory of Human Motivation," *Psychology Review* 50 (1943): 378–379.

5. George L. Frunzi and Patrick E. Savini, *Supervision: The Art of Management*, 4th ed. (Upper Saddle River, N.J.: Prentice Hall, 1997), 148.

6. Caruth, *Compensation Management*, 27.

7. Ibid., 29–31.

8. Frederick S. Hills, Thomas J. Bergmann, and Vida G. Scarpello, *Compensation Decision Making*, 2d ed. (Fort Worth: Dryden Press, 1994), 342–343.

9. Caruth, *Compensation Management*, 31–34.

10. Bob Nelson, "The Ironies of Motivation," *Planning Review*, January–February 1999, 26–31.

11. Wayne Cascio, *Managing Human Resources*, 5th ed. (Boston: Irwin–McGraw-Hill, 1998), 405.

12. Caruth, *Compensation Management*, 34–35.

13. Ibid., 34.

14. Barbara Parus, "Designing a Total Rewards Program to Retain Critical Talent in the New Millennium," *ACA News*, February 1999, 21.

15. Joseph H. Boyett and Jimmie T. Boyett, "Four Essentials for Motivating Employees in a Changing Environment," *Innovative Leader*, October 1999, 2.

16. Cascio, *Managing Human Resources*, 345.

4

JOB ANALYSIS

Broadly defined, job analysis is the process of collecting, interpreting, and reporting pertinent facts about the nature of a specific job. This process encompasses determining the duties and responsibilities that comprise the job; identifying the skills, abilities, knowledge, experience, and other factors required of a worker to be able to perform the job; and preparing job descriptions and job specifications.[1]

Job analysis is the most fundamental of all human resource management activities because all other personnel functions, especially compensation, depend to a large extent on the successful execution of this one activity. Job analysis is a crucial step in the development of a compensation program. The information gathered, synthesized, and reported through this process will form the basis upon which significant compensation program decisions will be made. Consequently, it is important that job analysis be done carefully and accurately.

OVERVIEW OF THE JOB ANALYSIS PROCESS

Before considering the job analysis process in detail, an explanation of some of the terminology used in this activity is necessary. Three terms that warrant definition are *task, position*, and *job*.

A task is a duty; it exists whenever effort must be expended for a specific purpose such as typing a letter. A position is a group of tasks assigned to one employee. In any organization, there are as many positions as there are workers. A job, on the other hand, is a group of positions that are identical as far as their major or significant tasks are concerned. In a small organization, where every position differs from every other position, a position is also a job.[2]

Job analysis, in essence, consists of five major components: (1) identification of each job in the organization; (2) collection of information about the duties, responsibilities, and working conditions of the job; (3) delineation of essential job functions and marginal job functions; (4) determination of the human qualifications needed to perform the job; and (5) preparation of job descriptions and job specifications.

Job Identification

Before any job can be analyzed, it is necessary to determine what and how many jobs exist in the organization. To do this, a list of all positions is compiled. In a large organization the list would be assembled department by department; in a small organization, the list would be compiled for the total company. There are several ways this list can be constructed: by studying the organizational chart, by reviewing payroll records, by examining personnel directories, by talking to supervisors and managers, or by observing the actual work performed in each organizational unit. The final list of positions should equal the total number of employees in each department if it has been compiled department by department; or it should equal the total number of employees in the organization if it has been compiled in aggregate fashion.

Once the list of positions has been completed, the next step is to develop a list of jobs. If, for example, an organization has six employees who function as accounting clerks and they all perform the same duties, it is clear that "accounting clerk" constitutes one job. But, if an organization has three individuals designated as "engineer" and one performs electrical engineering duties, one carries out mechanical engineering duties, and the other performs chemical engineering duties, it is clear that there are three separate jobs, not one. Should any doubt exist as to whether two or more positions are actually similar in nature, they should be listed as separate jobs until further analysis can be done to clarify the situation.

After the tentative list of jobs has been completed, it is good practice to standardize job titles so that they conform to universally accepted and recognized titles. Frequently, organizations create job titles that are unique to the organization and have little or no meaning outside the institution. The *Dictionary of Occupational Titles*, a publication of the U.S. Department of Labor, contains a list of standardized, commonly used, and widely accepted job titles.[3] Wherever possible, these titles should be used.

Collection of Data Relative to
Job Duties and Responsibilities

After determining which jobs exist in an organization, the major task of analysis begins: ascertaining the specific duties, responsibilities, essential functions, and marginal functions of each job. Techniques for accomplishing this vital function are examined in subsequent sections of this chapter.

Determination of Needed Human Qualifications

One of the most difficult parts of job analysis is determining the skills, abilities, experience, and other qualifications needed to perform a job. A great deal of judgment, discretion, and expertise is required by the individual performing the job analysis. While input from supervisors and managers is helpful, there is a tendency for these individuals to describe the qualifications that an ideal job incumbent should possess. Employees, especially those who have been performing a job for a while, also tend to overstate the qualifications needed. The task of the job analyst is to sort through preferred qualifications and determine the minimally appropriate level of skills needed for successful job performance.

Preparation of Job Descriptions and Job Specifications

The final phase of job analysis is to prepare written documents that enumerate the duties, responsibilities, and functions of the job (job descriptions), and specify the skills, abilities, and other qualifications needed to perform the job (job specifications).

The following sections cover the purposes and uses of job analysis information. Later sections examine in greater detail how the information is gathered and reported.

PURPOSES AND USES OF JOB ANALYSIS

As a basic tool of human resource management, job analysis provides information that can be used in a number of ways to satisfy organizational purposes. The information provided through this activity can be used to do the following:

- Assist in human resource planning. Through job analysis, data relative to future skills needs are determined. The organization knows not only what jobs will be needed in the future, but also the qualifications individuals will need to fill these jobs successfully.
- Establish definitive criteria for making staffing decisions. Under the provisions of Title VII and the *Uniform Guidelines for Employee Selection Procedures* issued

by the Equal Employment Opportunity Commission in 1978, all selection standards and procedures used must be job related. Job analysis is the vehicle through which this is accomplished.

- Indicate the need for training of present as well as future job incumbents in the performance of job duties and responsibilities.
- Establish a basis for appraising the performance of employees in terms of actual job duties.
- Assist in the career planning and development process by identifying the qualifications employees must have to progress to positions of greater responsibility.
- Reallocate work from one job to another if the workload is too heavy in one job or if it could be performed better in another job.
- Correct unsafe or undesirable working conditions in a job before such conditions cause injury or illness to workers.
- Determine which jobs are exempt from the payment of overtime compensation and which jobs are not.
- Evaluate jobs relative to each other, thereby establishing a system of internal equity that can be used for compensation purposes.
- Establish groups or classes of similar jobs for compensation or performance-appraisal purposes.
- Create a factual basis for determining promotions, transfers, terminations, or demotions.
- Establish a basis that assists in research efforts attempting to distinguish successful from less successful employees.
- Protect the organization in the event of legal challenge. Courts have typically held that a job analysis made in good faith is admissible as evidence that an organization has attempted to validate certain of its personnel procedures and practices.[4]

This list is intended to be illustrative rather than exhaustive. However, it demonstrates that there are a number of reasons why all organizations should perform job analysis. Not the least of these reasons is the creation of a foundation, through development of job descriptions and job specifications, for an effective compensation program.

IMPACT OF THE ADA ON JOB ANALYSIS

The Americans with Disabilities Act of 1992 has had a significant impact on the preparation of job descriptions. This act requires that essential functions of a job be differentiated from marginal job functions. Essential job functions are those job duties that are intrinsic to the position. They are, in essence, the reasons a position exists. Evidence of an essential function in a particular job includes the following: (1) the employer's judgment of its essentiality, (2) written job descriptions that suggest the essential nature of a job function, (3) the amount of time a job incumbent spends performing the specified function, (4) the consequences of not requiring the employee to perform the function, (5) the work experience of previous employees in the job, and (6) the current work experience of employees in similar jobs.[5] Marginal functions are job functions that may be performed but are not key reasons for the execution of a job.

Since the enactment of the ADA it has become incumbent upon employers to separate essential job functions from marginal job functions inasmuch as the act precludes employers from discriminating against qualified individuals with disabilities who can, with or without reasonable accommodation, perform the essential functions of the job. As stated in Section 101(8) of the ADA, "Consideration shall be given to the employer's judgment as to what functions of a job are essential, and if an employer has prepared a written job description before advertising or interviewing applicants for the job, this description shall be considered evidence of the essential functions of the job."

Well-written, comprehensive job descriptions that separate essential job functions from marginal ones help protect an organization from charges of disability discrimination in hiring, compensation, promotion, transfer, or other employment descisions.

TYPES OF JOB ANALYSIS INFORMATION

A thorough, effectively performed job analysis can collect a wealth of information. The specific information generated depends largely upon its potential uses. As a general rule, it is preferable to collect as many job facts as possible so as not to overlook any important items. The following list presents examples of the types of data that can be gathered, by category.[6]

1. Job Duties
   - General purpose of the job.
   - Duties performed daily and the approximate time spent on each.
   - Duties performed only at stated periods, such as once a week or once a month, and the approximate time spent on each.
   - Duties performed infrequently or irregularly, such as fill-in for another worker, and the approximate time involved.
   - Most difficult or complex parts of the job and why they are difficult or complex.
   - Essential functions of the job, those duties that are the basic purpose of the job.
   - Marginal functions, or peripheral duties, that are not the primary reason for the job's existence.

2. Job Responsibilities
   - Nature and extent of responsibility for money, property, equipment, or other types of assets.
   - Nature and extent of responsibility for materials or supplies.

- Nature and extent of responsibility for people.
- Number of workers supervised, directly or indirectly.
- Job title of workers supervised, directly or indirectly.
- Nature and extent of access to or usage of classified, confidential, or proprietary information.
- Nature and extent of decision-making authority.

3. Machines, Equipment, Tools, and Materials Used
   - Machines and equipment operated and degree of proficiency required.
   - Tools used and degree of proficiency required.
   - Types of materials used, how they are used, and what is done to them.

4. Controls over Work
   - Type of instructions received on how work is to be performed and from whom they are received.
   - Tasks that must be checked by others and by whom and how they are checked.
   - Decisions that must be referred to supervisor.
   - Policies or procedures used.

5. Performance Standards or Output Expectations
   - Output requirements.
   - Quality requirements.
   - Time schedules, deadlines, or other time requirements that must be met.

6. Interactions with Others
   - Nature and frequency of contacts with coworkers or other organizational personnel.
   - Nature and frequency of contacts with people outside the organization.
   - Types of circumstances under which contacts within or outside the organization are normally made.
   - Number of people contacted in a typical workday.

7. Organizational Relationship
   - Job title of immediate supervisor.
   - Department and unit to which job is assigned.
   - Type of supervision received.
   - Type of supervision given.
   - Job from which individual is typically promoted to present job.
   - Job to which individual is typically promoted from present job.

8. Physical Factors and Job Environment
   - Percentage of time spent sitting, standing, and walking.

- Amount and type of physical exertion required.
- Environmental conditions in which work is performed.
- Typical work schedule, including overtime requirements.
- Job factors that produce fatigue.

9. Education, Training, Experience, and Personal Requirements
   - Minimum level of education needed.
   - Specialized courses required.
   - Licenses or certifications required.
   - Minimum level of experience required.
   - Types of jobs in which required experience is usually gained.
   - Personal requirements needed, such as oral or written communication skills, and mathematical or mechanical aptitude.
   - Other qualifications, skills, or characteristics.

Certainly, job duties, responsibilities, essential functions, and marginal functions are crucial items that must be identified as far as compensation programs are concerned, but it is also important to identify job qualifications as well as the relationships and contexts in which the job is performed.

TRADITIONAL JOB ANALYSIS METHODS

Over the years four traditional methods of job analysis have evolved: (1) questionnaires, (2) interviews, (3) observation, and (4) some combination of the preceding methods. These approaches, despite their deficiencies, are still the ones most commonly used by organizations.

Questionnaires

One of the simplest and quickest ways to collect a substantial amount of data on many jobs simultaneously is to administer a structured questionnaire to employees. Questionnaires are also the most economical data-collection method. With this approach each employee in a job—or if there are many employees performing the same job, a representative sample of employees— is given a questionnaire and instructed to provide certain kinds of information about his or her job. While the specific types of data requested depend upon how the organization plans to use the job analysis information, the worker is typically asked to elaborate on the kinds of things shown in the list of job information collected.

Administering a job analysis questionnaire to employees is done in one of three ways: (1) The job analyst meets with all employees of a work unit and explains how to complete the questionnaire; (2) the job analyst meets with work-unit supervisors to explain how to complete the instrument and the supervisors, in turn, explain it to their employees; or (3) the questionnaire is distributed with an accompanying memorandum that contains the instructions needed for completing it. From an effectiveness standpoint, the first approach would seem to be the best, since it offers the greatest opportunity to answer questions, provide clarification, and eliminate problems that may affect the quality or quantity of the information garnered by questionnaires. Once the employee completes the questionnaire, it is usually reviewed by his or her supervisor for completeness and accuracy, and then returned to the job analyst.

Designing a questionnaire that will produce the data needed for a thorough analysis of jobs is not an easy matter. The types of information needed, how the information will be used, and other factors must be considered before a sound instrument can be constructed. In many instances one questionnaire cannot be used for all the jobs in an organization; several may be required. It may be necessary, for example, to design one questionnaire for production workers, another for clerical employees, and another for technical personnel.

Obviously, the questionnaire approach to job analysis has some disadvantages: (1) It may interfere with normal work routine, since employees will typically complete it during working hours; (2) it may produce inaccurate information due to the tendency of employees to overstate the importance of their jobs; (3) it may generate insufficient data if employees completing the instrument are not verbally facile; (4) it may be viewed by some employees as an imposition or interference with their normal work; and (5) it may, if used on a large number of jobs at once, produce a mass of data for a job analyst to examine, interpret, synthesize, and report in meaningful fashion.[7] Nevertheless, the questionnaire remains the most widely used job analysis method.

Interviews

The second traditional method of conducting job analysis is to interview employees performing the work. When this method is used, a structured interview guide is utilized so that the same questions are asked of each job incumbent and the same areas are covered in every interview conducted. Such a guide is especially critical when several individuals will be doing the interviewing. In effect, the interview method is much like the questionnaire approach except that the information is given to the analyst orally instead of in writing.

Job analysis interviews may be conducted in several different ways. They may be held with an individual employee, a group of employees performing the same job, the supervisor of a section or department, the individual employee and then the supervisor, or a group of employees and then the supervisor.[8] The most common procedure is to interview the job incumbent individually and then verify the information received by interviewing the worker's supervisor.

Interviews can be a very effective means of collecting job analysis information because most workers enjoy talking about their jobs. A skillful interviewer can often probe a job in much greater depth than could ever be achieved through a questionnaire.

Interviews have certain limitations: (1) They are time consuming and therefore more expensive than questionnaires; (2) the quality of the information gathered is highly dependent upon the interviewer's skill; (3) they are often disruptive to the work routine because they take employees away from their assigned tasks; (4) they may be viewed as threatening by employees; and (5) even though the interviewer may be highly skilled, the quality and quantity of information obtained may suffer if the employee is not orally expressive.[9] Still, in most instances the information provided by interviews may be far superior to what can be collected by questionnaires.

Observation

Job analysis can also be conducted by observing employees as they perform their jobs. The analyst simply watches the worker and records information about the various tasks being performed and the kinds of skills used to perform them. In order not to miss infrequent or irregular tasks, it may be necessary to observe many work cycles over an extended period of time.

The biggest advantages of observation are that the analyst can see first-hand the conditions under which the work is performed, note the level of complexity or difficulty involved, and gain greater insight into the job than might be possible through other methods. On the other hand, relying solely upon observation as a job analysis method has serious drawbacks: (1) Observation requires a highly trained individual who can recognize task difficulties and variations of skill requirements; (2) many jobs are largely mental rather than physical and there is not really much to observe; (3) it is easy to overlook infrequently performed job duties that require greater skill and effort than those performed on a daily basis; (4) observation can be very time consuming and thus expensive; (5) observation can be threatening to employees; and (6) observation may disrupt normal work routine, not only for the worker being observed but also for others in the work unit who are uncomfortable with an outside observer in their midst.

Certainly, there is a place for observation in the collecting of job analysis information, but its place is secondary rather than primary.

Combination

Of all the traditional approaches to job analysis, a combination method is probably the best because it minimizes the disadvantages and maximizes the advantages of any one approach used by itself. Of the possible combination approaches, the two used most often are (1) questionnaires and interviews, and (2) questionnaires, interviews, and observations.

As indicated earlier, one of the advantages of the questionnaire is that it produces a great deal of data rather quickly. But the job analyst often encounters difficulty in analyzing or interpreting questionnaire data. Employees may use jargon, shoptalk, or technical terms that mean little to the analyst. In addition, employees may provide very sketchy information that has little or no value to an outsider. Interviews conducted with the employee's completed questionnaire in hand give the analyst an opportunity to seek clarification or obtain additional job information.

The interview itself can be conducted more expeditiously when workers have already supplied written material because the analyst does not have to cover every aspect of each job, but only those parts where additional explanation is needed. Interview time is likely to be 50-percent less when the discussion with the worker is conducted from a completed job analysis questionnaire.[10]

A job analysis that combines questionnaires, interviews, and observation of the job and physical environment collects the most complete information. Observation often reveals factors about a job that are not uncovered through questionnaires or interviews; for example, poor lighting, an inefficiently designed work station, excessive or irritating noise, or unusual physical motions required for task performance, items that may affect the subsequent evaluation and compensation of a job. Utilizing questionnaires, interviews, and observations provides the advantage of seeing a job from different perspectives; consequently, the information obtained in this fashion not only tends to be more complete, but also more valid for compensation purposes.

THE PRODUCTS OF JOB ANALYSIS

Two major written products result from job analysis: a job description and a job specification. The job description delineates duties, responsibilities, essential functions, and marginal functions; the job specification sets forth the human skills and qualifications needed to be able to perform a specific job. In actual practice job specifications are commonly included as a section in the description itself. However, it is beneficial from a conceptual viewpoint to envision these two end products as separate items that serve different purposes. By doing so, greater emphasis is placed on describing the job and accurately specifying the skills required for job performance.

Job descriptions and job specifications are crucial to compensation programs. Job descriptions and job specifications establish the factual basis for determining rates of pay and establishing performance standards, and for delineating career paths or progression ladders.

Job Descriptions

Writing a good job description is not a simple matter. A job description must be specific, concise, complete, accurate, meaningful, and readable.[11] Whoever writes the description—job analyst, manager, or supervisor—must have an understanding of the content needed for job evaluation and compensation purposes, the manner in which the information is to be presented, and effective writing techniques.

Content

The specific content of a job description varies from organization to organization depending upon the uses to be made of the description, the format selected, and the nature of the job being described. Despite content differences, three requisites must be satisfied: job identification, job definition, and job delineation.

Job identification consists of information that differentiates one job from another. Commonly used identifiers include job title, departmental location of the job, specific unit to which the job is assigned, exempt or nonexempt status, and title of the position to which the job reports. In large organizations additional identifiers may also be used; for example, job number, labor grade or job class, and number of job incumbents.

Careful thought should go into selecting a job title, since it is the primary job identifier. The title chosen should reflect as clearly as possible the nature of the work performed, be distinct enough to differentiate the job from other similar jobs, and be consistent with other titles used in the organization. Job titles, unfortunately, are often misleading. An executive secretary in one organization may be little more than a highly paid keyboardist, while a job with the same title in another organization may identify an incumbent who is an administrative assistant to a chief executive officer and does little or no keyboarding. As mentioned earlier, the *Dictionary of Occupational Titles* published by the U.S. Department of Labor can be of invaluable assistance in standardizing job titles. This book contains approximately 25,000 standardized job titles, as well as job descriptions. Each job title includes a numeric code that categorizes a job by different dimensions, such as major job category, subsection of the major category, the job's relationship to data, people, and things, and an alphabetical listing within the job category.[12] Wherever possible, an organization should use the titles and codes contained in the *Dictionary of Occupational Titles*.

Job definition is usually accomplished by means of a summary of the job that sets forth the purpose or nature of the job, why it exists, and how it relates to other organizational jobs. A good job summary provides, in two to four sentences usually, a succinct statement of the job's function, and assists in differentiating it from other jobs in the organization.

Job delineation is the actual heart of the job description; it is the section of the job description in which duties, responsibilities, essential functions, marginal functions, reporting relationships, and other tasks or functions are enumerated. It is, obviously, the longest part of the overall description. Sufficiently detailed information must be provided about actual job duties, but the temptation to be verbose or pompous must be vigorously resisted. The job should be described so that duties, responsibilities, essential functions, and marginal functions can be clearly understood by users of the job description.

Format

There is no universal job description format; nevertheless, the three requisites for job content—job identification, job definition, and job delineation—provide a reasonable indication of the basic format that should be followed. Variations in job description format are most frequently found in the job delineation portion. Duties, responsibilities, and functions are often subdivided into several sections to provide clarity and call attention to important job factors: financial responsibility, decision-making authority, controls over work, and interactions with others, for example. This is a sound practice because it not only clarifies duties, responsibilities, and functions, but also improves the readability of the job description.

Whatever format is used should be consistent from job to job for each particular group of jobs; for instance, all production jobs should be described according to the same format, and all managerial jobs should be described according to the same format. In addition, the format used should parallel the use for which the description is intended. Where the job description is to be used as the basis for job evaluation, each compensable factor in the job evaluation plan must be clearly addressed in the job description. Where the job description is to be used as a basis for performance evaluation, each performance factor must be indicated.

Writing Techniques

Many job descriptions used in contemporary organizations are poorly written; they are excessively wordy, imprecise, or difficult to read. A job description should be an action-oriented document that states precisely, concisely, and clearly the duties performed and responsibilities carried out in a particular job. Careful attention to clarity of expression is absolutely essential. The following guidelines should be observed when writing a job description:

- Start each duty or responsibility statement with an action verb, such as "analyze," "calculate," "compute," "file," "issue," "prepare," "reconcile," "sort," "tabulate," or "transmit." Words of this kind identify what is actually done in a job (see Figure 4.1 for a list of suggested action words to use in job descriptions).
- Avoid imprecise terminology. Words such as "handles," "coordinates," or "deals with" are vague and open to different interpretations by different readers.
- Avoid shoptalk, jargon, or acronyms wherever possible because they are confusing to people who are not intimately familiar with the job.
- Use short, easy-to-read sentences.

Figure 4.1
Selected Action Words for Job Descriptions

Accomplish	Contact	Help	Prescribe
Accumulate	Contribute	Identify	Prevent
Acknowledge	Control	Implement	Process
Acquire	Convert	Import	Procure
Adjust	Convert	Improve	Promote
Advise	Correct	Inform	Provide
Affix	Correlate	Initiate	Purchase
Allot	Correspond	Innovate	Quantify
Alter	Create	Insert	Question
Amend	Decide	Inspect	Rate
Analyze	Delegate	Integrate	Read
Answer	Delete	Interpolate	Receive
Answer	Deliver	Interpret	Recommend
Apply	Describe	Interview	Reconcile
Appraise	Design	Investigate	Record
Approve	Determine	Issue	Refer
Approve	Develop	Itemize	Register
Approve	Devise	Join	Regulate
Arrange	Dictate	Justify	Reject
Assemble	Dispatch	Lead	Relate
Assist	Display	List	Release
Assure	Disseminate	List	Remit
Attach	Distribute	Locate	Remove
Attend	Divide	Maintain	Report
Authorize	Edit	Make	Request
Balance	Elaborate	Manage	Require
Batch	Eliminate	Match	Rescind
Budget	Employ	Measure	Research
Build	Encourage	Merge	Revise
Calculate	Endorse	Modify	Route
Cancel	Enforce	Monitor	Scan
Check	Engage	Move	Schedule
Clarify	Establish	Negotiate	Search
Classify	Estimate	Notify	Secure
Close	Examine	Nullify	Select
Collate	Exchange	Observe	Sell
Collect	Exclude	Obtain	Show
Communicate	Execute	Occupy	Solve
Compare	Expedite	Operate	Sort
Compile	Extend	Organize	Specify
Comply	Extract	Originate	Standardize
Compose	Extract	Outline	Summarize
Compute	Facilitate	Participate	Tabulate
Concentrate	File	Perform	Terminate
Condense	Formulate	Permit	Transcribe
Conduct	Furnish	Persuade	Transmit
Confirm	Gather	Place	Update
Consolidate	Generate	Post	Verify
Construct	Give	Predict	Weigh
Consult	Guide	Prepare	Write

- Use a style that specifies *who* does *what*, *when* it is done, *why* it is done, *where* it is done, and *how* it is done.
- Be detailed, but not wordy. Verbiage not only tends to confuse, but may also imply a degree of complexity that does not exist in a job.
- Use an outline form. With the exception of the job summary, which is normally in paragraph form, a job description is not a narrative. Each job duty, responsibility, or function-identification statement should make a specific point.
- Enumerate each duty and responsibility in the general order of its overall importance to the job.
- Accurately differentiate essential functions from marginal functions.
- Keep the user in mind. In compensation the users of job descriptions are likely to be managers from different areas of the organization (the job evaluation committee) who are not familiar with the job that is being described. Select words and make statements they will understand.

Figure 4.2 presents a job description that follows the preceding guidelines. While the job described is one that is not specific to any organization, the same style and format can be used for almost any job.

Job Specifications

Job specifications outline the minimum qualifications, such as education, experience, or skills, a person should possess to perform a job satisfactorily. Job specifications should always reflect the minimum rather than the ideal qualifications for a particular job. In many instances there is probably a tendency for organizations to overstate qualifications. Because the information on job qualifications is usually gathered from supervisors or employees, organizations often overstate qualifications. Supervisors may describe the ideal candidate while employees may describe their own skills. Several problems can result if specifications are inflated. First, if specifications are set so high that they systematically eliminate minorities, women, individuals with disabilities, or other protected class members from consideration for jobs, the organization runs the risk of discrimination charges. Second, compensation costs will increase because ideal candidates expect to be compensated more than candidates with minimum skills. Third, job vacancies will be harder to fill because ideal candidates are more difficult to find than minimally qualified candidates.

Ascertaining the appropriate qualifications for a job is undoubtedly the most difficult part of job analysis. It requires a great deal of probing on the part of the job analyst as well as a broad understanding of the skills needed to perform varieties of work. Because of the problems associated with job specifications, it is preferable for an organization to underspecify rather than to overspecify qualifications.

Figure 4.2
Job Description

Human Resource Management Systems
Job Description

Position Title: Administrative Assistant   **Reports To:** Manager
Department: Operations   **Date Prepared:** January 10, 2000
FLSA Status: Non-Exempt   **Job Code:** HRMS-OP-AA-01

Purpose of Position: Provides standard assistance as information provider, gathering data, and performing data entry.

Essential Functions:

1) Acts as receptionist. Greets, assists, provides information, and interviews visitors to ensure effective flow of information and activity. Opens and routes incoming mail. Answers correspondence. Prepares outgoing mail.

2) Maintains inventory control and security. Maintains files. Retrieves information as requested. Answers questions in person or over the telephone. Proofs correspondence and reports. Copies and compiles data for records and reports. Prepares department reports for use as scheduled.

3) Operates office machines such as typewriter, adding machine, media machines, calculator, and copy machines. Operates computer terminal to input and retrieve data. Instructs others in using office equipment. Provides simple preventive maintenance of office equipment. Determines needs and makes recommendations for maintenance, repairs, and furnishings. Records information for service, purchase, or use to ensure accuracy. Engages in follow-up activities by telephone or correspondence to evaluate, finalize, and verify user satisfaction. Ensures efficient equipment operation.

4) Maintains file to ensure retention, freedom from errors, and easy access. Files records and reports, posts information to records, sorts and distributes information, etc. Verifies accuracy of material to be filed. Searches for and investigates information contained in files, inserts additional data on file records, completes reports, keeps files current, and supplies information from file data or removes files upon request. Keeps records of material removed, stamps material received, traces missing files, and types indexing information on folders.

5) Directs activity and provides supervision during absence of supervisor. Provides training and general direction for temporary staff in work procedures. Prepares work schedules, expedites workflow, issues written and oral instructions, and examines work to assure exactness, neatness, and conformance to policies and procedures.

6) Assists in analyzing financial information. Assists with the preparation of reports by detailing assets, liabilities, balance sheet preparation, profit and loss statements to summarize current and projected financial position. Receives funds, disburses funds, and records monetary transactions. Compiles collection, disbursements, bank reconciliation reports, withdraws cash from bank accounts, and retains custody of cash fund.

7) May temporarily perform other duties, as required, to maintain operations and services.

Marginal Functions:
Marginal Functions will vary with the specific assignment and depend on the particular unit or function for which the person is responsible. Consideration will be given on a case by case basis and reassignment of marginal duties will be made when appropriate.

Figure 4.3 shows the specifications for the position of administrator, human resources, as described in the earlier list of information collected in a job analysis.

OTHER JOB ANALYSIS METHODS

Although the majority of organizations in the United States use the traditional approaches to job analysis described in this chapter, there have been attempts to develop more systematic, standardized approaches to improve the quality and consistency of job analysis information. Three of these approaches—the Position Analysis Questionnaire (PAQ), the Job Analysis

Figure 4.3
Job Specification

Human Resource Management Systems
Job Specification

Position Title: Administrative Assistant
Department: Operations
FLSA Status: Non-Exempt

Reports To: Manager
Date Prepared: January 10, 2000
Job Code: HRMS-OP-AA-01

Knowledge, Skill, Abilities, and Other Requirements:
High school diploma or equivalent required and a minimum of 2 to 3 years general office working experience. Strong computer skills in WordPerfect or Windows helpful. Good communication skills, both written and oral, and organization skills essential.
- **Normal Ambulatory Requirements:** Ability to move in and around personal work space and to and from other areas of the office or building to attend meetings, deliver or retrieve materials, conduct interviews, or other activities outside of personal work space.
- **Normal Cognitive Requirements:** Ability to learn, remember, and integrate rules, policies, or practices guiding the performance of an activity.
- **Normal Speech/Communication Requirements:** Ability to communicate verbally with supervisors, coworkers, and customers to gather information and/or explain procedures.
- **Normal Written Communications Requirements:** Ability to continually record information such as draft correspondence/reports/documents/policies/procedures, conduct interviews recording information, prepare case narratives, or prepare other lengthy documents using handwritten or mechanical means.
- **Normal or Corrected Reading Vision Required:** Ability to read with attention to details.
- **Normal or Corrected Hearing Required:** Ability to hear and understand speech to interact with coworkers/supervisor/customers on a routine or frequent basis with the use of amplifying equipment/hearing aids.

Supervision of Personnel:
None

Physical/Mental/Environment:
- **Physical Demands:** Normal sitting, standing, walking, and carrying.
- **Environment/Hazard Demands:** Pleasant working conditions.
- **Travel Demands:** Moderate travel requirements, such as out-of-town meetings or training sessions.
- **Lifting Demands:** May lift office equipment and supplies on occasion.

Schedule (JAS), and Functional Job Analysis (FJA)—are described in this section. While other new approaches have also been developed, PAQ, JAS, and FJA are the most widely recognized and frequently used nontraditional job analysis methods.

Position Analysis Questionnaire

The PAQ was developed at Purdue University. It is the result of more than ten years of research by psychologists who studied thousands of jobs.[13] The PAQ is a structured job analysis questionnaire that uses a checklist approach to identify job elements. There are 194 job descriptors that relate to job-oriented or worker-oriented elements. Proponents of the PAQ believe that the ability of the checklist to identify job elements, behaviors required of job incumbents, and other job characteristics makes it possible to use this procedure for virtually any type of job.[14]

The 194 job elements used in the PAQ are grouped into twenty-seven division job dimensions and five overall job dimensions. These thirty-two dimensions are further divided into six major job activities: information input, mental process, work output, relationships with other persons, job context, and other job characteristics. Each job descriptor is evaluated on a specified scale, such as "extent of use," "importance of job," "possibility of occurrence," and "applicability."

Computer scoring allows each job studied to be analyzed very quickly relative to the thirty-two different job dimensions. The score derived represents a profile of the job that can be compared with standard profiles to group the job into known job families; that is, jobs of a similar nature. In essence, the PAQ identifies significant job behaviors and classifies jobs. Using the PAQ, job descriptions can be prepared based on the relative importance and emphasis given to various job elements.

The PAQ is completed by an employee or employees familiar with the job being studied, typically an experienced job incumbent or the immediate supervisor. Job analysts then prepare the profiles and job descriptions. As can be deduced from this brief description, the PAQ is a comprehensive, complex form of job analysis that requires an individual trained in its use if it is to produce the desired results.

Department of Labor Job Analysis Schedule

For many years the U.S. Department of Labor has worked on the development and refinement of a systematic means of analyzing and classifying job content: the Job Analysis Schedule.[15] Many federal, state, and local government agencies as well as private enterprises use this approach or some variation of it. The JAS is an instrument for gathering data on five categories that can be used to define satisfactory job performance: worker functions; work fields; machines, tools, equipment, and work aids; materials, products, subject matter, and services; and worker traits.

Worker functions describe what workers do in the performance of a job with data, people, and things. The JAS includes a scale of values that ranks the complexity of worker functions. The twenty-four identifying activities for the three worker function areas are shown in Figure 4.4. The highest combination of the three areas establishes the relative importance of the job. Normally, reading down a column, each successive function includes each lower function. For example, in the column "Data," if the highest activity identified is compiling, it is assumed that the job also requires computing, copying, and comparing. Note that the numerical values assigned to the functions are the reverse of what might be expected in a typical value scale. With the JAS, the lower the numerical value, the higher the level of activity.

The work fields, which are classified into ninety-nine different categories, describe the mechanical, technological, or socioeconomic requirements of the job. The category of machines, tools, equipment, and work aids identifies the instruments and devices of a mechanical nature that are used to carry out the job. The category of materials, products, subject matter, and services describe the type or kind of materials worked on, the end products, the knowledge required to be used in performing the job, and the nature of the services rendered. Worker traits are primarily concerned with job specifications. They are divided into five components: training time, aptitude, temperament, interests, and physical demands. Obviously, effective use of the JAS requires a highly trained and skilled job analyst.

Figure 4.4
Job Analysis Schedule Worker Functions

Data	People	Things
0 Synthesizing	0 Mentoring	0 Setting up
1 Coordinating	1 Negotiating	1 Precision Working
2 Analyzing	2 Instructing	2 Operating–Controlling
3 Compiling	3 Supervising	3 Driving–Operating
4 Computing	4 Diverting	4 Manipulating
5 Copying	5 Persuading	5 Tending
6 Comparing	6 Speaking–Signaling	6 Feeding–Offbearing
	7 Serving	7 Handling
	8 Taking Instruction and Helping	

Functional Job Analysis

This approach to job analysis, a modification of the JAS, is a comprehensive approach that concentrates on the interactions among the work, the worker, and the work organization.[16] Functional Job Analysis is a worker-oriented approach to job analysis that identifies what a worker actually does rather than what the worker is responsible for.

FJA utilizes a modified version of the worker-functions scales contained in the job analysis schedule. In fact, the two scales are almost identical, except that FJA adds "no significant relationship" to the data, people, and things categories of worker functions and reverses the numerical coding.

The basic premises and fundamental elements of FJA are as follows:

1. A distinction is made between what gets done and what a worker must do to get it done. As far as job analysis is concerned, it is probably more important to know the latter. For example, an airline pilot does not fly passengers; he or she performs a multitude of tasks to take an airplane from one location to another.

2. What a worker does in a job is related to only three basic elements: data, people, and things. These are, in fact, the materials as well as the results of all work that is performed in any organization.

3. In relation to data, people, and things, workers function in unique ways. In essence, data draw on mental resources; people draw on interpersonal resources; and things draw on physical resources.

4. Every job requires that a worker relate to data, people, and things.

5. Although worker behavior or task performance can be described in an almost infinite number of ways, there are only a few definite and identifiable functions connected with data, people, and things. These basics are those shown in Figure 4.4.

6. The functions performed by workers proceed from the simplest to the most complex. For instance, the least complex form of people would be serving, while the most complex would be monitoring. Consequently, if an upper-level function is required, all of the lower-level functions are also required.

7. The three hierarchies for data, people, and things provide two measures for a job: level and orientation. Level is a measure of complexity in relation to data, people, and things. Orientation is a measure of involvement with data, people, and things.[17]

Proponents of FJA claim that, in addition to being a useful means of analyzing jobs, it also establishes criteria that can be used to evaluate the worth of a job (set compensation rates) and appraise the performance of workers in each job. As with the other newer approaches to job analysis, FJA is more complex than traditional methods and requires a well-trained job analyst.

NOTES

1. Donald L. Caruth and Gail D. Handlogten, *Staffing the Contemporary Organization*, 2d ed. (Westport, Conn.: Quorum Books, 1997), 102.

2. Donald L. Caruth, *Compensation Management for Banks* (Boston: Bankers Publishing, 1986), 37.

3. U.S. Department of Labor, *Dictionary of Occupational Titles*, 4th ed. (Washington, D.C.: U.S. Government Printing Office, 1991).

4. Caruth and Handlogten, *Staffing*, 104–105.

5. Joan Ackerstein, *The Americans with Disabilities Act: What Supervisors Need to Know* (Burr Ridge, Ill.: Business One Irwin/Mirror Press, 1994), 22.

6. Caruth, *Compensation Management*, 256–262.

7. Ibid., 40.

8. Ibid.

9. Ibid., 41.

10. Ibid., 43.

11. Ibid., 44.

12. U.S. Department of Labor, *Dictionary*.

13. Ernest J. McCormick, Paul R. Jeanneret, and Robert Mecham, "A Study of Job Characteristics and Job Dimensions as Based on the Position Analysis Questionnaire (PAQ)," *Journal of Applied Psychology* (August 1972): 347–368.

14. Joseph Tiffin and Ernest J. McCormick, *Industrial Psychology*, 6th ed. (Englewood Cliffs, N.J.: Prentice Hall, 1974), 53.

15. U.S. Department of Labor, Manpower Administration, *Handbook for Analyzing Jobs* (Washington, D.C.: U.S. Government Printing Office, 1972).

16. Caruth and Handlogten, *Staffing*, 118.

17. Ernest J. McCormick, "Job Information: Its Development and Application," in *Staffing Policies and Strategies*, ed. Dale Yoder and Herbert S. Heneman (Washington, D.C.: Bureau of National Affairs, 1974), 458.

5

JOB EVALUATION: NONQUANTITATIVE TECHNIQUES

Job evaluation is a systematic procedure for determining the worth of a job within an organization relative to all other jobs in that organization. Its basic purpose is to establish a system of relationships between jobs that recognizes their similarities, differences, and organizational contributions. Job evaluation creates a hierarchy of jobs and establishes an internally equitable structure of jobs that reflects their value to the institution.[1] It provides, as a result, an objective basis for attaching monetary rates to jobs.

The focus of job evaluation is essentially an internal one. It is not ordinarily concerned with how jobs are valued in the labor market. Job evaluation is primarily concerned with determining the relative worth of jobs within the confines of a particular organization. The process of job evaluation may involve a simple comparison of one job to another or it may entail the comparison of a job to a set of predetermined criteria. Regardless of the specific approach used, job evaluation replaces totally subjective judgments of job value with reasonably objective assessments of job worth.

There are four traditional approaches to job evaluation: ranking, classification, the point method, and factor comparison. Ranking, the simplest of the four methods, involves taking all of the jobs in an organization and arranging them in rank order of their importance, from the most important job to the least important job. Classification creates a number of job grades or classes—

similar to a series of pigeonholes—and assigns each job to one of these pre-determined classes. The point method defines the key factors in all jobs and assigns point values to different degrees of every factor; each job is then compared with the factors and points are assigned to the job based on the degrees of each factor used in the job. Factor comparison defines key job factors and then compares a job with other jobs one factor at a time. In addition to these approaches, other proprietary methods have been developed by consultants and are used in a number of contemporary organizations.

Ranking and classification are usually referred to as nonquantitative techniques since no attempt is made to establish specific quantitative differentials between the values of jobs. The point method and factor comparison are normally described as quantitative methods because they provide quantitative expressions that differentiate the value of a job from other jobs.

CONSIDERATIONS IN SELECTING A METHOD

All job evaluation approaches have the same objective: an accurate assessment of a job's worth. Some methods go about it in very simple ways, while other methods employ complex procedures. Studies, however, have shown that there is a fairly high degree of correlation between the results produced by different job evaluation schemes. In other words, different methods generally tend to produce similar results.[2] Since there is a commonality in the end results generated by the various methods of job evaluation, an organization should carefully examine its own situation and compensation program goals to select a specific approach to job evaluation that is appropriate for what it wants to accomplish. Among the factors that an organization should consider and weigh carefully are cost, installation time, longevity, ease of application, and acceptance by managers and employees.[3]

Cost

One of the primary considerations in selecting a job evaluation method, especially in small organizations, is cost. What kind of expenditure will a particular approach involve? Unfortunately, there are little data available that address the comparative costs of different job evaluation methods. There are costs associated with designing the system (if a proprietary plan is not used), implementing it, and administering it. Consulting fees may be required if an organization deems it advisable to use outside assistance or chooses a proprietary method. In implementing the program there is a considerable investment of management and employee time; while these are not out-of-pocket expenses, they do represent a sizeable investment in job evaluation. The question, then, is how much an organization wants to spend or how much it can afford to spend on job evaluation. It is possible to make a generalization about job evaluation costs: The more complex a plan is, the more it will cost. Complex approaches to job evaluation, such as the point method or factor comparison, entail greater expenditures for design and implementation; simpler approaches, such as ranking and classification, involve lower design and implementation expenditures. The willingness or the ability of a firm to spend money for a job evaluation plan is, consequently, a major consideration in choosing a particular approach.

Installation Time

A second consideration in the selection of a job evaluation method is installation time. How long will it take to design and implement a particular approach? There is no hard and fast answer to this question. A number of variables influence installation time: size of the firm, number of jobs to be covered, availability of managers and supervisors to participate in the job evaluation process, amount of training required for the evaluators, and size of the compensation staff devoted to the effort. Another generalization can be made relative to installation time: The simpler the approach, the faster it can be installed. Where rapid installation is a major concern for an organization, ranking may well be the best approach, since it requires little in the way of design or training time. The point method and factor comparison—more complex approaches to job evaluation—require considerably more design and training time.

Longevity

Another consideration in the selection of a specific job evaluation approach is the expected life of the plan. How long can the system be expected to remain viable and serve the needs of the institution? Will it be a permanent approach or will it outlive its usefulness in a relatively short period of time? The usefulness of ranking, for example, deteriorates as an organization grows and the number of jobs increases. Ranking tends to become cumbersome and inconsistently applied in the long run. Seldom is it a permanent solution to a firm's job evaluation needs; at best it is a stopgap measure with a short life span. Classification, point, and factor comparison methods are all designed to accommodate increases in the number of organizational jobs as well as changes that may occur in the contents of specific jobs; thus, their longevity is much greater than the simple ranking approach. Because of these differences in longevity among the plans, an organization should examine its anticipated growth in jobs prior to deciding on a specific job evaluation technique. One of the authors once installed a job evaluation point that, with periodic modifications, was used by an organization for eighteen years.

Ease of Application

The degree of ease with which a job evaluation plan can be applied to a company's jobs is also a factor that needs to be weighed when choosing a job evaluation system. Ranking is probably the easiest method to apply in small institutions, but is much more difficult to use in a larger organizations. Factor comparison, a much more complex approach, tends to be difficult to use in any institution, regardless of size. Classification is possibly the second easiest method to apply. Application of the point method is less complex than factor comparison but more difficult than classification; it is the third easiest method to apply. Ease of application, however, must be weighed against other selection criteria, since it cannot be assumed that the most easily applied plan will of necessity be the best plan to use in a particular institution.

Acceptance

In many instances a major factor in the selection of a job evaluation technique is degree of acceptance of the technique by those who will use it, as well as by those who will be affected by its use. The easier a plan is to explain and the more objective it appears to be, the greater its acceptance will be, generally speaking.

Point plans are relatively easy to understand because they have the appearance of precision and objectivity. Point plans, consequently, enjoy a relatively high degree of acceptance by managers and employees. Factor comparison, on the other hand, is very difficult to explain; consequently, it tends not to be as readily accepted as the point method. Ranking, while easy to explain, often appears to be very subjective, a factor that hinders its acceptance by employees. Classification stands somewhere in the middle as far as acceptance is concerned; the approach is easy to explain, but some degree of subjectivity is inherent in the methodology. Any approach to job evaluation, however, will probably be accepted by an organization's personnel if the approach is sufficiently explained and is used consistently. A firm should always consider how its employees might react to a particular job evaluation approach; it should also consider the amount of communication required to explain a particular method and gain acceptance for its use.

Use of Job Evaluation Committees

Another issue that must be addressed before job evaluation begins is whether committees will be used in the evaluation process. If the organization does not have or is not planning to hire a job evaluation or compensation specialist, it will have to rely upon an evaluation committee. Where the organization has an in-house compensation specialist, it has a choice of how jobs will be evaluated: by the specialist or by a committee. In most instances, it is probably more advantageous to use a committee.[4]

Why use a job evaluation committee? First, job evaluation is not a simple matter. It is a decision-making process that benefits from the collective judgment of knowledgeable people throughout the organization. Second, job evaluation's impact on compensation expenditures specifically and human resource practices generally is too great for it to be entrusted to one or two specialists, no matter how extensive their expertise might be. Third, employee as well as managerial acceptance of the program is often enhanced by relying on nonspecialists to do the evaluations because nonspecialists are usually perceived by employees to be one of "us" and not one of "them." Use of a committee provides the benefit of collective judgment as well as the psychological advantage of being "home owned" and "home operated," so to speak.

Size and composition of the committee are very important. A typical committee is usually composed of five to seven members. If membership is less than five, the differing perspectives essential to sound collective decision making are not adequately represented. If membership is greater than seven, the committee tends to become somewhat unwieldy: There are too many divergent viewpoints, sessions take longer without corresponding improvements in results, and scheduling a convenient time when all members can be present becomes more difficult.

Ideally, the members of the committee should come from various areas of the organization. It may not be possible or practical to have every major area represented, but representation should be as broad based as possible.

If an organization has a job evaluation specialist or a human resource manager, that person would normally chair the committee but may or may not have a vote in the proceedings. The functions of the chairperson are to see that each job is evaluated fairly and to keep the meetings running smoothly; it is not his or her function to unduly influence committee members in their decisions about jobs. When the specialist is a voting member of the committee, his or her vote may sway other members. The results tend to be more objective when the specialist is precluded from directly influencing the final outcome. When there is no human resource person in the organization, as in the case of a very small company, the committee would select its own chairperson.

Job evaluation committee membership is normally assigned on a rotating basis, with no member serving longer than two years at a time. Rotation should be staggered so that the committee does not lose all of its experienced members at any one time. Assignment to the job evaluation committee is an important responsibility and it is essential that this importance be conveyed to each member.

Most of the committee's work will be during the implementation phase of job evaluation, when all of an organization's jobs have to be evaluated. Lengthy sessions are usually required. Committee members must expect to devote a great deal of time to the initial job evaluations. Later, the committee will only be required to meet when new jobs have to be evaluated or when there are requests for reevaluations of existing jobs.

Thorough training of committee members is imperative, especially at the outset of the evaluation process. Each member must understand the system being used and the procedures by which jobs are evaluated. Initial training may be provided in one of several ways: (1) by the job evaluation specialist, (2) by the human resource manager, (3) by a functional area manager assigned the responsibility of implementing job evaluation, or (4) by an outside consultant. Public seminars on job evaluation sponsored by training organizations or universities are also helpful in training evaluators. As original members rotate off the committee and new ones are added, training is normally accomplished in a one-on-one fashion, with the chairperson or human resource professional familiarizing the new member with the system and its mechanics.

THE RANKING METHOD

With some of the essential background considerations now out of the way, we can look at the specific approaches that can be used to evaluate jobs in an organization. In the remainder of this chapter we will examine job ranking and job classification.

Job ranking involves compiling a list of all of an organization's jobs in the order of their importance or value from highest to lowest.[5] In using this approach, evaluators are normally asked to keep the whole job in mind when making their assessments of a job's rank. Each evaluator makes his or her own independent judgments and the results are then averaged to produce a final ranking during a committee session.[6]

Let's look at an example to illustrate how ranking works. Assume that a small retail clothier has the following ten jobs to be ranked:

1. Cashier
2. Salesperson
3. General Accountant
4. Merchandise Stocker
5. Manager
6. Secretary
7. Accounts Payable/Receivable Accountant
8. Custodian
9. Alterations Specialist
10. Warehouse Attendant

Further imagine that a committee of five people has been selected to perform the evaluations. Each committee member, working from job descriptions of the ten jobs, would compile his or her own rankings of the jobs. When the entire committee meets, the rankings of the individual members would be presented, averaged, and a final ranking calculated. Table 5.1 shows how the ten jobs were ranked by each of the evaluators and the final results as determined by averaging.

Table 5.1
Job Ranking Results

| Job | Committee Member Evaluations | | | | | | Final |
	A	B	C	D	E	Average	Ranking
Custodian	9	9	10	10	10	9.6	10
Warehouse Attendant	10	10	9	9	9	9.4	9
Merchandise Stocker	8	8	8	7	8	7.8	8
Cashier	6	7	7	8	7	7.0	7
Salesperson	7	6	6	6	5	6.0	6
Alterations Specialist	5	4	5	5	6	5.0	5
Secretary	4	5	3	4	4	4.0	4
Accounts Payable/Receivable Accountant	3	2	4	3	3	3.0	3
General Accountant	2	3	2	2	2	2.2	2
Managers	1	1	1	1	1	1.0	1

Usually the evaluators arrive at their rankings by using a procedure known as *alternation*. With this procedure an evaluator decides which job is the most important and assigns it a 1. He or she then decides which job is the least important and assigns it the lowest ranking—in our example, a 10. The evaluator next selects the second most important and the second least important jobs and gives them a ranking of 2 and 9, respectively. This procedure is repeated two jobs at a time until all jobs have been assigned a rank.

Job rankings may also be determined in a more scientific or objective fashion by using a paired comparison matrix instead of the alternation method.[7] Table 5.2 shows a completed matrix for the same ten jobs. To use the matrix the evaluator compares each job listed on a row with each job shown in the columns. For example, the evaluator would compare the job of Cashier with Salesperson, General Accountant, Merchandise Stocker, and so forth. Next, the evaluator would compare Salesperson with Cashier, General Accountant, and so forth. If the job in the row is more important than the job in the column, the rater places a 1 in the box. If the job in the row is less important than the job in the column, the rater places a 0 in the box. After all jobs have been compared, the rows are totaled. The job receiving the highest score is the most important and the job receiving the lowest score is the least important, and so on.

Occasionally, two jobs will end up with the same ranking, which simply means that the raters were unable to distinguish one job from the other as far as overall importance is concerned. When this happens it is not necessary to force one of the jobs into a higher or lower rank. They should be left at the same rank for calculation purposes.

Advantages

As a means of job evaluation, there are several advantages to ranking.[8] The most prominent of these are the following:

- It is an inexpensive job evaluation method. There is little or no cost involved in designing a system.
- Ranking does not require the use of outside consultants or job evaluation specialists.
- Ranking can be installed very quickly. All that is needed as preliminary work is a good set of job descriptions for the evaluators to use.
- Ranking is easy to use. Evaluators do not have to be trained to any great extent.
- Because people have a natural tendency to rank jobs in an organization, ranking gives legitimacy to an already natural process.
- No specialized knowledge is required. Ranking can be implemented by operating managers whose area of expertise is not compensation or human resource management.
- Ranking is easy to explain to employees.
- Ranking is an improvement over a totally subjective approach to determining job worth.

Table 5.2
Paired Comparison Matrix

	Custd	Ware Att'd	Merch Stock	Cashier	Sales	Alter	Secretary	AP/AR	Gen Acct	Manager	Total	Ranking
Custodian	-	0	0	0	0	0	0	0	0	0	0	10
Warehouse Attendant	1	-	0	0	0	0	0	0	0	0	1	9
Merchandise Stocker	1	1	-	0	0	0	0	0	0	0	2	8
Cashier	1	1	1	-	0	0	0	0	0	0	3	7
Salesperson	1	1	1	1	-	0	0	0	0	0	4	6
Alterations Specialist	1	1	1	1	1	-	0	0	0	0	5	5
Secretary	1	1	1	1	1	1	-	0	0	0	6	4
AP/AR Accountant	1	1	1	1	1	1	1	-	0	0	7	3
General Accountant	1	1	1	1	1	1	1	1	-	0	8	2
Manager	1	1	1	1	1	1	1	1	1	-	9	1

- Ranking is well suited to small organizations with a limited number of jobs needing an inexpensive, fast, and uncomplicated means of determining the relative value of the organization's jobs.

Disadvantages

Ranking, however, is deficient in several ways as a job evaluation method.[9] The major shortcomings of this approach are as follows:

- There is a lack of data to justify the final results of ranking. Jobs are simply compared and then placed in the order of their apparent importance. Normally no back-up information is available to support how the ordering was actually determined.
- Ranking is somewhat inflexible. As new jobs are added to an organization or as existing jobs change, all jobs have to be reranked.
- Ranking is subject to bias on the part of the evaluator. Raters are often influenced by such factors as the personality or experience level of the incumbent jobholder. Also, the rate of pay currently assigned to the job tends to influence an evaluator's ranking of jobs.
- Because there are usually no factual data to support how the ranking was determined, employee acceptance of this approach may be low. Viewed from an employee's perspective, ranking appears to be very subjective. Moreover, results are difficult to explain objectively.
- Ranking provides no clear identification of differentials between jobs. Equal differentials are often assumed to exist between adjacently ranked jobs. In reality, the differentials between jobs are seldom equal.
- Ranking is very imprecise. At best, it is an approximation of how jobs compare with each other. It does not recognize subtle differences between jobs that may be important in a particular organization.
- Ranking is not easy to use if there are many jobs to be ranked. It works best when there are only a few jobs involved—roughly eight to twenty—and the differences between jobs are fairly easy to recognize. But with more than twenty jobs the laboriousness of ranking increases tremendously. The method becomes extremely cumbersome to use and the results become increasingly imprecise.

In short, ranking is an inexpensive and quick way for an organization with only a few jobs to implement a formal job evaluation program. The larger the organization, the less useful ranking is in determining the worth of jobs. Ranking is a usable approach—certainly it is better than no formal system at all—but it is not recommended for organizations that have more than twenty jobs or for smaller organizations that anticipate rapid growth in the number of jobs they have.

JOB CLASSIFICATION

This method of job evaluation involves slotting jobs into a number of groups or classes. Figuratively, it is akin to sorting items into a series of pigeonholes.

In this case, however, each pigeonhole is a niche that represents similar jobs. Unlike ranking, classification does not attempt to create a definite ordering that differentiates each job from every other job; rather, it seeks to differentiate a group of similar jobs from other groups of similar jobs.[10] In classification these groupings are known variously as pay grades, job grades, labor grades, job classes, or job levels.

The biggest single user of the job classification technique is the federal government. Its General Schedule classification system covers several million government workers employed in almost every field or occupation imaginable. State and local governments also rely extensively upon job classification to evaluate their jobs.

The heart of the classification system is the series of descriptions that define each class, job grade, or pigeonhole. These descriptions must be specific enough to address individual job content, but also general enough to cover a wide variety of jobs. The following are three job class descriptions from a typical classification system. Note the language used in these class descriptions. On the one hand it is precise enough to identify work details in specific jobs, but on the other hand it is general enough to fit jobs of all kinds:

Grade 1. Includes all classes of positions the duties of which are to be performed, under immediate supervision, with little or no latitude for the exercise of independent judgment, (1) the simplest routine work in office, business, or fiscal operations, or (2) elementary work of a subordinate technical character in a professional, scientific, or technical field.

Grade 5. Includes all classes of positions the duties of which are (1) to perform, under general supervision, difficult and responsible work in office, business, or fiscal administration, or comparable subordinate technical work in a professional, scientific, or technical field, requiring in either case, (A) considerable training and supervisory or other experience, (B) broad working knowledge of a special subject matter or of office laboratory, engineering, scientific, or other procedure and practice, and (C) the exercise of independent judgment in a limited field; (2) to perform, under immediate supervision, and with little opportunity for the exercise of independent judgment, simple and elementary work requiring professional, scientific, or technical training equivalent to that represented by graduation from a college or university of recognized standing but requiring little or no experience; or (3) to perform work of equal importance, difficulty, and responsibility, and requiring comparable qualifications.

Grade 9. Includes all classes of positions the duties of which are (1) to perform, Under general supervision, very difficult and responsible work along Special technical, supervisory, or administrative experience which has demonstrated capacity for sound independent work, (B) thorough and fundamental knowledge of a special and complex subject matter, or of the profession, art, or science involved, and (C) considerable latitude for the exercise of independent judgment; (2) with considerable latitude for the exercise of independent judgment, to perform difficult and responsible work, requiring (A) professional, scientific or technical training equivalent to that represented by graduation from a college or university of recognized standing, and (B) considerable additional professional, scientific, or technical training or experience which has demonstrated capacity for sound independent work; or (3) to perform other work of equal importance, difficulty, and responsibility, and requiring comparable qualifications.[11]

The biggest obstacle in using the classification method is writing the descriptions that define each job class.[12] This activity can only be accomplished by someone skilled in analyzing, recognizing, and defining those factors that finitely differentiate one group of jobs from another group of jobs. Consequently, the classification method of job evaluation is seldom used in business or industry because the time and expense involved in developing effective descriptions of job classes is enormous. The reason for classification's widespread use in government institutions is the ability of this approach to cover a broad range of jobs—manual, operative, clerical, technical, administrative, and managerial—within a single method of job evaluation.

When classification is used, the procedure for evaluating jobs is relatively simple once the descriptions of job classes have been developed. Each evaluator—in the public sector typically a specialist in job classification—reads the job description, compares it with appropriate job class definitions, and assigns the job to a particular job class or slot. If a committee is used, assignments to classes are compared and the job is slotted into the class favored by the majority of committee members.

A key question in developing a classification system is deciding how many classes or grades will be needed to cover all of the jobs that an organization might have. Since many government entities often use no more than twenty classes, it is reasonable to expect that any private-sector organization, even one of extremely large size, would require no more than eighteen and possibly fewer classes. Eight to twelve classes would appear to be adequate for the majority of companies. Fewer than eight classes would suggest that sufficient differentiation between jobs has not been determined. More than twelve suggests that artificial differentiations between jobs have been developed. The intent of the classification approach is not to create a multiplicity of classes that confuses the assignment of jobs to a particular grade, but to develop the minimum number of classes that will enable an organization to distinguish similar jobs from dissimilar jobs.

Advantages

Classification offers the following advantages as a method of job evaluation:[13]

- Inasmuch as managers and employees probably tend to classify jobs anyway, this approach adds a degree of formalization to what is a basic human tendency.
- Classification facilitates the establishment of lines of progression. The lines do not have to be identified from specific job to specific job, they need only be identified from class to class.

- Classification places jobs into classes as the jobs are evaluated. Other approaches, such as the point method and factor comparison, evaluate the jobs first and then for convenience group them into classes. Thus, classification saves a step in the development of a job structure.

- New jobs can be easily accommodated by a classification plan. They can be evaluated and slotted into the existing system readily. Also, jobs that change in content can be reclassified without difficulty.

- Classification plans can be designed so they cover all of an organization's jobs. Other approaches to job evaluation often utilize separate evaluation plans for different types of jobs: one plan for clerical jobs, one plan for production jobs, one plan for managerial jobs, and so on.

- Despite its operational simplicity, classification is still more objective than job ranking.

Disadvantages

An organization contemplating use of the job classification method should be aware of its limitations. The major limitations are as follows:[14]

- Writing class descriptions is a demanding task and should be undertaken only by someone who is a job analyst or compensation specialist. Even when done by professionals, developing class definitions may prove to be very difficult work.

- Classification suffers from an inherent potential for manipulation. Employees may use inflated language to describe their job duties in order to justify assignment of the job to a higher class. Where supervisors or managers actually write the job descriptions, there is an even greater potential for overstatement of job duties in language that is appropriate for a higher class. In other words, it is possible to "beat the system" if one is semantically proficient.

- With classification there is a lack of detailed supporting information to justify the evaluation of a job. The job is compared with a general class description, and if it seems to fit, it is assigned to the class. Data that clearly indicate why the job was placed in a certain grade are not available.

- Frequently, a job may overlap the descriptions of two classes. The question, which may be difficult to resolve objectively, is what class does the job belong in, the higher or the lower one? Operationally, this is one of the biggest difficulties in using a classification plan to evaluate jobs.

In essence, classification has the ability to cover a tremendous variety of jobs under one evaluation plan, but writing descriptions that adequately define classes is not an easy assignment to accomplish.

NOTES

1. Donald L. Caruth, *Compensation Management for Banks* (Boston: Bankers Publishing, 1986), 50.

2. Ibid., 51.

3. Ibid., 51–53.

4. Ibid., 54–55.

5. George T. Milkovich and Jerry M. Newman, *Compensation*, 6th ed. (Boston: Irwin–McGraw-Hill, 1999), 112.

6. Caruth, *Compensation Management*, 57.

7. Milkovich and Newman, *Compensation*, 113–114.

8. Caruth, *Compensation Management*, 57–59.

9. Ibid., 59–60.

10. Frederick S. Hills, Thomas J. Bergmann, and Vida G. Scarpello, *Compensation Decision Making*, 2d ed. (Fort Worth: Dryden Press, 1994).

11. Caruth, *Compensation Management*, 61.

12. Ibid., 61–62.

13. Ibid., 62–63.

14. Ibid., 63–64.

6

JOB EVALUATION: QUANTITATIVE TECHNIQUES

The ranking and classification approaches to job evaluation are frequently described as *whole job* methods in that they do not attempt to assess the importance of specific factors involved in job performance.[1] Rather, they consider the job in its entirety. Either of the whole job approaches, as a result, may ignore or minimize significant features of jobs. Ranking and classification can also be thought of as top-down or macro approaches to job evaluation.

The two methods of job evaluation examined in this chapter are normally referred to as *job factor* approaches because they identify and then evaluate jobs in terms of specific elements that comprise those jobs. The point method and factor comparison can be thought of as bottom-up or micro approaches to job evaluation.

The point method and factor comparison are also quantitative job evaluation techniques. Each of the two methods attaches numerical values to specific job components and the summation of these values provides a quantitative assessment of a job's relative worth. Either method provides greater precision in the job evaluation process than is possible with ranking or classification.

THE POINT METHOD

The most widely used approach to job evaluation in the private sector is the point method.[2] The popularity of this procedure results from the ease with which it can be understood and administered. However, unlike ranking, the development of an effective point plan is a complex process that usually requires the services of a compensation specialist.

Developing the Plan

The development of a point plan involves four steps:[3]

1. Selection of compensable factors.
2. Definition of each factor.
3. Definition of each degree of each factor.
4. Determination of the relative value of each factor and assignment of points.

Selection of Compensable Factors

Compensable factors are elements that describe and differentiate one job from another; they are those components of a job that an organization actually pays for when it compensates an employee.[4] Compensable factors may be determined through job analysis, committee decision, or examination of factors used by other organizations in their job evaluation plans. Regardless of how they are determined, compensable factors should be

- Job related; that is, they should accurately describe, reflect, and differentiate significant components of work performed in various jobs.
- Sufficient in number to permit distinction between degrees of each factor used in particular jobs.
- Clearly distinguishable from each other so that there is no overlap in meaning from one factor to another.
- To some degree in most, if not all, jobs to be covered by the plan.
- Acceptable to those who will use or be affected by the job evaluation plan.

Point plans generally use between four and ten compensable factors, with practically all plans including the essential four factors: education, experience, responsibility, and working conditions.[5]

The specific number of factors used is not normally a critical issue. There should be a sufficient number so that accurate distinctions can be made between jobs, but there should not be so many that overlapping between factors occurs. It has been found that having a large number of compensable factors does not improve the accuracy of job evaluation, but does increase the difficulty of using the system. Generally speaking, eight to twelve factors appear to be adequate for any point plan.

Definition of Factors

Once compensable factors have been selected, the next task is to define each factor. These definitions are very important because they form the basis for evaluating jobs. Definitions must be precise; they must be clear; they must have the same connotations for all evaluators. If not, evaluation errors will occur. The following are some typical factor definitions:

- *Education.* Formal education and training, or the equivalent, which a person must have as the necessary preparation for performing satisfactorily the duties of a job. Consider only the requirements of the jobs, not the person who may be performing it.

- *Experience.* The length of time typically required by a person to acquire the skill needed to perform satisfactorily the duties of the job. Where previous experience is necessary, time spent in related work or in lower positions, either within the organization or with other institutions, is considered as contributing to the total experience required to perform the jobs.

- *Job Complexity.* The difficulty of job duties. This is the amount of judgment required in making decisions, analyzing problems, planning activities, and determining courses of action. The extent to which initiative and creativity are required to perform the job.

- *Monetary Responsibility.* The responsibility for gain or loss to the company as a result of actions or decisions which affect the company from a cost standpoint. The loss may involve receipt of money, disbursement of funds, furniture and equipment, materials, labor, one's own time, the time of others, purchases, investments, and so forth.

Definition of Each Degree of Each Factor

The third step in the development of a point plan is to determine the number of degrees of each factor and write definitions for each degree of every factor. Each factor must be subdivided into several gradations so that the amount of the factor existing in a job can be judged accurately.[6] It is not necessary, or even desirable, for each factor to be divided into the same number of gradations or degrees. Some factors can be divided into as many as seven or eight degrees, while some factors may have only three or four degrees. Variations between degrees should be clearly discernible in order to facilitate recognition of differences by evaluators. As a rule, the less critical a factor is in terms of the total range of jobs to which it will be applied, the fewer degrees it will have.[7] Similarly, the more critical the factor, the more degrees it will have. In most office situations, for example, working conditions are not of great importance as a job factor; thus, there might be only three or four degrees for this factor. Experience, on the other hand, is usually crucial in most jobs; consequently, this factor is commonly divided into seven or eight gradations.

After the appropriate number of degrees for each factor have been determined, definitions of each degree are developed. The following are illustrative degree definitions for mental demands, a compensable factor used in many clerical and administrative job evaluation plans:

- *1st Degree.* Minor concentration required.
- *2nd Degree.* Some concentration required because of job content.
- *3rd Degree.* Concentration needed at all times. Job is subject to some distractions or interruptions.
- *4th Degree.* Close concentration and attention required. Job is subject to frequent distractions or interruptions.
- *5th Degree.* Intense concentration required because of technical or creative nature of the work. Job is subject to numerous distractions or interruptions. Frequent shifting from one task or project to another is required.

Determine Relative Value of Each Factor and Assign Points

Next, the relative weights of each factor and the specific values of each degree must be established. Factor weights are important because they reflect the organization's feelings about what it is paying for in a job.

While factor weights may be determined statistically, the most prevalent approach is to use the judgment of a committee. The committee reaches its decisions by proceeding through four steps. First, each member ranks the factors in order of importance and the total committee then agrees on a final ranking. Second, each member is asked to allocate 100 percent of value among the factors and the committee agrees on the assigned weights. Third, the committee decides on the total points to be used in the plan and points are assigned to each factor according to the previously determined weights. Fourth, each member distributes the factor points horizontally across the factor degree and the committee reaches accord on the distribution.[8] Figure 6.1 illustrates the steps used in this approach.

One of the problems in determining factor weights is that there are no magic formulas. Each organization must decide for itself how it will weight whatever factors it chooses to use in its job evaluation plan. Review of the plans of other firms, however, may be beneficial in providing a point of departure.[9]

Another problem in developing a point plan is deciding on the total number of points to be used. There are no standards in this area either. In practice, the total number of points used in a plan may vary from as low as 500 to as high as 2,000. This problem, fortunately, is not particularly critical. A high number of points provides a more recognizable differential between jobs than does a low number of points. Therefore, it seems advisable to use a sufficient number of points to provide adequate differentiation. As a rule of thumb, 1,500 points seems to work well for most plans.[10]

Figure 6.1
Assignment of Factor Weights

Step 1 Factor Ranking		
Compensable Factors	Rank	
Education	3	
Experience	1	
Responsibility	2	
Working Conditions	4	

Step 2 Factor Weighting	% Weight
Compensable Factors	20
Education	40
Experience	30
Responsibility	10
Working Conditions	100

Step 3 Point Allocation by Factor	Points
Compensable Factors	
Education	100
Experience	200
Responsibility	150
Working Conditions	50
	500

Step 4 Point Allocation by Degree	Degrees					Maximum
Compensable Factors	1	2	3	4	5	Points
Education	25	50	75	100	--	100
Experience	40	80	120	160	200	200
Responsibility	30	60	90	120	150	150
Working Conditions	10	15	30	50	--	50
						500

A final problem that must be addressed is that of allocating factor points to the various degrees of that factor. Once more, there are no hard and fast rules that apply in all cases. Arithmetic or geometric progressions are commonly used. In an arithmetic progression, point increases are in equal amounts from the lowest degree to the highest degree; for example, 25, 50, 75, 100. In a geometric progression, increases are in equal percentage amounts; for example, 10, 20, 40, 80. It is not unusual to find progressions that are neither arithmetic nor geometric. The specific approach used in assigning points to degrees is not overly crucial as long as it is one with which the organization feels comfortable.[11]

Evaluation Procedure

Once the complexities of developing the point plan are over and done with, the procedure for evaluating jobs is relatively simple. In fact, it is not greatly different from the method used in ranking or classification. If a committee is used to evaluate jobs, each evaluator, working independently, reads the job description, compares it with factor and degree definitions, and decides which degree of each factor best fits the job. When the committee meets, evaluations are compared and a consensus evaluation is generated. Because of the number of individual judgments that must be made on each job evaluated, it is helpful to use a worksheet such as the one shown in Figure 6.2. With the worksheet each evaluator simply circles the appropriate degree for every factor and totals the points assigned. The worksheet not only saves time but also provides documentation of the evaluation process.

When several jobs are being evaluated, as in the initial round of evaluations, there are two ways that evaluators can perform their assignments. First, an evaluator can compare each job with factor and degree definitions one job at a time. Second, an evaluator can compare each job with factor and degree definitions one factor at a time. In the first approach each job is evaluated individually before moving on to the next job. In the second approach each

Figure 6.2
Job Evaluation Worksheet

Job Title: _____

Department: _____

Factors	Degrees						
	1	2	3	4	5	6	7
1. Education	20	40	60	80	100	120	
2. Experience	35	70	105	140	180	225	275
3. Job Complexity	20	40	60	80	100	120	
4. Supervision Received	5	20	35	50			
5. Monetary Responsibility	25	50	75	100	125		
6. Contact With Others	25	50	75	100	125	150	
7. Confidential Data	5	20	35	50	65		
8. Mental Demands	10	20	30	40	50		
9. Working Conditions	5	15	25	35			
10. Supervisory Responsibility	0	25	50	75	100	125	

Total Points: _____

Evaluator: _____ Date: _____

job is evaluated simultaneously factor by factor. Compensation theorists maintain that the second method assures a more accurate evaluation because jobs are not only compared with factor and degree definitions, but also with each other. While it is difficult to argue with the theory of a factor-by-factor evaluation approach, the practicality of this method is another matter. Evaluating jobs factor by factor involves a great deal of paper shuffling as well as discipline—it is extremely difficult to think of a job in terms of only one factor. In practice it is much easier to accomplish evaluations job by job.

Advantages

The popularity of point plans, as attested to by their widespread use, would seem to suggest that this method of job evaluation has distinct advantages over other methods.[12] Some of the most prominent advantages are the following:

- Point plans are much more objective than either ranking or classification.
- Point plans are easy to use and understand.
- The numeric precision of a point plan leads to greater acceptance by managers and employees. Job evaluation results have the appearance of being exact.
- A point plan is flexible. It can be designed for application to a wide variety of jobs.
- Point plans have a fairly good life expectancy. They can accommodate changes in existing jobs or the addition of new jobs easily.
- A point plan analyzes job components rather than the overall job, thereby producing more accurate ratings than either ranking or classification, which look at the whole job.
- The rating scales used in a point plan tend to reduce evaluation errors and alleviate the influence of bias on the part of evaluators.
- Job classes can be developed readily on numerical differences between jobs.
- Point plan evaluation procedures provide documentation to support evaluation decisions.
- Point plans tend to increase in accuracy and consistency with use as evaluators gain greater understanding of factor and degree definitions.

Disadvantages

The major disadvantages associated with point plans are as follows:[13]

- There may be some difficulty involved in developing the point scales. Frequently, outside assistance is required to help formulate the details of a point plan; consequently, there is normally a higher cost associated with developing a point plan than there is with job ranking.
- Installation time may be longer than with ranking because of the need for working out the details of factors, degrees, and points.

- The operating details of the plan are not always easy to explain to employees or managers. Factors, degrees, weights, and point values may not be readily understood.
- The combination of compensable factors selected for use on a particular plan may not be the most appropriate combination for that specific organization.
- Because jobs are compared with a fixed standard rather than with each other, some subtle yet important distinctions between jobs may be overlooked.
- With a point plan evaluations may appear to be more precise than they actually are; subjective judgments may simply be masked by quantification.
- Despite the attempt to eliminate bias, evaluations may be influenced by the evaluators' consideration of the job incumbent or by preconceived notions relative to the job.

FACTOR COMPARISON

By far the most complex approach to job evaluation is the factor comparison method.[14] This method requires considerable training of evaluators and because of its complexity it is the least used job evaluation method. Factor comparison is a hybrid approach to job evaluation. It contains aspects of job ranking as well as aspects of the point method. It is similar to ranking in that jobs are compared with other jobs, but it is also similar to point evaluation in that jobs are compared with a set of compensable factors.[15]

Five compensable factors are normally used in this method: mental requirements, physical requirements, skill, responsibility, and working conditions.[16] Because these factors are considered to be found universally in all jobs, factor comparison does not require the development of separate plans to cover different kinds of jobs. A single comparison scale can accommodate managerial, administrative, technical, and clerical jobs.

Developing the Plan

There are six steps involved in the development of a factor comparison plan:[17]

1. Define compensable factors.
2. Select key jobs.
3. Rank key jobs by factors.
4. Allocate money rates for key jobs across factors.
5. Compare key job factor and money rankings.
6. Plot key jobs on factor comparison scale.

Define Compensable Factors

The first step in factor comparison is the easiest one to accomplish. Inasmuch as factor comparison utilizes five universal factors that are allegedly present in all jobs, there is no difficulty in deciding which or how many factors to use. The only real task is to write definitions of the factors that will fit a particular organization. The definitions are usually very broad in nature and resemble the factor definitions used in a point evaluation plan. Often an institution implementing a factor comparison plan simply borrows the definitions from another organization.

Select Key Jobs

The second step is to choose a representative number of key jobs that will serve as benchmarks. A key job or benchmark job is one that is (1) stable in content and changes little over time; (2) well-known and easily recognized by managers in various labor market institutions; (3) susceptible to clear, concise description; (4) a good reference point as far as level of difficulty and responsibility is concerned; (5) accepted in the labor market for setting compensation rates; (6) representative, when taken together with other key jobs, of the complete range of the organization's jobs; and (7) currently compensated at what is considered to be an accurate rate of pay.

The selection of key jobs is extremely important because the entire factor comparison method is built around key jobs. Key jobs serve as reference points and must be representative of the full range of jobs to be evaluated. The exact number of jobs selected to serve as benchmarks depends upon the diversity of jobs to be covered by the plan. Typically, ten to fifteen jobs are selected.

For purposes of illustration, assume that a machine shop has identified five key jobs: tool and die maker, lathe operator, milling machine operator, general machinist, and expeditor. These five jobs will now be used to demonstrate how a factor comparison job evaluation plan is developed.

Rank Key Jobs by Factors

Each key job is next ranked on each factor. Where a committee is used, committee members do this independently and then merge the results into an average or collective ranking of jobs factor by factor. Table 6.1 shows the factor rankings for each of the five illustrative key jobs. Tool and die maker ranks first in mental demands, followed in order by lathe operator, milling machine operator, general machinist, and expeditor. Rankings for the other four factors are shown in the appropriate columns.

Allocate Money Rates for Key Jobs Across Factors

The next step, performed independently by committee members and then combined into an overall committee consensus, is to apportion the hourly rate currently paid each job across the five factors. This is done by estimating how much of the hourly rate is associated with mental requirements, how much is associated with physical requirements, and so on. In this step the evaluator is trying to answer the question, "What are we really paying for in

Table 6.1
Average Ranking of Key Jobs by Factors

Job	Mental	Skills	Physical	Responsibility	Working Conditions
			Factors and Rank		
Expeditor	5	5	1	5	1
Tool and Die Maker	1	1	5	1	5
Milling Machine Operator	3	3	3	3	4
General Machinist	4	4	2	4	2
Lathe Operator	2	2	4	2	3

this job?" Table 6.2 shows the hypothetical money allocations for the five key jobs used in this example.

Compare Key Job Factor and Money Rankings

In this step the two sets of judgments made on each key job are compared. The factor rankings are, in effect, vertical comparisons, while the money rankings are horizontal comparisons. If a job is assigned the same ranking in both comparisons, the job is considered to be a key job, since the judgments validate each other. If the two rankings are fairly divergent, the job is adjudged not to be a key job and is eliminated from further consideration in the development of the factor scale (any job eliminated at this point will be evaluated later). Where the rankings vary only slightly, adjustments are typically made on the monetary side to bring the rankings into agreement with each other. Table 6.3 shows how the rankings of the five example key jobs compare with each other.

Plot Key Jobs on Factor Comparison Scale

The next step in developing a factor comparison plan is the construction of a factor comparison scale, such as the one depicted in Figure 6.3, that will be used to evaluate the organization's remaining jobs. The scale is simply the monetary rate allocated to key job factors in an earlier development step.

Table 6.2
Average Distribution of Present Hourly Pay

Job	Mental	Skills	Physical	Responsibility	Working Conditions	Present Hourly Rate
			Factors and Rank			
Expeditor	1.56	2.30	3.80	1.00	2.88	11.54
Tool and Die Maker	4.56	5.60	1.40	4.88	1.82	18.26
Milling Machine Operator	4.22	4.12	1.82	3.84	1.90	15.38
General Machinist	3.00	3.54	2.88	1.96	2.08	13.46
Lathe Operator	4.45	4.70	1.70	4.08	1.96	16.43

Table 6.3
Comparison of Factor and Monetary Rankings

Job	Mental		Skills		Physical		Responsibility		Working Conditions	
	F	$	F	$	F	$	F	$	F	$
Expeditor	5	5	5	5	1	1	5	5	1	1
Tool and Die Maker	1	1	1	1	5	5	1	1	5	5
Milling Machine Operator	3	3	3	3	3	3	3	3	4	4
General Machinist	4	4	4	4	2	2	4	4	2	2
Lathe Operator	2	2	2	2	4	4	2	2	3	3

Evaluating Nonkey Jobs

The factor comparison scale is the means by which all remaining jobs—
the nonkey jobs—are evaluated. Essentially, this is accomplished by comparing the factors in nonkey jobs with the factors of key jobs as identified by
the reference points in the scale. For example, assume that the job of tool crib
attendant is to be evaluated. The evaluator reads the job description, examines the first factor on the scale (mental demands), and locates two key jobs
between which the mental demands of tool crib attendant fall. As shown in
Figure 6.3, the two benchmarks for mental demands are general machinist
and expeditor. At this point the evaluator rereads the two descriptions for
these jobs to determine which one is closest to tool crib attendant as far as
mental demands are concerned. The evaluator then slots the job at what is
considered to be an appropriate rate; in the example, $4.10. The same proce-
dure is repeated for the remaining four factors (see Figure 6.4). With the
evaluation completed, the monetary rate for the job is determined by totaling
the dollar values assigned to each factor. In the case of tool crib attendant the
wage rate is $16.20. This same procedure is repeated for every job evaluated.

Advantages

Specific advantages of the factor comparison method of job evaluation
include the following:[18]

- Each plan is custom made for each organization, using that organization's own
  jobs and rates of pay. Such tailoring produces a job evaluation plan that closely fits
  the organization and its situation.
- Factor comparison can accommodate changes in jobs or the addition of new jobs;
  thus, the longevity of a plan is fairly good.
- The dual comparison used—jobs to jobs and factors to factors—tends to enhance
  the accuracy of the evaluations.
- Because factor comparison uses only five factors, the possibility of overlap between factors is greatly reduced.
- Evaluation is done in monetary rates; thus, job pricing is accomplished as a job is
  evaluated rather than as an additional step.

Figure 6.3
Factor Comparison Scale

$ Rates	Mental	Skills	Physical	Responsibility	Working Conditions
				Factors	
5.60		-Tool and Die Maker			
5.00				-Tool and Die Maker	
		-Lathe Operator			
	-Tool and Die Maker			-Lathe Operator	
4.00	-Lathe Operator -Milling Machine Operator	-Milling Machine Operator -General Machinist	-Expeditor	-Milling Machine Operator	
					-Expeditor
3.00	-General Machinist		-General Machinist		
		-Expeditor			-General Machinist -Lathe Operator -Milling Machine Operator -Tool and Die Maker
2.00	-Expeditor		-Milling Machine Operator -Lathe Operator -Tool and Die Maker	-General Machinist	
1.00				-Expeditor	

- Factor comparison is an improvement over ranking and classification because compensable factors are explicitly identified.

Disadvantages

As a means of job evaluation, factor comparison suffers from the following limitations or disadvantages.[19]

- The factor scale is time consuming to develop; thus, installation cost is greater with this method than with other approaches.

Figure 6.4
Factor Comparison Scale (with Tool Crib Attendant)

$ Rates	Mental	Skills	Physical	Responsibility	Working Conditions
				Factors	
5.60		-Tool and Die Maker			
		-TC Attendant			
5.00				-Tool and Die Maker	
		-Lathe Operator			
	-Tool and Die Maker -TC Attendant -Lathe Operator			-Lathe Operator	
4.00	-Milling Machine Operator	-Milling Machine Operator	-Expeditor	-Milling Machine Operator -TC Attendant	
		-General Machinist			
3.00	-General Machinist		-General Machinist		-Expeditor
		-Expeditor			-General Machinist -TC Attendant -Lathe Operator
2.00			-Milling Machine Operator -Lathe Operator -TC Attendant -Tool and Die Maker	-General Machinist	-Milling Machine Operator -Tool and Die Maker
	-Expeditor				
1.00				-Expeditor	

- Factor comparison is a difficult method of evaluation to explain to managers or employees. Because it is difficult to explain, it may not be readily accepted.
- Development of the plan is a cumbersome process.
- Extensive training may be required before evaluators can use the system effectively.
- The universal factors used may not be the most appropriate set of factors to use in all cases.
- As market rates change, the whole system has to be changed if it is to remain accurate.
- Evaluators may be influenced by current rates of pay for particular jobs when they distribute money rates; if so, bias may be introduced into the evaluations.

PROPRIETARY JOB EVALUATION METHODS

In addition to the generic approaches to job evaluation described in this and the previous chapter, various consulting firms have developed their own special proprietary methods of evaluating jobs within an organization and establishing a salary structure.[20] Normally, these methods are variations and refinements of either the point method or factor comparison approach and combine evaluation with marketplace pricing so that internal and external equity are established in quick succession. Inasmuch as there are a number of such systems available, no attempt will be made to single out one or two of these approaches. The reader who is interested in obtaining more information on proprietary systems is referred to the Appendix, Compensation Web Sites, which shows Web sites for several consulting firms.

NOTES

1. Donald L. Caruth, *Compensation Management for Banks* (Boston: Bankers Publishing, 1986), 65.

2. George T. Milkovich and Jerry M. Newman, *Compensation*, 6th ed. (Boston: Irwin–McGraw-Hill, 1999), 117.

3. Caruth, *Compensation Management*, 66.

4. Milkovich and Newman, *Compensation*, 118–119.

5. Caruth, *Compensation Management*, 69.

6. Milkovich and Newman, *Compensation*, 124–126.

7. Caruth, *Compensation Management*, 67.

8. Ibid., 69.

9. Ibid.

10. Ibid.

11. Ibid.

12. Ibid., 72.

13. Ibid., 72–73.

14. Frederick S. Hills, Thomas J. Bergmann, and Vida G. Scarpello, *Compensation Decision Making*, 2d ed. (Fort Worth: Dryden Press, 1994), 220.

15. Ibid.

16. Ibid.

17. Caruth, *Compensation Management*, 74–79.

18. Ibid., 79–81.

19. Ibid., 81.

20. Ibid., 81–84.

7

COMPENSATION SURVEYS

A compensation survey is a systematic attempt to obtain relevant information on wages and salaries, benefits, compensation policies, and pay practices from other institutions competing in the same labor market for similar personnel.[1]

The terms *systematic attempt* and *other institutions* merit further elaboration. *Labor market* is so crucial to understanding compensation surveys that it is addressed in detail in a following section.

Systematic attempt means that the compensation survey must be well thought out, carefully planned, logically organized, and properly conducted to yield valid results.[2] Haphazardly soliciting data from acquaintances in other institutions or asking convention attendees about the salaries their firms pay are not compensation surveys and will not provide the kind of hard data that are needed for establishing a sound pay structure in an organization. A compensation survey must follow a master plan that specifies what information is to be obtained, from whom it is to be collected, and how it is to be gathered. Only by approaching the survey in such a systematic, logical, and orderly fashion will valid, usable information be amassed.

Other institutions refers to organizations in the industry and organizations outside the industry that compete for the same kind of human resource talent or skills.[3] For example, a bank conducting a compensation survey would need to survey not only banks but other institutions that employ similar clerical and administrative personnel: mortgage loan companies, credit unions, consumer loan firms, and insurance companies, to mention a few. If a bank did not include other types of organizations in a compensation survey it would be ignoring firms that may exert strong influence on compensation levels within a particular labor market. Organizations compete with other similar organizations for qualified human resources, and they also compete with a host of nonsimilar institutions. This competition for skills is particularly true for lower-level positions in organizations where skills are generic and easily portable from industry to industry or from firm to firm. Consequently, a compensation survey that accurately reflects conditions in the labor market must include a representative sample of all types of organizations that employ people with skills similar to those used in the surveying institution.

A compensation survey is a complex endeavor that must be done carefully and thoroughly to assure a sound salary structure and an effective compensation program. It should not be approached lightly.

THE PURPOSE OF SURVEYS

Compensation surveys serve three basic purposes.[4] The primary purpose, of course, is to determine going rates of pay for particular jobs so that the surveying organization can initially develop and then continually maintain a salary structure that is congruent with the labor market. If internal rates of pay are too low, an organization will be unable to attract or hold sufficient numbers of qualified employees. If internal rates of pay are too high, the organization will be spending more than it should on compensation and profitability will be adversely affected. Consequently, it is necessary to periodically ascertain what other institutions are paying to attract, hold, and motivate employees of similar skills in comparable jobs.

The second purpose of a survey is to determine if the organization's indirect compensation—its benefits package—is in line with other labor market competitors. Since indirect compensation constitutes a large portion of the total compensation package, a firm must assure itself that it is as competitive in this area as it is in the area of direct compensation. The compensation survey collects information that helps assure competitiveness in indirect compensation.

The third purpose of a compensation survey is to determine if an organization's pay policies, procedures, and practices are consistent with those of other competing labor market institutions. Among the items in this area that might be examined through the survey are periodicity of merit pay increases, handling of cost-of-living adjustments, performance appraisal methods, length of probationary periods, updating of job descriptions, and job evaluation techniques.

In short, a compensation survey enables an organization to (1) compensate its jobs at rates that are consistent with the rates paid by other organizations, (2) provide benefits comparable to those offered by other employers, and (3) keep its pay policies, procedures, and practices up to date. By accomplishing these three things, a company is better able to attract, hold, and motivate sufficient numbers of qualified employees to perform the work of the institution.

DEFINING THE LABOR MARKET

One of the key concepts in compensation surveys is that of labor market.[5] This term is expressed more appropriately, perhaps, as relevant labor market, since a single market does not exist for all of the jobs in any organization.

What is a labor market? A labor market, defined very simply, is that geographical area from which an employer usually recruits workers. While it is relatively easy to define what a labor market is conceptually, in practice it is often quite difficult to determine just how much geography to include. The actual geographical extent of a labor market is influenced by at least three factors: (1) the specific occupations, qualifications, or skills involved; (2) the time or distance employees are willing to commute to a particular job; and (3) the distance employees are willing to relocate to change jobs.

Occupations, Qualifications, or Skills

Many of the jobs within any organization do not require high levels of skill for their performance. The ability to read, write, type, follow instructions, operate a personal computer, and so forth are basic or generic skills that are fairly widely distributed in the general employment-seeking population. Thus, an employer could reasonably expect to find people who possess basic skills in just about any localized area. This means that the extent of the labor market for individuals possessing generic skills is very limited in its geographical scope. A department store, for example, could normally expect to find salespeople, order clerks, or data-input personnel residing within close proximity to the store. As a general rule, the more basic a skill is, the more geographically restricted the labor market is for that skill.

Much the same argument can be made for occupations such as computer operator, secretary, or accountant. While the numbers of people within these occupational groupings is not as great as those possessing only minimal qualifications, the geographical area from which people in these occupations can be recruited will nevertheless be roughly the same area in which individuals of lesser qualifications are sought.

Commuting Distance

Especially important for determining the extent of the labor market for many of a firm's jobs is the distance from the workplace or the time a person is willing to spend commuting to and from work. While this is a highly personal matter and one that may well vary from one part of the country to another, it must always be considered in determining the appropriate labor market area to survey.

How much time are most people willing to spend commuting to a job? There is no definitive answer to this question. Some compensation specialists suggest that it may be as much as ninety minutes each way. Others suggest that it might be as little as thirty minutes. Although it cannot be proven—but can be used as a general rule of thumb—the average person is probably willing to spend approximately sixty minutes to get to work and approximately sixty minutes to return home. Fortunately, commuting time or distance as a factor that influences the extent of a labor market is one of the easiest factors to determine for clerical or nonprofessional jobs. For an organization in a metropolitan area all that is needed is a large Zip code map and a handful of pushpins. Using the organization's current personnel roster, a pin representing the home address of each employee is placed in the appropriate Zip code. The result is an identification of commuting time and distance for present employees—in effect, this is the labor market from which the firm currently draws most of its employees.

Relocation Distance

The distance that people are willing to move in order to change jobs is a second factor influencing the relevant labor market. Generally speaking, the more specialized the occupation or profession, the more likely it is that a person would be willing to change his or her place of residence in order to accept another job; the less specialized the occupation or the more basic the job skill is, the less likely a person would be to move in order to change employers. In terms of labor market extent this means that the amount of geography involved for positions such as senior electrical engineer, benefits administrator, controller, or manufacturing manager may be fairy extensive. Consequently, if the compensation survey fails to include the full geographical area within which people are willing to relocate, salary data obtained may be inaccurate.

As the preceding discussion suggests, an organization does not have a single labor market with which to contend; it has several. Thus, the term *relevant labor market* takes on even greater significance when an organization plans and subsequently conducts a compensation survey. The relevant market may not be the same for clerical jobs and for managerial jobs. For survey purposes, therefore, it is often necessary to identify and define the appropriate labor market on the basis of job or occupational groupings. This means that in most cases a single compensation survey will not suffice. Several surveys may need to be conducted to secure accurate data.

The Four Possible Labor Markets

There are four possible labor markets that an organization, especially a large one, may need to consider when designing and conducting a compensation survey: (1) local, (2) regional, (3) national, and (4) international.

The local labor market is that relatively small geographical area bounded by approximately sixty-minutes commuting time from the firm's location. This is the primary market from which an organization recruits the majority of its employees. The regional market is comprised of an area within a state, such as South Texas, or an area inclusive of several states; the Far West or the Southeast, for example. The national labor market consists of the entire United States. Two or more countries, one of which is normally the United States, constitute an international labor market.

Because of the types of jobs being surveyed, there is often some overlap in relevant labor markets. Table 7.1 shows an example of some typical banking jobs and the four possible labor markets that might be relevant to each job. Admittedly, this illustration is an oversimplification; its purpose, however, is merely to suggest that careful thought must be given to identifying appropriate labor markets before a survey is initiated.

DESIGNING THE SURVEY

For the sake of simplicity, assume that our only concern is designing a survey to be used in the local labor market. Since the principles of design are essentially the same for any survey and because most organizations are primarily concerned with a local market for the vast majority of their jobs, this concentration on a single type of survey will be less confusing than attempting to address the design of several surveys simultaneously.

Effective survey design must deal with five basic questions: (1) What types of organizations will be included in the survey? (2) How many organizations will be surveyed? (3) What specific organizations will be contacted? (4) What information is needed? (5) Which of the surveying firm's jobs will be included in the survey? Answering each of these questions may sometimes be difficult.

What Types of Organizations Will Be Included?

As emphasized previously, the compensation survey must not be limited only to firms of a similar nature. Rather, it should, if it is to be an accurate

Table 7.1
Relevant Labor Markets by Selected Positions

Position	Relevant Labor Market			
	Local	Regional	National	International
Teller	X			
Consumer Loan Officer	X	X		
President (Small bank)	X	X	X	
President (Large bank)			X	
Manager, Foreign Exchange			X	X

reflection of what is happening in the labor market, include a sample of other types of organizations that compete for the same kinds of skills as does the surveying organization.[6]

Faced with a plethora of dissimilar enterprises in the labor market, where does the survey designer start? How does he or she begin to ascertain the types of institutions that need to be included in the survey? The best way to do this is by identifying within the organization certain generic jobs; that is, jobs that are common to different organizations within the local labor market. Institutions that are unlike the surveying organization often compete for the same skill sets. To omit these organizations in a survey may produce distorted labor market data.

The authors, for example, have worked with a small municipality in designing its compensation survey and interpreting the results for a number of years. This municipality surveys twenty-two other cities to determine compensation rates for jobs that are city-specific, such as building inspector, police officer, firefighter, park superintendent, and so on. But it also surveys nine other local institutions—two banks, one county government, one electric utility, one university, and four manufacturers—for compensation rates on generic jobs, such as custodian, accounts payable clerk, secretary, and maintenance technician. This municipality recognizes that there are some jobs where compensation information is best obtained from like institutions, but there are also jobs where individuals can move freely between industries and are not confined to working only for a city. Accordingly, information should be collected from all organizations that compete for the same kind of talent.

How Many Organizations Will Be Surveyed?

Once we know the types of organizations to be included in the survey, the next concern is determining the appropriate number of organizations to survey. Obviously, surveying all of the companies within a relevant labor market is out of the question because of cost, time, and so forth. On the other hand, surveying only a few institutions may produce distorted data uncharacteristic of the marketplace. What, then, is an appropriate number and how is this number ascertained?

Unlike other surveys, a compensation survey is seldom a statistically random sample in which the number of participants and their specific identities are determined through mathematical formulae. Instead, it is a judgmental sample that seeks to obtain relatively accurate data by surveying organizations that are believed to be representative of the marketplace. Further complicating a determination of the precise number of organizations to survey is the problem of anticipated response rate to the survey. Normally, not all firms surveyed will respond.

The question of how many organizations to survey, therefore, hinges on answering two additional questions: (1) How many responses are needed to assure adequate representation? (2) How many of the institutions surveyed are likely to reply to the request for compensation information? Unfortunately, there are no definitive answers to either of these crucial questions. There are, however, some rules of thumb that can be used for guidance.

Depending on the specific labor market involved, between fifteen and thirty usable responses from representative institutions are believed to provide sufficiently reliable compensation survey data: fifteen responses in a relatively small labor market and thirty responses in a more extensive one.[7] The response rate is more difficult to ascertain in advance. The type of industry involved and the manner in which the survey is conducted appear to influence the willingness of selected institutions to respond.

It has been suggested that a firm should survey a minimum of thirty labor market institutions to obtain a reasonably adequate amount of compensation information (30 companies × 0.50% response rate = 15 responses). Remember, these numbers are strictly guidelines and not hard and fast rules. If more data can be collected, they probably should be.

Now that the types of institutions that need to be surveyed have been identified and some indication of the number that will have to be included in a sample of the labor market has been determined, we will turn our attention to identifying the specific institutions that will be surveyed.

Which Specific Organizations Will Be Contacted?

There are several factors to be considered in selecting the particular firms to be included in the survey: industry comparability, organization size, similar jobs, location, and contacts in other institutions. The representativeness of the sample and the response rate are influenced by all of these items.

Industry Comparability

The majority of specific institutions sampled should be other similar firms or organizations so that labor market comparability within the specific industry can be ascertained. The surveying firm needs to be able to compare itself with other firms that compete with the organization or perform work that is very similar to the work it performs.

Organization Size

Institutions of about the same size as the one conducting the survey, as measured by numbers of employees, will need to be included in the survey, since they are potential labor market competitors of equal stature. But large firms should also be included because they frequently exert considerable influence on compensation levels and practices in the local labor market, especially if their pay scales tend to be higher than market average.

Similar Jobs

Organizations asked to participate in the survey must have jobs similar in nature to those of the organization conducting the survey. If jobs are not similar, valid comparisons of salary data cannot be made.

Location

Institutions within close physical proximity to the surveying firm are prime candidates for inclusion in the survey because they are subject to the same commuting time and traffic patterns. Moreover, their visibility tends to make them competitors, not only for people to be hired in the future, but also for current employees who might change jobs for compensation-related reasons.

Contacts in Other Institutions

All other factors being equal, when the person conducting the survey knows someone in another organization, especially a human resource specialist or compensation manager, the chances of receiving a response to the survey are much greater than they are when no one is known and the survey must be sent blindly. Consequently, the extent of contacts the surveyor has often influences the selection of institutions to be surveyed. This, however, should not be the major criterion for choosing institutions, since one person's contacts may not be representative of the total labor market.

Each of the foregoing factors must be carefully weighed to arrive at the representative sampling of specific institutions that will reflect current labor market conditions.

What Information Is Needed?

Compensation surveys may run the gamut from very simplistic requests for minimum and maximum rates of pay for only a few jobs to extremely complex, multipage questionnaires seeking a wide variety of pay data as well as detailed information on compensation practices. Therefore, an organization has to carefully determine the specific types and quantities of information that it realistically needs for the purposes it has in mind. The temptation to collect extraneous information should be strongly resisted because of the additional time and cost involved.

The minimum amount of information normally solicited in a survey includes salary ranges for selected positions, identification of major forms of indirect compensation, and specification of practices, particularly in those areas where the surveying institution feels that its present practices may be deficient.

Typically, the first survey that an organization conducts will tend to be much more comprehensive than subsequent surveys. When a compensation program is initiated it is often necessary to examine policies, procedures, and practices of other institutions in fairly detailed fashion. Once the program is operational, periodic spot checks of selected areas will enable an institution to keep its program competitive.

In assessing its survey information requirements an organization should also note that the amount of information sought from respondents might affect the response rate. Generally speaking, the more information requested, the lower the response rate will be.

Which Jobs Will Be Included in the Survey?

The final issue to be resolved in designing a compensation survey is to determine the specific jobs that will be used for collecting salary information. It is impractical to try to obtain pay data on each job that an organization has. It is also unnecessary because a limited number of key jobs can be used effectively to represent the full spectrum of all jobs in an institution. A key job is one that serves as a benchmark or point of reference for other jobs within the same general group or class. A key job is characterized by the following:

- A well-known, relatively stable content not subject to rapid change.
- Content that is susceptible to clear, concise definition.
- An easily recognizable title indicative of the work performed.
- Ability to represent a certain level of education, experience, and so forth so that when combined with other key jobs the full range of positions to be covered by the salary plan is depicted.
- Several employees incumbent in the position so that, as a group, all key jobs used account for a sizable proportion of the organization's total workforce.
- Supply and demand factors that are relatively stable and have not been affected recently by dramatic shifts in the labor market.
- Equivalency or high similarity in content to jobs in other institutions.
- Traditional usage by other labor market organizations in their compensation surveys.

In addition, a job that has a high turnover rate or one that is hard to fill may be included as a key job because it represents an area of known or suspected compensation problems.

How many key jobs should be used in a compensation survey? Unfortunately, there is no definitive answer to this question. What is requisite in a survey is coverage of the full range of jobs in an organization. This means, obviously, that the more jobs an organization has, the more key jobs its survey will have to include to assure the collection of data that accurately reflect the full spectrum of jobs. Twenty to thirty jobs seems to be typical for the majority of surveys. In an organization's initial survey it is preferable to err on the side of including too many jobs rather than too few. If the number of jobs used turns out to be too high, it can be reduced in subsequent surveys.

In addition to deciding which and how many key jobs will be used in the survey, there is the problem of assuring comparability between the surveying institution's jobs and those of the respondents. Only a comparison of like jobs will produce valid salary data. It is customary to use succinct job summaries along with job titles so respondents may make intelligent determinations of job comparability. These abbreviated descriptions of jobs, no longer than three to five sentences as a rule, can be taken from the job summary portion of the job description.

CONDUCTING THE SURVEY

Once the survey has been designed, consideration must next be given to how it will be conducted and what actions are necessary to assure a sufficient response rate.

Survey Methods

There are four generally used procedures for conducting a survey: (1) telephone, (2) personal interview, (3) mailed questionnaire, and (4) some combination of the first three approaches. Each of these methods has certain advantages and disadvantages.[8]

Telephone

A telephone survey is normally used when a minimum amount of information on a very small number of jobs is all that is needed. If the jobs are easily identifiable, readily recognizable, and highly standardized, a telephone survey can provide data very quickly. If information is desired on a large number of jobs, the jobs are subject to variations in content from firm to firm, or extensive information on benefits, procedures, policies, and practices is required, the telephone survey may not be a very useful means of collecting compensation data. The primary advantage of the telephone survey is speed and the primary disadvantage is the limited amount of information that can be collected.

The survey respondent, on the other hand, may feel that the telephone procedure is disruptive, since it requires immediate attention and response to information requests. Use of this method is recommended only for periodic spot checks or situations where salary data on one or two jobs are needed immediately.

Personal Interview

The most effective technique for obtaining compensation information is the face-to-face interview. This method permits in-depth discussion of job similarities and differences and clarification of informational requests, thus assuring the highest degree of validity possible. The major drawbacks of personal interviews are that they are time consuming and costly. In addition, there is the problem of scheduling interviews with survey participants: Difficulties in arranging interview appointments may extend the collection of information over a lengthy period.

Personal interviews work best where there is a small number of organizations to be surveyed, the labor market is geographically limited, and contacts—human resource managers or compensation specialists—within the organizations to be surveyed are known personally by the individual conducting the survey.

Personal interviews are very beneficial in field testing a compensation questionnaire before it is used for the total survey group. Two or three preliminary interviews may reveal the need to modify questions, delete items, or incorporate additional informational requests. Another potential benefit of the personal interview is that it may establish lines of communication and cooperation that lead to greater sharing of information between organizations in the future.

Mailed Questionnaire

The most widely used means of obtaining compensation information is the mailed questionnaire. The principal advantages of this method are that it (1) allows a greater number of institutions to be included in the survey, (2) permits respondents to complete the questionnaire at their convenience, (3) enables the surveying institution to collect more data than with either the telephone survey or personal interview, (4) permits full coverage of the geographical extent of the labor market, and (5) is less time consuming and costly than other survey methods. Disadvantages of the questionnaire approach include (1) a lower response rate than with telephone or personal interview methods because the questionnaire can be easily ignored or discarded, (2) inaccuracy of data because respondents may not carefully compare jobs or may misinterpret questions, and (3) response time—respondents may delay completing the questionnaire even when a response date is specified.

Combination

Occasionally, a combination of the three survey methods is used. A mailed questionnaire may be sent to the majority of firms to be surveyed, personal interviews may be conducted with a limited number of organizations where close contacts are already established, and the telephone may be used to collect information from organizations that have only one or two of the key jobs used in the survey. A combination approach would theoretically maximize the advantages of each individual approach while minimizing the disadvantages. In reality, however, a combination approach seems to add more complexity to the survey procedure and necessitates greater coordination of efforts.

Assuring a Sufficient Response Rate

One of the greatest challenges in conducting a compensation survey is assuring a response rate that is high enough for compensation decisions to be made with some degree of confidence based on the data received from the survey.[9] Two simple measures can significantly increase the response rate. Organizations being surveyed are much more likely to respond if they are promised a summary of the results of the survey and if they are assured that their responses will be treated with strictest confidence. The offer of a summary report and the guarantee of confidentiality are normally made in a cover letter accompanying the survey questionnaire. In addition, the cover letter typically explains the nature and purpose of the survey, the number of institutions involved, and so on.

Summary of Results

Responding to a survey can be a time-consuming activity. Consequently, it is quite natural for a potential survey participant to ask, "What's in it for me?" before agreeing to provide the requested information. The promise of a good summary of the survey results, to be delivered in timely fashion after the conclusion of the survey, is the inducement that most often encourages participation. Even though they may not have a current need for salary information, all organizations tend to be interested in compensation data. Moreover, there may be a future need for such information. Participation in a survey, by establishing cooperation and communication, makes it easier for a responding organization to obtain the data it requires when an actual need does arise. While courtesy and positive public relations suggest that an organization participate in a compensation survey, it is mutual need, either in the present or in the future, that typically motivates survey participation.

The summary of survey results sent to participants should include data on each question asked. The data should be presented in the form of averages, percentages, arrays, and so forth so that no specific organization can be identified by other participants. A good summary report helps assure continuous participation of respondents in subsequent surveys conducted by an organization.

Confidentiality

All survey respondents must be assured of complete confidentiality and the surveying institution must take steps to protect the privileged nature of reported data. Reporting results in summary form helps, as does coding the survey questionnaires. It is common practice to assign a code number to each organization; the code number is the only piece of identifying information to appear on the survey instrument itself. The person conducting the survey retains the master code list, thereby eliminating the possibility of unauthorized personnel being able to identify respondents.

The coding system need not be elaborate; a two- or three-digit code works very well. With a two-digit code each organization is simply assigned a number from 01 through the number of the total institutions being surveyed, such as 27 or 32. When a three-digit code is used, the first digit usually designates the type of institution and the last two digits designate the specific institution. Coding by institutional type is beneficial because it allows for easy arrangement, computation, comparison, and reporting of results by types of labor market competitors.

Codes are also useful for presenting information in the summary report. Where an array of salary data is provided, for example, individual salary figures for jobs can be shown by code number for each reporting organization. Thus, each company—informed of its code number when it receives the summary report—is able to compare itself to every other surveyed institution and the usefulness of the data to respondents is enhanced.

Cover Letter

A good cover letter is essential when conducting a survey by mail. It should include the following: (1) an identification of the organization conducting the survey; (2) a statement of the purpose of the survey; (3) a general description of the survey population—23 manufacturing companies, 12 hospitals, and so on; (4) a guarantee of confidentiality; (5) an assurance that each respondent will receive a summary report of the findings in timely fashion; and (6) a specific date by which responses should be returned—normally two to three weeks after the anticipated date that surveyed organizations will receive the questionnaire.

A preliminary letter may also help when surveys are conducted by telephone or personal interviews. The letter alerts potential respondents to the fact that they will be contacted. Thus, when the telephone call requesting the information or an appointment comes it does not come as a surprise.

INTERPRETING THE DATA

After all data have been received from survey respondents, the task of tabulating, analyzing, interpreting, and presenting results begins.[10] There is no uniform procedure for accomplishing this task. Diversity in data analysis appears to be the rule rather than the exception. The judgment of the analyst is often as critical as the statistical approaches used.

There are, essentially, two types of data to be tabulated and interpreted: *salary* and *other*. The salary data component is self-explanatory. Other data include information collected on indirect compensation, policies, procedures, and practices. The analysis of salary data tends to be more complex and more subject to the exercise of judgment than the analysis of the second-survey (other) data component. The following sections examine both of these areas.

Salary Data

Salary data can be analyzed in a variety of ways, but the primary purpose is always to establish some measure of central tendency.[11] The two most commonly used measures of central tendency are the *mean* (the simple average of all values in a given set of data) and the *median* (the middle value in an array of all values in a given set of data). Both mean and median can be affected by the *range* of values—the difference between the lowest and the highest value— in a set of data. The calculation and interpretation of salary data for an organization's internal use must, therefore, concern itself not only with computing a measure of central tendency, but also with examining the range of the data so that distortions in the mean or median caused by extremely high or low figures are minimized.

The mean is the measure of central tendency used most often in the statistical analysis of salary data.[12] The analysis starts with the development of a numerical array of reported salaries for each key job. In a true array, minimum salaries are shown from lowest to highest and maximum salaries are also shown from lowest to highest. In survey data analysis, however, it is customary to keep reported salaries—lows and highs—together by respondents; consequently, a modified array is used. The modified array normally lists salaries from lowest to highest for minimum salaries only. Table 7.2 shows such an array for the job of customer service representative.

After the array is completed, an average minimum and an average maximum salary is calculated. For internal analysis purposes, the surveying organization's salary figures are then inserted so that a comparison can be made with all surveyed institutions and the labor market averages. Looking at the minimum salaries in Table 7.2 we see that minimum salaries are in the survey range from $1,417 per month to $1,708 per month; maximum salaries range from $1,842 to $2,272; the average minimum salary is $1,572, and the average maximum salary is $2,078. The surveying organization's minimum and maximum salaries are $1,554 and $2,020, respectively.

This is an example of the type of data normally provided to survey respondents in the summary report, with one exception: The surveying organization's own salary figures are sometimes omitted. Recipients of the report are thus able to make their own interpretations of the data and perform any additional analyses they feel are important or that will make the data more meaningful to them.

Because the surveying firm is concerned with interpreting the data in light of its own needs—specifically the establishment of an internal salary structure that is competitive with the labor market—further analytical computations may be necessary. (These computations will not, of course, be included

Table 7.2
Salary Data Array, Unadjusted Averages (Key Job: Customer Service Representative)

Respondent	Monthly Minimum	Monthly Maximum
223	1,417	1,842
301	1,458	1,896
214	1,542	2,050
213	1,542	2,050
302	1,583	2,106
305	1,583	2,058
219	1,600	2,128
221	1,608	2,139
306	1,667	2,272
224	1,708	2,227
Unadjusted Averages	1,554	2,078
Surveying Firm's Salary	1,554	2,020
Difference	-18	-58

in the report of findings sent to survey respondents.) For example, rather than calculate a simple average that may be distorted by salaries that seem to be somewhat inconsistent with the overall market, for internal uses an adjusted average is often employed instead. In the previous example we see that the minimum salaries reported by respondents 223 and 301 appear to be out of line with the data reported by other institutions, as well as with the average for all that is actually reflective of the marketplace. For the purpose of determining an average minimum salary that is a more accurate reflection of the marketplace, these figures should probably be excluded from the calculation of an average. On the maximum side the salaries reported by respondents 306 and 224 seem to be inconsistent with other reported salaries. These figures, too, should possibly be eliminated in the calculation of a truly representative average. In Table 7.3 the aforementioned salary figures are omitted from the calculation of a new average—the adjusted average.

Comparing both examples, we can see why it may be desirable to use a selected average instead of a simple average. With unadjusted salaries the organization's minimum salary is $18 less than the survey average and the maximum is $58 less than the survey average. Based on these numbers one might reach the conclusion that the organization is extremely competitive in its starting salary but slightly less competitive in its maximum salary.

The picture changes somewhat when the adjusted numbers in the second example are examined. The organization's minimum salary is $25 less than

Table 7.3
Salary Data Array, Adjusted Averages (Key Job: Customer Service Representative)

Respondent	Monthly Minimum	Monthly Maximum
214	1,542	2,050
213	1,542	2,050
302	1,583	2,106
305	1,583	2,058
219	1,600	2,128
221	1,608	2,139
Unadjusted Averages	1,579	2,092
Surveying Firm's Salary	1,554	2,020
Difference	-25	-72

the selective average and the maximum is $72 less. While these numbers are clearly not extreme, they suggest that the organization may not be as competitive as first thought. If the organization sets its salary scale based on the averages in the first example, it could find its ability to attract sufficient numbers of personnel to the customer service representative job slightly impeded, since a potential employee stands a good chance of getting a better starting salary elsewhere. At the same time, the organization might want to reconsider its maximum salary because the selected average suggests a greater discrepancy than the pure average did. Obviously, a great deal of judgment is required to determine which averages to use.

Judgment plays a major role in computing the selected average. For example, why wasn't the $1,542 salary of respondent 214 eliminated along with the $1,417 and $1,458 figures? The answer is that, in the opinion of the analyst, $1,542 represents a more realistic market low than the other two numbers. Another analyst may have reached a different conclusion. (This example deliberately uses amounts that are close together to illustrate the part judgment or "feel" for the data plays in the computation of a selected average.)

The real purpose of the selected average is to eliminate obvious misfits in the data—misfits that occur because a respondent's job is not comparable to a survey key job or because a respondent's salary scale is not in line with the majority of labor market institutions—so that a really meaningful interpretation of reported salaries can be made. In most cases, data that do not fit are clearly evident and the decision to eliminate those data is an easy one to make. On the other hand, marginal data—our $1,542, for example—require a great deal of thought before a decision is made to include or exclude those data from the calculation of an average.

Certainly, this brief discussion of interpreting salary data has not addressed all of the problems and questions that may arise. It has shown, hopefully, that careful thought and sound judgment are needed in addition to a calculator or computer.

Other Data

While several variations are possible in tabulating and presenting the myriad of other compensation data collected in a survey, the most common approach is a tabular format depicting the number of responses and the percentage distribution of answers to each item on the survey questionnaire.[13] Table 7.4 shows a very abbreviated version of a typical tabulation. Since respondents may inadvertently omit an answer or choose not to answer a question, it is important to show the number of responses to each particular item or to include a "no response" column in the tabulation.

Table 7.4
Other Compensation Data

	Percent of Responses	% Yes	% No
Life Insurance?	32	100	0
100% company paid?	32	41	59
Employee pays part?	32	59	41
Health insurance?	32	100	0
100% company paid?	32	68	32
Employee pays part?	32	32	68
Dental insurance?	32	53	47
100% company paid?	17	41	59
Employee pays part?	17	59	41
Pension plan?	32	100	0
Noncontributory?	32	56	44
Contributory?	32	44	56
Profit Sharing?	31	100	0
Noncontributory?	31	58	42
Contributory?	31	42	58
Tuition reimbursement?	32	75	25
Company cafeteria?	30	37	63
Free parking?	32	47	53
Annual cost-of-living adjustment?	31	13	87
Probationary employment period?	32	94	6
30 days or less?	30	67	33
31 to 60 days?	30	17	83
Over 60 days?	30	17	83

The interpretation of other compensation data is much more clear-cut than the interpretation of salary data. The majority of labor market institutions either offer a particular form of indirect compensation or they do not, they either have a particular policy or they do not, and so forth. The difficult part of the interpretation comes in deciding at what point an organization should implement a compensation practice or policy that a majority of the survey group has but the organization does not have. This is, again, entirely a matter of judgment. Certainly, if 75 percent of the surveyed institutions provide dental insurance but the surveying firm does not, the firm is not competitive in this aspect of indirect compensation. But what if the reported percentage is 50 percent? The organization is at least as competitive as half of the reporting organizations. Should the company consider providing dental insurance or should it wait until three-fourths of the market does? Or should it be a trendsetter and provide this benefit before it becomes widespread in the labor market in order to garner a distinctive competitive edge in recruitment or retention? Answers to these questions are policy decision deeply rooted in management's compensation philosophy and have to be made on an individual basis, organization by organization.

USING OUTSIDE SURVEYS

Rather than conduct its own compensation survey, many organizations elect to use one or more of the numerous surveys conducted by outside organizations. These surveys, sometimes referred to as *canned*, *packaged*, or *third party* surveys, are conducted by a variety of institutions, government agencies, trade associations, consulting firms, and so on. Such surveys may be classified broadly as either published or proprietary surveys.

Published compensation surveys are those that are readily available as public documents or those that may be purchased for a nominal fee. Proprietary surveys usually entail a more substantial fee or a membership requirement. As substitutes for a company-conducted examination of salaries and compensation practices, each type has particular advantages and disadvantages.

Published Surveys

While published surveys are available from many sources, the major source of publicly available information on compensation is the U.S. Bureau of Labor Statistics.[14] The Bureau of Labor Statistics conducts the National Compensation Survey (NCS) and the Occupation Employment Statistics Survey (OES). Recently redesigned, the NCS provides data on employee salaries, wages, and benefits. The OES provides information on salaries and wages by occupation. Data from the NCS are available for eighty-one metropolitan areas and seventy-three nonmetropolitan areas. The OES provides information for the nation, states, and all metropolitan areas, as well as Washington,

D.C., Puerto Rico, Virgin Islands, and Guam. The Bureau of Labor Statistics, through its modernized surveys, hopes to create a comprehensive statistical survey that provides employers with information to fit their changing needs.

The Federal Reserve System also conducts compensation surveys within each of its districts. This information is generally available through the district offices.

In addition to surveys conducted by government agencies, many professional organizations, such as the Administrative Management Society, conduct annual surveys of salaries within their areas of specialization.

Advantages of Published Surveys

Published surveys offer certain benefits for organizations that decide not to conduct their own independent surveys.[15] Among these benefits are the following:

- Time. Information reported is in final form, ready for use. The time-consuming activities of designing the survey, conducting it, calculating results, and reporting findings are eliminated.
- Cost. Expenses are greatly reduced because there is little or no out-of-pocket expenditure to obtain the survey results.
- Sample size. A large number of respondents is generally included, thus assuring a statistically sound sample size.

For a small firm that is unable to conduct its own in-house survey, published compensation data offer a viable alternative to obtaining needed salary information.

Disadvantages of Published Surveys

Published surveys are not without their disadvantages.[16] Some of the major drawbacks are as follows:

- Timeliness. The data may be several months to a year old before they are published; if so, the data may be inaccurate. Moreover, current published surveys may not be available when an organization has a specific need for compensation information.
- Inappropriate labor market. A national or regional survey may not be relevant for the local labor market in which a company competes for human resources.
- Nonkey jobs. Published surveys may include few, or none, of a particular company's key jobs. Accurate comparison of jobs may therefore be difficult.
- Limited data. Reported results may contain irrelevant data while omitting information that is urgently needed by an organization.

Comparing the advantages and disadvantages of using published surveys, it can be seen that there is a trade-off involved. Published surveys save time and money but may not provide the information needed on particular jobs or for a specific labor market.

Proprietary Surveys

In addition to compensation surveys available on either a widespread or limited public basis, there are a number of private surveys conducted each year by trade associations, employers' cooperatives, and consulting firms. The results of these surveys normally are available only to organizations that are members of the particular group or that are clients of the consulting firm. A fee may also be charged for a copy of the report.

Advantages of Proprietary Surveys

Using proprietary surveys offers an organization several advantages.[17] The most prominent are the following:

- Time. All the time-consuming activities of conducting an independent survey are eliminated. In addition, the report is invariably user oriented, so that its utility to an organization is considerably enhanced.
- Timeliness. Report data are normally very current. Furthermore, proprietary surveys are likely to be conducted and the final report made available at the same time each year.
- Sample size. Proprietary surveys are apt to include a sufficiently large number of respondents, so statistical soundness is assured.

Disadvantages of Proprietary Surveys

Some of the drawbacks of using proprietary surveys are as follows:[18]

- Cost. A membership fee or a charge for the report may be involved. Admittedly, this is not substantial in most cases, but it is a factor to be considered.
- Inappropriate labor market. Depending upon the particular survey, a national or a regional labor market may be the one studied, instead of the local market from which the organization draws most of its personnel. If this is the case, the resulting data may be inappropriate for a particular firm in a specific locale.
- Nonkey jobs. Occasionally a proprietary survey may not contain sufficient numbers of a company's key jobs, thereby making it difficult to set a pay scale that covers all jobs.
- Lack of control. Unless the survey is a cooperative one, an organization has no control over what data are collected, which institutions are surveyed, the labor market selected, and the format in which results are reported. Relevance of the data, consequently, may be impaired.
- Change in participation. A fault in some surveys is that participants change significantly from year to year, causing the consistency of the data to suffer.

Most of the disadvantages of proprietary surveys are not major ones, but they are factors to be weighed before placing total reliance on these surveys. By and large, proprietary surveys are definitely superior to and far more usable than publicly available data. Consequently, they should be carefully considered as a feasible alternative when a compensation survey need arises.

In summary, outside surveys may serve an organization's needs adequately. Advantages and disadvantages of published and proprietary surveys should be carefully compared with the benefits and problems of conducting an independent survey. If an outside survey is used, it is imperative that it fills the specific needs of the firm and provides relevant information.

RESURVEYING THE LABOR MARKET

A compensation survey is not a one-time activity. Once initiated, the survey must be repeated at regular intervals. Inflation, recession, changes in labor supply and demand factors, shifts in labor market boundaries, innovations in compensation methods and practices, and so forth necessitate staying abreast of the labor market. To assure salary competitiveness with other organizations, the survey should be repeated at least annually. The follow guidelines should be followed when resurveying the labor market:[19]

- Conduct the survey at the same time every year. For example, if the initial survey is conducted in July, subsequent resurveys should also be conducted in July. Distortions in data may result from surveys conducted at inconsistent points in time from year to year. If in one year a survey is conducted after other labor market organizations have revised their compensation rates, but the following year the survey is conducted at a time before rates have been adjusted, erroneous interpretation of the data, and consequently an inaccurate salary scale, may result.

- Use essentially the same group of respondents each time. Drastic changes in the composition of the survey group from year to year can affect the reported data. Periodically it is necessary to add new organizations to the survey group as well as delete others, but these changes must be made slowly so that the quality of the data is not unduly impacted. For instance, in an original survey group of thirty respondents, two might be deleted from a subsequent survey because they submitted incomplete data or were found not to be labor market competitors, while three other organizations might be added. Considering the size of the group, this would not be a major change.

- Use the same key jobs in each survey. The same key jobs should be used in every survey to maintain consistency. Changes in key jobs should be made gradually.

- Employ the same statistical techniques for analyzing the data. Do not use a simple mean for computing salary averages one year and switch to a selected average the next year and back to a simple mean the following year. Inconsistencies in statistical analysis produce distortions in data that result in salary scale inaccuracies.

- Carefully monitor the compensation survey questionnaire. Delete requests for information that are no longer needed or useful. Add new items when additional information is required. Review the questionnaire for unnecessary complexity, eliminate ambiguity, and make every effort to keep the instrument as simple as possible.

Adhering to these guidelines will produce consistent and accurate results in each resurvey of the labor market.

NOTES

1. Robert L. Mathis and John H. Jackson, *Human Resource Management*, 8th ed. (Minneapolis–St. Paul: West, 2000), 395.

2. Donald L. Caruth, *Compensation Management for Banks* (Boston: Bankers Publishing, 1986), 85.

3. Ibid.

4. Ibid., 86.

5. Frederick S. Hills, Thomas J. Bergmann, and Vida G. Scarpello, *Compensation Decision Making*, 2d ed. (Fort Worth: Dryden Press, 1994), 266–269.

6. Ibid., 269–271.

7. Caruth, *Compensation Management*, 92.

8. Ibid., 97–99.

9. Ibid., 99–101.

10. Ibid., 101–105.

11. Ibid., 102–105.

12. Ibid., 102.

13. Hills, Bergmann, and Scarpello, *Compensation Decision Making*, 283–285.

14. See "National Compensation Survey, Overview," 10 January 2000, available <http://stats.bls.gov/comover.htm>, 1–3; "National Compensation Survey, Frequently Asked Questions," 10 January 2000, <http://stats.bl.gov/comfaq.htm>, 1–3; and "National Compensation Survey, Contacts," 10 January 2000, <http://stats.bls.gov/comconta.htm>, 1–2 for a complete overview of the National Compensation Survey.

15. Caruth, *Compensation Management*, 109.

16. Ibid.

17. Ibid., 112.

18. Ibid., 112–113.

19. Ibid., 113–114.

8

JOB PRICING

Job pricing, an essential task regardless of the specific method of job evaluation used, brings together and integrates all of the previously performed activities of compensation system development: job analysis, job evaluation, and compensation surveys.[1] In addition, job pricing takes into consideration basic concepts of motivation, especially perceived equity.

Job pricing can be defined as the process by which monetary rates are attached to jobs so that a system of internal equity established through job evaluation acquires the added dimension of external equity. It is through job pricing that the internal values of organizational jobs are aligned with external rates of pay the labor market suggests are appropriate for those jobs.[2]

There is, unfortunately, no formula for taking the various bits and pieces of information generated through job evaluation and salary surveys and calculating precisely or automatically job prices that are internally and externally equitable. Consequently, as with other compensation system development activities, job pricing should be approached carefully and deliberately, with a view to establishing consistency and equity throughout the pay structure. This chapter will examine the role of both statistics and judgment in producing an appropriate set of monetary rates for an organization's jobs.

THE MECHANICS OF JOB PRICING

For simplicity of illustration, it will be assumed that only one job structure is being priced. In reality, most organizations, even small ones, have two or more job structures; one for clerical jobs and one for managerial jobs, for example. The procedures are the same, however, for pricing any structure. There are six steps involved in setting monetary rates for jobs: (1) establish pay policy guidelines, (2) construct market and organization pay lines, (3) determine job classes, (4) develop salary rate ranges, (5) resolve *red circle* and *green circle* rate discrepancies, and (6) formulate pay increase policy.[3]

Establish Pay Policy Guidelines

Pay policy guidelines set forth the organization's philosophy on internal compensation rates relative to pay rates in the labor market. These policies deal with the issue of compensation levels and answer the question, "What should be the organization's compensation level in light of the compensation level extant in the overall market?" Pay policy guidelines may, in fact, be established formally or informally when the initial decision is made to implement a systematic compensation program. Whether originated earlier in the process or at this later state, pay policies constitute the actual starting point for setting compensation rates.

An organization has four choices relative to its compensation levels: (1) pay what the market is paying, follow; (2) pay in excess of what the market is paying, lead; (3) pay less than the market is paying, lag; or (4) some combination of follow, lead, and lag.

Follow the Market

Perhaps the most common policy for many organizations is to set pay levels that are commensurate with market rates. This practice assures that an organization is at least as competitive paywise as other labor market institutions; therefore, an organization's chances of attracting, holding, and motivating human resources are equally as good as those of other firms that compete for similar talent. Such a policy also keeps compensation costs at a reasonable level; a firm is neither paying more nor less than is reasonably required to obtain sufficient people.

Lead the Market

A second policy alternative is to establish internal pay rates that are in excess of prevailing market rates. While there are different formulae that may be employed to express the degree of leadership desired, the most commonly used one is a percentage; for example, "It is the organization's policy to pay 5 percent above average labor market rates for similar jobs." Such a policy positions a company as a compensation leader and stipulates the amount of leadership desired.

Why would an institution adopt a compensation leadership policy? There are five likely reasons: (1) to assure an abundant supply of job applicants, (2) to increase the likelihood of selecting highly qualified candidates, (3) to decrease personnel turnover, (4) to increase employee productivity, and (5) to prevent unionization attempts.

Obviously, a policy of leadership will raise compensation costs in the short run. Before implementing such a policy an organization should carefully examine the benefits it hopes to gain. It should also determine the amount of compensation leadership it wishes to exercise. In some cases compensation leadership may pay significant dividends in the long run by attracting high-caliber employees; thus, this is a policy deserving careful study by any organization. If adopted, results should be monitored closely and continuously to determine if anticipated benefits are actually realized.

Lag the Market

Another policy alternative is to pay less than the market is paying. Typically, this policy, as in leading the market, is expressed in terms of a percentage.

There are times when lagging the market is an appropriate policy to follow: when there is an excess of qualified people available or when the organization is experiencing a profit squeeze, for example. It is also an inexpedient policy at other times—when labor supply is tight or profitability is unusually high—that can produce deleterious results, such as high turnover, poor performance, and job dissatisfaction.

If used as a pay policy guideline, the amount of lag between an organization's pay levels and those prevalent in the market should not be too great. While the question of how much to lag the market cannot be answered in the abstract, anything more than a 10-percent lag would appear to be questionable.

Combination

A final alternative to compensation competitiveness is some combination of following, leading, and lagging market pay levels. Typically, this policy is used where different forces affect various segments of the pay structure dissimilarly. An example will illustrate why a combination pay policy is sometimes advisable.

Assume that an organization is confronted with the following conditions: an abundant supply of people to fill entry-level positions that require no previous experience, a shortage of qualified applicants to fill middle-level positions such as senior accounting clerk, and a number of long-tenured employees at the upper end of the compensation structure. These three different conditions suggest the propriety of using a combination of pay policy guidelines. First, the abundance of people to fill lower positions could be addressed by a policy decision to pay less than market rates for the lower part of the job structure. Second, the difficult in finding people to fill middle-level positions necessitates paying at least market rates for these jobs. Third, the presence of many long-tenured personnel at the upper end suggests paying more than market rates to assure continued job satisfaction as well as to reward these employees for their loyalty and long service to the organization. Therefore, a combination of guidelines may be required to deal with these conditions effectively. If adopted, a combination policy must be examined regularly to ascertain whether the circumstances that prompted its use still exist. When conditions change, the guidelines should be changed.

Establishing pay policy guidelines is a decision for top management, but compensation personnel who are familiar with internal and external conditions should be relied upon for their suggestions about the feasibility or desirability of various alternatives.

Construct Market and Organization Pay Lines

The second step in job pricing is to construct trend lines that show the progression through the series of pay rates for key jobs in the labor market, as well as the progression through the rates that an organization is actually paying for each key job. The purpose of this analysis is to illustrate graphically how an organization's current compensation plan compares with the market.[4]

It is here that graphics and statistical techniques become involved in job pricing. This aspect of the pricing process may appear to be rather complex because of the requisite calculations and charts. It is not really as difficult as it first appears, especially in light of software packages available to handle the statistical computations and graphics.[5] Even when done manually, constructing pay lines is not overly complicated, although it may be somewhat time consuming. A simple illustration in a more or less step-by-step fashion will demonstrate what is involved. Inasmuch as the point plan of job evaluation is the most commonly used method of determining internal equity, the illustration will assume that this is the procedure employed by the organization in the example. When ranking, classification, and factor comparison are used for job evaluation, the procedure for job pricing is essentially the same.[6]

Table 8.1 shows the raw data that form the basis for the example. As can be seen in the table, the organization has evaluated its jobs and assigned a point value to each; a labor market survey has also been conducted using twenty-five key jobs that represent a wide range of point values. For each key job, the average salary in the marketplace, the organization's average salary, and the number of job evaluation points are shown. With these data several graphic and statistical analyses can be performed.

The first step in analyzing the data is to construct a scatter diagram relating survey salary figures for each key job to the job evaluation points that have been assigned by the organization. The resulting graph is shown in Figure 8.1. The scatter diagram of market salaries relative to job evaluation points provides a general verification of the accuracy of the organization's job evaluation efforts. In the example shown it can be seen clearly that there is a fairly good relationship between points and salaries; in general, the higher the number

Table 8.1
Survey and Organization Salaries with Job Evaluation Points

Job	Survey Average	Organization Average	Job Evaluation Points
1	1,950	1,790	100
2	1,900	1,820	150
3	2,100	1,940	140
4	2,120	1,990	320
5	2,200	2,090	250
6	2,360	2,120	300
7	2,250	2,190	380
8	2,460	2,220	500
9	2,620	2,380	460
10	2,680	2,430	550
11	2,700	2,400	500
12	2,800	2,540	620
13	2,920	2,620	720
14	2,970	2,580	630
15	2,740	2,600	710
16	3,170	2,860	945
17	3,030	2,900	975
18	3,080	2,800	885
19	3,100	2,950	1,075
20	3,220	3,000	1,110
21	3,260	2,980	1,808
22	3,380	3,050	1,150
23	3,640	3,200	1,320
24	3,360	3,100	1,255
25	3,450	3,250	1,360

of points assigned to a job, the higher the market rate of pay. The scatter diagram tends to support the validity of the organization's evaluations.

The second step is to compute a trend line—usually called a *salary curve* or a *wage curve*, even though it is likely to be a straight line—to the data in the scatter diagram. The trend line, shown in Figure 8.2, establishes the average relationship between salaries and points and indicates the general progression existing between jobs. There are two ways of fitting this line to the data: by eyeball or by the statistical technique of least-squares. Eyeball is the easiest approach and, depending on the array of the data, may be accurate enough for analysis purposes. To use this method, a compensation analyst simply looks at the data closely and draws a line through it so that an approximately equal number of dots are above and below the line drawn.

Figure 8.1
Scatter Diagram: Market Rates and Job Evaluation Points

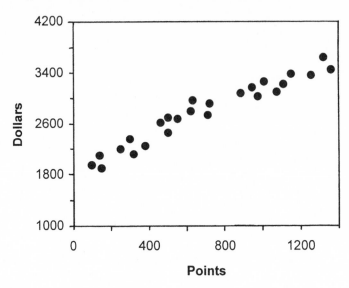

Figure 8.2
Salary Trend Line: Market Rates

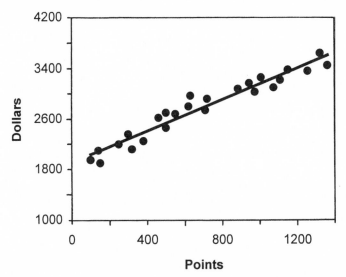

Least-squares is a statistical technique that produces a mathematically accurate trend line by minimizing the sum of the squares of the vertical deviations from the line.[7] (An explanation of the least-squares method and the procedures for calculating a mathematically precise trend line can be found in any business statistics textbook.) The line in Figure 8.2 was calculated by the least-squares technique. The eyeball approach will suffice in many cases, but if there is any doubt, or the data contain unusual variation, the least-squares method is recommended.

Next, these two steps are repeated using the organization's salary data and assigned job evaluation points.[8] Figure 8.3 shows the resulting scatter diagram and trend lines.

At this point in the analysis of the data, some idea of the progression in salaries as viewed by the labor market and some idea of the progression of salaries within the organization has been determined. What remains to be done is to compare the market trend line with the organization's trend line. This comparison is depicted in Figure 8.4.

Comparison of the two trend lines clearly shows that the organization is consistently below the market at all levels of its compensation structure. The deviation from market is less at lower job levels, but gradually increases at higher levels. Now the organization is in a better position to evaluate its pay policy guidelines in terms of what is actually occurring in the labor market. Based on Figure 8.4 it is obvious that if the expressed policy of the organization is to be a pay leader or to be competitive with the labor market, internal pay rates will need to be adjusted upward as the compensation system is finalized. If the policy of the organization is to lag the market, it is currently doing just that; however, the question of whether the actual amount of lag matches the desired amount of lag will need to be answered. Comparison of the two trend lines enables the organization to objectively assess its position

Figure 8.3
Salary Trend Line: Organization

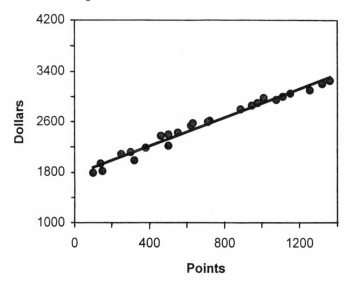

Figure 8.4
Salary Trend Comparison: Market and Organization

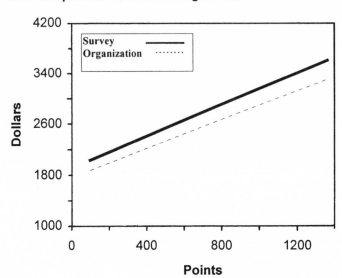

vis-à-vis the market and to determine what adjustments are necessary to bring actual pay rates into alignment with market rates in light of the organization's expressed pay policy guidelines.

From an operational standpoint, all of the data and calculations presented in Figures 8.1 and 8.4 can be displayed on one graph. This was not done here because the resulting graph tends to become very busy and also because it is easier to follow the analysis step by step when several charts are used.

Determine Job Classes

Job classes are convenient groupings of jobs that are approximately equal in difficulty or importance as determined through job evaluation.[9] Except for difficulty or importance, these jobs may have little else in common. Whether jobs are grouped into classes as part of the job pricing process depends to an extent upon the method of job evaluation used. The point plan and factor comparison method require the creation of job classes. The classification approach establishes job classes as part of constructing the evaluation system. Ranking may or may not utilize job classes, depending on the number of jobs that have been ranked to develop a compensation system. Commonly, the determination of job classes is considered to be part of the pricing process. One of the key features of a job class is that all jobs within that class are covered by the same range of pay. Precise amounts paid to specific jobholders will vary because of seniority, performance, or other factors; however, each job in the class is subject to the same minimum and maximum rates of pay.

There are several reasons why job classes are commonly used in compensation systems. First, it is much more convenient to price ten or twelve job classes than it is to set individual rates for fifty or sixty different jobs. Second, it is easier and less costly to administer job classes as opposed to individual job rates. When individual rates are used, even small changes in job content or duties may necessitate changes in salary. Third, many jobs are by nature very similar or closely related. To attempt to differentiate between them on some extremely finite basis is, for all practical purposes, extremely difficult or artificial. Job classes eliminate this problem.

Constructing job classes on some reasonable basis and determining the appropriate number to use is a matter that warrants thoughtful consideration of several factors. First, there is no optimum number of job classes that is appropriate for any given salary structure. In practice, it is not uncommon to find as few as six classes or as many as thirty used for pay structures that are essentially similar. What is known, however, is that there must be sufficient classes to recognize not only the similarities among jobs, but also to reflect the differences between jobs. Creating too many classes requires a precise differentiation among jobs that is probably not realistic; too few classes tends to blur the distinctions between jobs. The matter of the appropriate number of classes often boils down to a question of management policy and the needs of the organization. What is acceptable to top management? What is administratively feasible? What do employees perceive as fair? What adequately recognizes differences in job worth to the organization? There are no conclusive answers to these questions. There are, on the other hand, a few considerations to assess in deciding the number of classes that may be reasonable for a particular salary structure.

Typically, there are natural clusters of jobs that can be identified from the scatter diagrams of salaries and job evaluation points. Figure 8.1—the comparison of market rates and points—shows, for example, seven potential job clusters: one from 0 to 200 points, another from 200 to 400 points, and so forth. Based on the data presented, it would seem that seven job classes may be the appropriate number for the compensation structure in question. Figure 8.5 shows the identification of these classes more clearly. Additional verification of the appropriateness of these seven classes is obtained when the organization's internal rates and points (Figure 8.3) are compared with market rates and points (Figure 8.1). Scatter diagrams will not always identify such clear-cut clusters of jobs, but they will offer an excellent starting point for the identification of classes.

Another potential indicator of the correct number of job classes is industry practice. How many classes do other comparable organizations use for similar salary structures? This information, which can be obtained from the compensation survey, allows an organization to draw upon and benefit from the

Figure 8.5
Tentative Job Classes

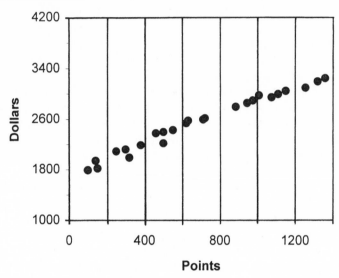

knowledge of organizations that may have more experience in administering compensation systems. This is not to suggest that the number of classes other institutions use is the precise number a given organization should use. Industry practice does, however, provide general guidance as to what may be an appropriate number of classes.

The number of pay structures that are to be used is another factor that influences the number of classes to be established. If an organization has decided to use only one pay structure to cover all of its jobs below the level of top management, more classes will be required than if it has decided to use multiple pay structures. This is true because there is a greater dissimilarity of jobs in the first instance and a greater similarity in the second instance.

A final consideration in determining the number of job classes is assuring some degree of consistency between classes. Figure 8.5 shows that the tentatively identified classes are consistently established at intervals of 200 job evaluation points. Job classes should have a reasonable degree of uniformity or some logical basis for distinguishing between them. This does not mean that all classes must consist of the same precise number of job evaluation points, but it does suggest that order and progression should dictate the cutoff points between classes. In some job class structures the point spread between classes decreases in the upper levels of the structure. For example, the point spread in classes one through six might be 200 points, while the spread in classes seven through ten might be 150 points. This is perfectly acceptable because it has a consistency to it. (A decreasing point spread is often used to afford better differentiation between higher-level jobs.) On the other hand, a job class system that consists of a 200-point spread for one class, a 300-point spread for the next class, and a 250-point spread for the following class defies logic, consistency, and uniformity.

While there is no magical formula for determining the precise number of classes to use, as a practical matter eight to fourteen classes would appear to be adequate for any pay structure. Some critics may claim that this is an insufficient number. The entire job classification system of the federal government, covering a multitude of jobs, contains only eighteen job classes. Thus, it would seem that any other organization should require no more than eighteen classes in any given pay structure.

Once all of the foregoing considerations have been take into account, a decision on the exact number of classes can be made. Each of the evaluated jobs can then be slotted into the appropriate class. Once this has been done, salary ranges for each job class can be set.

Develop Pay Grades or Pay Ranges

A salary rate range or class range is the difference between minimum and maximum rates of pay for a given job class. The range reflects the worth of a job, expressed in dollars, to an organization. Salary ranges permit organizations to recognize individual differences in performing a job and reward employees on the basis of these differences.[10] For the employee, salary ranges identify the amount of potential progression, in dollars, extant in a job. A range establishes a salary floor—no less than the minimum will be paid for performing a job within a particular class—and a salary ceiling—no more than the stipulated maximum will be paid for performing any job within a given class.

To construct salary ranges requires consideration of two sets of factors: (1) what is happening in the labor market, and (2) the internal needs and requirements of the organization. When conducting the compensation survey it is desirable to collect information on minimum and maximum salaries for key jobs, in addition to midpoint or average salary data. The minimum and maximum data enable a company to construct high and low market pay lines as well as an average pay line. Comparing the three pay trend lines offers some insight into rate ranges existing in the marketplace.

Figure 8.6 shows what these three pay lines might look like. The average market pay line is the same as the one previously shown in Figures 8.2 and 8.4. For the sake of simplicity, the data used to compute the market high lines and the market low lines have not been shown. The job classes can now be superimposed on the market pay lines, as illustrated in Figure 8.7. The intersections of the low, average, and high pay lines with the median point value of a job indicate the minimum, midpoint, and maximum dollar values for each job class as viewed by the labor market. The ranges for each class can

Figure 8.6
Market Pay Lines: High, Low, and Average

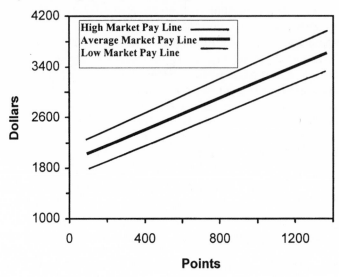

Figure 8.7
Job Class Rates Determined by Market Pay Lines

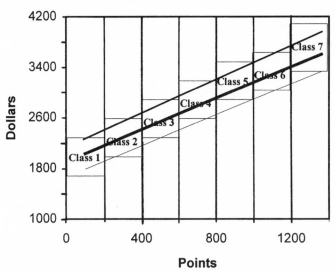

now be drawn in, also as indicated in Figure 8.7. Thus, on the basis of market data and internal evaluation of an organization's jobs, a fully priced job structure now exists.

In actual practice, job pricing seldom goes as smoothly as in this illustration. Frequently, market data may indicate a good deal of overlap between classes. If so, then the question of how much overlap should exist between classes has to be addressed.

A pay structure probably should contain no more than a three-class overlap; that is, the same salary should not be possible in more than two adjacent job classes. This means that one class should not overlap the next highest class by more than 50 percent. Excessive overlap of salary ranges can have a negative impact on employee morale, inasmuch as employees may view promotion to the next salary class as offering little or no advantage. On the other hand, if there is no overlap between classes employees may feel that promotion to the next class represents too much of a challenge.

Some organizations do not use high and low market pay lines to set rate ranges; they rely only on the average market pay line. Utilizing only the average pay line leaves the compensation specialist and management free to experiment with various range possibilities while attempting to maintain some degree of alignment with market pay. Figures 8.8 through 8.10 illustrate three salary range possibilities. Figure 8.8 shows a structure with no overlap between classes and a constant dollar salary range for each class. Figure 8.9 depicts a 50-percent class overlap from one class to the next class and an increasing dollar range. These illustrations are only three of the various possibilities that exist for constructing a salary structure.

Figure 8.8
Salary Structure: No Overlap, Constant Dollar Range

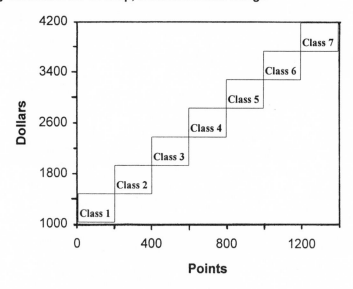

Figure 8.9
Salary Structure: 50-Percent Overlap, Constant Dollar Range

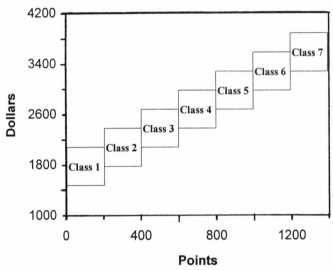

Figure 8.10
Salary Structure: 50-Percent Overlap, Increasing Dollar Range

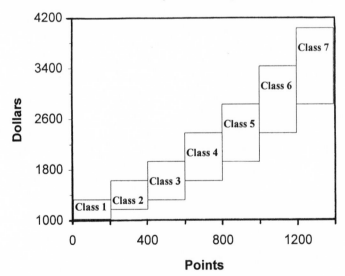

Internal considerations sometimes necessitate experimenting with pay ranges. For example, when ranges are initially constructed, a key factor in their design may be to assure that almost all of an organization's employees fit, salarywise, into the structure. If a significant number of employees fall outside of the classes that are established, problems can result. Also, if an organization has many long-tenured employees, ranges may have to be adjusted so that the majority of these employees are not positioned at or very near the top of the range.

Once the salary ranges have been finalized—and any reevaluations or adjustments of the class structure have been accomplished—the major work of job pricing is completed. There are still, however, two major issues to resolve before the compensation system can be implemented; namely, how to handle *red circle* and *green circle* rates and how to provide for periodic pay increases.

Establish Red Circle and Green Circle Rate Policies

A red circle rate is a salary currently being paid that falls outside the top limit of the pay range established for a job class. A green circle rate is a salary currently being paid that falls outside the lower limit of the pay range established for a job.[11] Red and green circle rates are fairly common problems when an organization's first formalized compensation system is installed. Without a mechanism—the compensation survey—for staying in tune with the marketplace, it is easy for individual pay rates to be set either too high or too low. Figure 8.11 illustrates a red and green circle rate situation. Correcting this problem requires the development of a compensation policy for dealing with overpaid and underpaid employees.

Figure 8.11
Red and Green Circle Rates

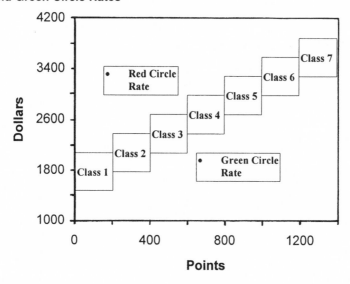

The Overpaid Employee

There are three common approaches to handling the employee who is paid above the established class maximum: (1) promote the employee to a job in a higher class, (2) freeze the rate until general increases in the salary structure bring the employee's rate into line with the job class, or (3) reduce the rate.

From a motivational standpoint, the first alternative is the most attractive. Promotion, even without an immediate increase in pay, is likely to be viewed positively by the employee. Yet promotion is not always a viable alternative. The employee may not be promotable. There may be no job openings to which the employee can be promoted. The employee may be promotable but there may be other employees who are more promotable. The situation calls for the development of a general policy that will apply to all overpaid employees; therefore, what the organization does for one employee, it must or should try to do for all overpaid employees.

The second alternative is to freeze the pay rate at its current level and wait for general increases in the salary structure to bring the rate into line with the established job class rate. In most instances, this is a simple, feasible solution to handling the problem. It does not jeopardize the employee's pay nor distort the organization's promotion system. The risk involved in this approach is the negative effect it may have on employee morale and motivation.

The third possibility is to reduce the rate to bring it into line with the class rate. This may be accomplished by an immediate cut in pay or by periodic reductions in pay over time. The negative effects of these actions are too great to warrant consideration of this approach as a viable alternative to handling the problem of overpaid employees. Where overpayment exists, it is due to mistakes made by management, not the employee. Reductions in pay in such a situation penalizes employees unfairly for a problem they did not create.

A reasonable policy for overpaid employees would probably be one that seeks to promote the employee if possible, but freezes the employee's salary at the current rate if promotion is not possible. Frozen salaries are generally brought back into line with class rates within a year or two, as periodic adjustments are made to the entire salary structure.

The Underpaid Employee

There are two ways of dealing with employees who are paid below the established class minimum: (1) bring the salaries to minimum immediately, or (2) bring the salaries to minimum by a series of planned adjustments over a period of time, such as one year. Bringing salaries immediately into line with the minimum rate for a class is theoretically the correct method of dealing with underpaid employees. Most of the time this instant adjustment poses no great difficulty because underpaid employees may not be underpaid by any great amount. In addition, immediate adjustments may have a very positive effect on employee morale or attitudes.

The situation changes greatly if the employee is significantly underpaid. Where the amount of increase necessary to bring an employee to class minimum is substantial, there is merit in making the necessary adjustments in increments, since a large one-time increase in pay may well create in an employee's mind the expectation of a large increase in later periods. When such increases are not forthcoming, motivation and morale may suffer.

A realistic policy for handling underpaid employees should concern itself with the need for immediate action while simultaneously addressing the magnitude of the adjustment required. An example of such a policy might be as follows: Adjustments not exceeding 10 percent of the employee's salary will be made immediately. Adjustments over 10 percent, but not exceeding 20 percent, will be made in two steps: an immediate 10-percent adjustment and the remaining adjustment at the end of six months. Adjustments of over 20 percent will be made in three steps, and so on. All adjustments necessary to bring employees into the class range will be accomplished in a maximum of twelve months.

Establish Increase Guidelines

The final step in pricing job structure is development of a system whereby periodic increases in salary can be awarded to employees.[12] The purpose of this system is to enable individuals to progress on some basis through the rate range established for a particular job. Two basic methods are generally used to provide for advancement through the salary range: (1) periodic step increases, and (2) merit progression. Both of these approaches create a basis for recognizing an employee's contribution to the organization and awarding pay increases based on this contribution.

Step Increases

The simplest procedure for handling periodic salary increases is to establish a series of definite pay steps through which an employee advances, depending upon tenure in a job. Each step represents a specific period of time, usually one year, spent performing the job. Therefore, the longer an employee is in the job, the higher that employee's rate of pay will be. Step increases provide for fixed dollar adjustments in salary. These adjustments are often referred to in practice as *scheduled increases* or *annual increases*. The theory underlying step increases is that the more time a person spends performing a particular job, the more competent that person will become; consequently, those who have been in a job the longest are the most competent performers and should receive higher rates of pay than those individuals who have been on the job a shorter length of time.

An example will illustrate how the values of steps are determined. Assume that a decision has been made to use six steps, the minimum salary for the job class in question is $2,000 per month, and the maximum salary is $3,000. In this case the step increase guide would be as follows:

> Step 1 = $2,000
> Step 2 = $2,200
> Step 3 = $2,400
> Step 4 = $2,600
> Step 5 = $2,800
> Step 6 = $3,000

The value of each step increase is calculated by using the following formula:

Salary Range ÷ Total Number of Steps – 1 = Incremental Step Increase Value

Thus, in the example, the numbers are

$$\$500 \div 6 - 1 = \$200$$

Adding the incremental increase to the total value of the preceding step gives the total value of a succeeding step.

The difficulty in developing a step increase guide is not in performing the computations; rather, it is in determining the number of steps to be used in the system. How many steps are appropriate? Unfortunately, there are no definitive guidelines for deciding how many steps are expedient for any given job structure or any given job class. Some plans use as few as three; some plans use as many as ten; others use a variable number, with fewer steps for lower job classes and more steps for higher job classes. The number of steps to be used and whether the same number of steps will be used for each job class within the pay structure are management policy decisions that merit careful attention. Class ranges, job tenure, and employee motivation need to be considered before action is taken.

The range of the class affects the number of steps because, generally, the greater the spread between minimum salary and maximum salary, the greater the possibility that each step increase represents a meaningful pay raise to the employee. In the preceding example, the percentage increases received by employees as they progress through the six steps are as follows:

> Step 1 = N/A
> Step 2 = 10.0%
> Step 3 = 9.1%
> Step 4 = 8.3%

Step 5 = 7.7%
Step 6 = 7.1%

Each adjustment in pay denotes a pay raise that is likely to be of significance to an employee. If, however, the class range is only $200 and six steps are used, progression from one step to the next loses much of its significance:

Step 1 = $1,000 (N/A)
Step 2 = $2,040 (2.0% increase)
Step 3 = $2,080 (2.0% increase)
Step 4 = $2,120 (1.9% increase)
Step 5 = $2,160 (1.9% increase)
Step 6 = $2,200 (1.9% increase)

One of the keys to determining the appropriate number of steps is to examine the significance of moving from one step to the next. It should be representative of real progress and viewed by the employee as such. If it is not, the number of steps contemplated is too many and should be reduced, or the monetary amount is too little and should be increased.

Job tenure is a second factor to be considered in arriving at an appropriate number of step increases in a pay plan. If an organization is growing rapidly and employees tend to move from a lower job to a higher job quickly, fewer steps may be required, since most employees will not stay in one job long enough to reach the top of the range. On the other hand, where organizational growth is stable or where the institution has a significant number of long-tenured employees, a greater number of steps may be required to provide some degree of perceived progression opportunities and prevent employees from reaching the tops of their job classes too quickly.

A third factor to weigh is employee motivation. This is not really a separate factor, since it is inextricably entwined with both class range and job tenure. It is, however, an element that deserves special deliberation. Perceived equity and expectancy theory are especially relevant to deciding how many steps to use. If for example, the class range is small and the number of steps used results in percentage pay increases that seem insignificant, employees are not likely to be motivated to perform at anything more than a barely acceptable level; the payoff, monetarily speaking, is just not there. On the other hand, if the number of steps is limited and employees reach the top of the range quickly only to find themselves stuck there, motivation and performance may suffer. It is crucial, therefore, to consider the contemplated number of steps from the viewpoint of the employees who will be affected. What will their reactions be? Will they perceive the number and amount of pay increases to be fair? Is the number of steps apt to reduce or increase performance? These and other similar questions should be answered thoughtfully.

From a practical standpoint, the use of different numbers of steps for specific segments of the pay structure, rather than a uniform number of steps for the entire structure, seems to be a realistic approach. First, lower job classes are typically comprised of entry-level or slightly higher jobs that can be mastered rather quickly. Moreover, most employees do not intend to make careers of these jobs; they normally expect to move up to higher-level jobs within the organization itself or with another institution. Since replacements are more easily found at lower levels, there is no great need to reward longevity beyond a certain limited point. Therefore, no more than five steps may be appropriate for the lower segment of the structure. Second, jobs within the middle classes take more time to master, replacements are typically harder to find, and retention of employees is usually more important. Under these conditions, rewards for job tenure acquire more significance. This segment of the structure may require as many as seven or more steps. Third, jobs within classes at the upper end of the spectrum take much more time to master, are considered career positions by both incumbents and the organization, are often difficult to fill when vacancies occur, and are typically held by long-tenured employees or employees who expect to become long-tenured. Consequently, it may be advisable to provide as many as ten steps at this level of the structure. While there is no exact number of steps that should be used in a plan, somewhere between five and ten is usually considered appropriate.

As a method of providing for progression through a salary range, the step increase approach offers several advantages: (1) ease of administration—the precise amount of the increase and the point at which it will be awarded are fixed; (2) communication to employees—the number of steps, the amount of increase, and the length of time required to merit a raise can be explained quite easily; (3) measurement—since increases are determined by seniority or *time in* grade, there is no need for establishing elaborate methods to differentiate levels of employee performance because pay is determined by the calendar; and (4) budgeting—estimated salaries for the coming year are easy to determine because who is due a raise, when it is to be given, and the amount to be given can be identified precisely.

There are, however, some serious disadvantages to using the step increase approach: (1) implied entitlement—automatic increases may suggest to employees that raises are theirs whether they have actually earned them or not; (2) no consideration of performance—seniority is the ruling factor rather than how well an employee performs the job; (3) negative motivational impact—since pay increases are based on job tenure there is no incentive to perform at a high level; and (4) inflexibility—managers do not have the ability to reward exceptional employees because everyone is locked into the same system.

Merit Progression

The second method of handling periodic salary increases is to base pay adjustments on the level of performance demonstrated by employees. These adjustments are variously referred to as *merit increases, merit pay, perform-ance increases*, or *performance-based pay*.

The theory behind this approach is that better performers should receive larger salary increases than poorer performers. In other words, merit progression is based on the principle that pay increases should be earned by measurable accomplishments on the job and not be granted simply on the basis of seniority. For merit progression to work successfully it is necessary for the organization to define various levels of performance, establish standards reflective of each level, and develop measures to indicate the actual level of performance achieved by an employee. These three tasks as well as others associated with performance appraisal are addressed in detail in Chapter 11.

Merit progression customarily relies on percentage increases in pay rather than fixed dollar amounts to determine the specific adjustment in pay that an employee will receive. The actual percentage increase received is directly related to the level of performance demonstrated. There are two basic approaches to handling the percentage increases: (1) constant percentages used throughout the salary range, and (2) variable percentages for different segments of the salary range.

Constant percentages of merit increase for the entire salary range require the development of only one set of merit pay guidelines. If, for example, an organization has identified five levels of performance, its merit percentage increase schedule might be as follows:

Level of Performance	*Percent Increase in Pay*
Clearly outstanding	10.0
Excellent	8.0
Good	6.0
Below expectations	2.0
Unsatisfactory	0.0

In applying these guidelines, any employee who is performing at the excellent level, regardless of where he or she currently is within the salary range, would receive a salary increase of 8 percent; any employee, regardless of position within the range, who is demonstrating good performance would receive a pay raise of 6 percent. The rationale of using constant percentages is that performance of an equal nature should be recognized on an equal basis and percentages rather than constant dollar amounts do this fairly. Moreover, employees—applying the concept of perceived equity to their salary increases—generally convert their raises into percentages for comparison with the raises of other employees. With constant percentages, a specific level of performance always merits the same percentage of increase, a situation that typically suggests equity to employees.

There are, though, two serious drawbacks to using this system of determining merit increases: (1) Employees at the upper half of the range receive greater dollar increases because their base salary is larger, and (2) excellent and outstanding performers may progress through the range so quickly that they soon reach the maximum salary and can progress no further. These points should be carefully considered before adopting this particular method.

It is not uncommon to find two separate sets of merit-increase percentages used in merit progression plans: one set for use below the midpoint of the range and one set for use above the midpoint. This is normally done to allow employees to reach the midpoint quickly, but then slow progression down so that employees do not reach the top of the range too soon. Another reason is to keep the actual dollar amounts of increases above and below the midpoint more in line with each other. A graphic example will illustrate the impact of using variable percentages. Table 8.2 shows a comparison of constant per-cent increases with variable percent increases. The data shown are based on these four assumptions: (1) the class range is $2,000 to $3,000, with a mid-point of $1,500; (2) the employee receives clearly outstanding performance evaluations at each appraisal; (3) clearly outstanding receives a constant 12-percent increase in the first instance, but a variable percent increase in the second instance of 12 percent below midpoint and 8 percent above midpoint. As Table 8.2 shows, using a constant percentage allows the employee only three full pay increases before reaching the class maximum, whereas the vari-able percentage increase guidelines permit four full pay adjustments before the top of the class is attained. Either approach enables the employee to reach the midpoint rapidly, but the variable percentage plan allows the employee one more full pay increase before topping out. In short, variable percentages increase the longevity of the class range.

The major drawback to a two-tier increase system revolves around em-ployees' perceptions of equity. The fact that the same level of performance merits different percentages of pay increases at different points in the struc-ture might seem unfair when viewed through the eyes of employees. While compensation specialists have a logical explanation—namely, that once the

Table 8.2
Merit Increase Comparisons

Constant 12% Increase			12% Below, 8% Above Increase		
Raise #	$ Increase	Salary	Raise #	$ Increase	Salary
-	-	2,000	-	-	2,000
1	240	2,240	1	240	2,240
2	269	2,509	2	269	2,509
3	301	2,810	3	201	2,710
4	190*	3,000	4	217	2,927
-	-	-	5	73**	3,000

*Represents 6.8-percent increase.

**Represents 2.5-percent increase.

expected level of job proficiency, as represented by the salary midpoint, has been reached additional gains in proficiency do not come rapidly—this argument may be difficult for employees to grasp. Undoubtedly, many employees may view the variable percentage approach as inconsistent or unfair. If so, perceived inequity in compensation is likely to be the result.

As a means of permitting advancement through a pay range, merit progression has several significant advantages, especially when compared to step increases: (1) recognition of performance—employees who perform at higher levels receive greater financial rewards than those who perform at lower levels; (2) motivational impact—because performance is recognized, employees may be stimulated to put forth greater effort; (3) flexibility—managers have greater latitude to recognize and reward differences in performance between employees; and (4) no implied entitlement—employees know that each pay increase is subject to actual performance and must be earned again in each succeeding evaluation period.

Merit progression is not without certain disadvantages: (1) lack of control over performance by the employee—there are many jobs where an employee has limited control over the tangible end result produced; (2) performance measurement—where no tangible end product results from an employee's efforts, precise measurement of performance levels is not an easy task; (3) perceptions of pay and performance linkage—employees must be able to see, and the organization must be able to demonstrate, that there is a direct connection between performance and pay and that increases are not affected by favoritism or other extraneous factors; (4) reliance on money as a motivator—merit progression places considerable emphasis on the role of money as a motivator and may neglect psychological aspects of the total compensation package; (5) employee uncertainty—unlike step increases, merit progression does not assure an employee that he or she will receive an increase of a certain amount or any increase at all; and (6) percentage differentials—when a two-tier system of increases is used there are potential problems of communicating the fairness of the system.

Once the pay increase policy and accompanying guidelines have been formulated, the salary structure is ready for implementation and use.

OTHER APPROACHES TO JOB PRICING

While perhaps the majority of organizations still use the traditional approach to job pricing described, three newer approaches have been developed. These are direct market pricing, broadbanding, and skill/competency-based pay.

Direct Market Pricing

Direct market pricing involves matching a large percentage of an organization's jobs with jobs in the labor market. It extends well beyond surveying the market with a set of key jobs. The intent is to match as many as possible of the organization's jobs with like jobs in the market. Direct market pricing deemphasizes internal consistency. Its focus is on achieving external equity. Rates for unique organizational jobs that cannot be found in the market are determined by comparing them to survey jobs in terms of their value to the organization and then slotting them into an appropriate pay level.

Broadbanding

Broadbanding provides organizations with a new approach to job pricing. Broadbanding involves the creation of a few, typically three to eight, comprehensive job grades rather than a number of smaller sized grades. Figure 8.12 shows a comparison of a traditional pay structure with nine job classes and a broadbanded structure that has collapsed the nine job classes into three. Note that each band has a minimum and maximum salary and a 50-percent overlap.

Broadbanding accommodates today's flatter organizational structure by eliminating narrowly defined jobs. Broadbanding emphasizes skill development and provides employees with more freedom to move laterally or up or down within a job grade. For example, an employee on occasion may desire to downshift to a less stressful or demanding position. Broadbanding allows employers to ease employees downward without penalizing them by imposing drastic cuts in pay. Broadbanding recognizes that in today's organizations employees may have to perform not just one, but several different jobs.

Broadbanding, according to one survey, is one of the fastest growing compensation systems in this country.[13] More and more companies are creating a few broadly defined pay grades as opposed to the numerous narrowly defined pay grades used in traditional job pricing approaches. Broadbanding gives supervisors and managers more latitude in making pay decisions. It is also less cumbersome than traditional compensation systems. On the other hand, there are some potential problems associated with implementing broadbanding. Sufficient time, for example, must be invested to determine whether it is appropriate for a particular organization. Training must be provided so that employees can fully understand the system. The conversion must use carefully planned phasing for a successful transition from a traditional pay grade approach to broadbanding.

Skill/Competency-Based Pay

Under a skill/competency-based pay structure workers are paid not simply for the job they may be performing presently, but on the basis of the number of other jobs they can perform or on the basis of the depth of knowledge they have acquired.[14] Such pay schemes are the result of organizational downsizing and restructuring. As organizations become leaner it is crucial that employees be able to perform several jobs. In skill/competency-based structures it is important

Figure 8.12
Traditional and Broadbanded Pay Structures

Traditional Pay Structure

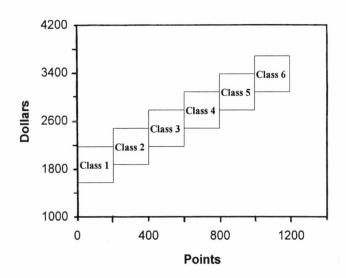

Broadband Pay Structure

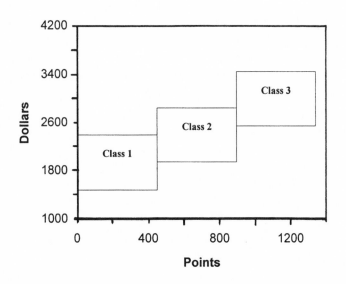

that the skills or competencies desired be identified, means of measuring skills and competencies be determined, means of acquiring them be identified, and pay increases be predicated upon their acquisition. Needless to say, there is a great deal of complexity involved in designing these systems.

MULTIPLE PAY STRUCTURES

How many pay structures should an organization have? Is a single structure sufficient to cover all jobs or should multiple structures be designed? These are complex questions that do not have precise answers.[15]

The type of job evaluation plan used has a direct bearing on the number of compensation structures. The classification approach, for instance, can be used effectively to evaluate all of any organization's jobs, from the highest to the lowest. Simple ranking can also accomplish the same result. The point plan and factor comparison are more realistically utilized for evaluating jobs where there is a common thread of responsibility, skill, and so on running through each of the jobs within some broad grouping, such as manual, clerical, or managerial.

Size of the organization also plays a role in determining how many structures may be necessary. Common sense would suggest that a company with only ten jobs should be able to use a single structure, whereas an organization with five hundred jobs might find it difficult to do so.

The different pay needs of different occupational groupings should be considered when deciding the number of pay structures required. The pay needs of executives and the basis on which they expect those needs to be fulfilled is quite different from those of rank-and-file employees.

Each organization must evaluate its own requirements in light of these factors. In general, it would seem that at least three structures are necessary for large institutions: one for top management; a second for other officials, managers, and high-level professionals; and a third for all other personnel. Each of these three structures may require its own separate job evaluation system and performance appraisal program.

UPDATING THE PAY STRUCTURE

Surprisingly, there is a lack of material in most compensation texts concerning the need to revise the salary structure, when to do so, how to go about it, and how to address problems that may be encountered when revision is undertaken. Most of what is presented addresses the evaluation of new jobs that are created from time to time or the reevaluation of existing jobs that undergo significant changes in content; in other words, the maintenance of internal equity. Revision of the pay structure is concerned with maintaining external equity. Once established, a pay structure cannot be expected to endure for an indefinite period of time. The following section considers factors that suggest the need for revision of the pay structure, when to revise, how to revise, and problems that may arise when the structure is revised.[16]

Need for Revision

The pay structure must be adjusted periodically because of (1) changes in labor supply and demand, (2) inflation, (3) changes in the organization's ability to pay, (4) changes in the organization's competitive position, and (5) increases in the number of long-tenured employees.

A labor market is not static; it is dynamic, with changes constantly taking place in the availability of people with certain skills as well as the demand for people having those particular skills. It is necessary to revise the pay structure to keep up with these changes in human resource supply and demand. Over the past decade, the demand for labor has been so high that many firms find they must pay well in excess of the required minimum wage just to attract enough people to fill entry-level positions.

Inflation is an economic reality. Too few dollars chasing too few goods—the classical definition of inflation—exerts an upward pressure on the price of everything, including the price of human resources. This inflationary pressure compels an institution to periodically adjust its pay structure upward. While inflation today appears to be under control, there is no guarantee that it will remain so indefinitely.

Not as important as labor supply and demand or inflation but nevertheless a factor that influences the need for adjusting pay levels is an organization's ability to pay. In times of poor organizational health, ability to pay may be a compelling reason to revise a pay structure downward. Likewise, a positive change in an organization's financial condition may suggest an upward revision of pay structures.

The institution's competitive position may also suggest the need for pay structure revision. To maintain high levels of performance in the face of increasing competition from other organizations, some companies may find it necessary to adjust salary levels upward to attract highly skilled personnel who can deliver the type of products and services the organization must offer to compete effectively.

A final consideration suggesting the need for revision is the seniority of an organization's employees. Some organizations, especially small to medium-size ones, frequently have a stable, long-tenured workforce. Where this occurs, employees are continually at or near the top of their salary scales. In order to continue to provide some degree of satisfaction with pay—and certainly to avoid the risk of pay dissatisfaction—upward structural adjustments are required periodically.

In general, economic forces, aided by internal organizational considerations, necessitate periodic revision of the pay structure.

When to Revise

Pay levels and compensation practices in an organization's labor market(s) should probably be reexamined at least annually. This is not to say, however, that the pay structure must be revised every year, although in light of today's economic realities an annual revision is apt to be advisable.

Based on the yearly examination of the labor market, an organization can compare its pay structure with that of the marketplace. When a significant deviation from stipulated pay policy occurs, revision is in order. Calculation of market pay lines and comparison with internal pay lines will indicate the amount of an existing deviation and suggest whether it is significant enough to warrant changes in the pay structure.

A point to keep in mind when examining an organization's current position vis-à-vis the market is that the data may represent past market conditions. A 5-percent variance from market rates at the time of the compensation survey could well become a 10-percent variance by the time of the next survey. Therefore, a revision to the pay structure must consider not only what is currently happening in the labor market but also what may occur before the next resurvey.

In most instances, it appears that annual adjustments to the pay structure are necessary to maintain viability in compensation.

How to Revise

Adjustments to the pay structure deal with the entire structure and not with individual job rates or rates for one or two job classes. Revision of the structure means reviewing it and modifying it in its entirety. Piecemeal changes in some job classes but not in others, or elevation of some individual job rates but not others, produces distortion of the entire pay system.

The creation of the original pay structure sets into place a system of equity in which the relationship of each job class to every other job class is established. Assuming that this relationship is accurate, any periodic revisions of the structure must preserve the original relationship. (Of course, if the structure proves to be inadequate, a new one will have to be created, but this is an entirely different matter from adjusting an existing structure.)

When the need for revision is seen, good practice suggests that the entire structure be *floated*. This means that the same relative adjustments to minimum and maximum rates for all job classes are made, so that the relationship between pay rates of all classes is maintained as initially constructed. The minimum and the maximum pay rates of all job classes should be increased by 6 percent if a 6-percent elevation in overall compensation is indicated. In other words, the entire structure moves upward by 6 percent.

When revising, it is necessary to consider not only the amount of adjustment currently required to maintain pace with the labor market, but also to anticipate what adjustments the market will probably make before the organization revises its pay structure again. Obviously, revision always involves some element of second guessing the market. This is the most difficult part of the annual revision process: anticipating the movement of the market while the organization's new salary structure is in place. Certainly, judicious timing of surveys—such as just after the majority of competing labor market institutions have made their adjustments for the coming year—can assist in this regard, provided that surveys can be so timed. Economic forecasts, salary forecasts, and similar data available from a variety of sources can also assist. Likewise, the compensation specialist's feel for future market changes, gained through extensive experience, can help.

Because of the anticipatory nature of structural adjustments, a question arises as to whether the entire required adjustment should be made at once or whether it should be made in two or more stages. This question is a valid one. The answer can be found in commonly accepted compensation practice. The majority of organizations make a single annual adjustment. One adjustment per year simplifies the revision process and is in keeping with what most other institutions are doing. On the other hand, there are some organizations— typically because of declining profits or accelerating costs—that determine the amount of adjustment on an annual basis but implement it in six-month increments. While adding an administrative burden, this two-step approach offers two advantages: it tends to hold down compensation costs for a while, and it suggests to employees, because of the frequency of adjustments, that the organization is closely attuned to required changes in compensation.

Problems in Revision

There are certain problems that may arise when a pay structure is adjusted. Attempting to anticipate the future has already been discussed. Other problems include creation of new green or red circle rates, pay compression, and compensation costs.

Revising the salary structure upward may create new green circle rates because some employees are currently being paid less than the new class minimum. If the structure is revised downward—a highly unlikely occurrence today—red circle rates above the new class maximum may be created. These problems should be handled in accordance with an organization's established policies. Normally, problems of this nature are of small magnitude.

Pay compression is a much more common and serious problem.[17] Compression occurs when minimum rates of pay, either for individuals or some lower-level job classes, are elevated without a corresponding increase for presently employed personnel or for higher-level job classes.[18] By and large, compression occurs because the entire pay structure has not been adequately adjusted. Piecemeal revisions will likely produce pay compression.

The cost of revising the salary structure may also be a very real problem for organizations. Given that a revision in pay structure usually means higher labor costs, an organization must weigh the need for and the costs of revision against potential increases in productivity or profitability or it must examine its ability to pass increased labor costs along to customers. Ultimately, the decision concerning the amount of required adjustment and the amount of actual adjustment that can be afforded by an organization is one that only top management can make.

NOTES

1. Donald L. Caruth, *Compensation Management for Banks* (Boston: Bankers Publishing, 1986), 115.

2. Ibid.

3. Ibid., 115–116.

4. Ibid., 118.

5. Frederick S. Hills, Thomas J. Bergmann, and Vida G. Scarpello, *Compensation Decision Making*, 2d ed. (Fort Worth: Dryden Press, 1994), 308.

6. Caruth, *Compensation Management*, 118–119.

7. Ibid., 306.

8. Ibid., 120–125.

9. Ibid., 125–129.

10. Ibid., 129–136.

11. Robert L. Mathis and John H. Jackson, *Human Resource Management*, 8th ed. (Minneapolis–St. Paul: West, 1997), 399–400.

12. Caruth, *Compensation Management*, 139–147.

13. Larry Reissman, "Nine Common Myths About Broadbands," *HR Magazine*, August 1995, 79–86.

14. Wayne F. Cascio, *Managing Human Resources*, 5th ed. (Boston: Irwin–McGraw-Hill, 1998), 400.

15. Hills, Bergmann, and Scarpello, *Compensation Decision Making*, 320–321.

16. Caruth, *Compensation Management*, 147–151.

17. Cascio, *Managing Human Resources*, 404–405.

18. Mathis and Jackson, *Human Resource Management*, 400.

9

INDIRECT MONETARY COMPENSATION: THE ROLE OF BENEFITS

The second major component of a total compensation system is indirect monetary compensation or benefits. This component consists largely of items of monetary value that an organization provides to employees in addition to salaries and wages, the first component of a compensation system. Although payment is normally received *in-kind* as various protections and services, some forms of indirect compensation may actually result in direct monetary payments to employees.[1]

This portion of the compensation package was formerly referred to as *fringe benefits*. Inasmuch as the cost of these protections and services has reached an average of 27.5 percent of payroll costs for civilian workers in the United States, according to a 1999 study by the Bureau of Labor Statistics, the term *fringe* is no longer descriptive or accurate.[2] *Employee benefits, benefits, supplementary compensation, indirect compensation,* or *indirect monetary compensation* are more appropriate terms today for describing this part of the total compensation package.

Indirect monetary compensation is the most confusing and complex area of compensation program design, implementation, and administration.[3] A tremendous variety of options are available. There is a great amount of legality involved with some elements. There are tax considerations—for both employee and employer—to be assessed carefully. It is beyond the scope of this book to delve into benefits in great detail; thus, this chapter will concern itself with an overview of indirect compensation, highlighting some of the most commonly provided benefits.

THE ROLE OF INDIRECT COMPENSATION

What role do benefits play in the compensation package? Why do organizations provide a particular package or level of benefits? What prompts institutions to spend as much as they do on indirect compensation? The purposes of benefits are to (1) assist a firm in attracting sufficient numbers of qualified employees, (2) aid in retaining employees, (3) comply with federal or state legislation, (4) fulfill labor agreements, (5) avoid the potential for increased mandatory offerings of benefits, and (6) help discharge a company's social responsibility for the well-being of its employees and their families.[4]

Attract Employees

Often it is the tangible components of compensation—the direct and indirect portions—that initially attract employees to a particular organization. If these tangible components are not competitive with the labor market, an organization will be unable to create an adequate pool of applicants from which to select the qualified personnel it needs. An acceptable package of benefits helps assure a sufficient supply of human resources; an unacceptable package deters workers from seeking employment with a particular firm.

Retain Employees

Indirect monetary compensation helps a company retain the employees it hires. Benefits provide a sense of security; they improve an employee's general feelings of satisfaction about an organization. Furthermore, since most benefit packages are specifically designed to favor employees with longer service, indirect compensation tends to encourage people to stay with an institution. Retirement benefits, for example, increase with years of service; profit-sharing plans often provide for greater participation as time with the organization mounts. Benefits create "golden handcuffs" that bind an individual to an organization, since leaving for employment elsewhere would wipe out indirect compensation advantages or privileges an employee has accrued through length of service.

Comply with Legislation

Employers are required by federal law to contribute to Social Security funding and provide benefits such as workers' compensation. In addition, employers may be required to provide leave to employees under certain conditions or to extend the offer of lower-cost employee-paid health insurance coverage after an individual terminates employment.

Fulfill Labor Agreements

Under the National Labor Relations Act of 1935 employers are required to bargain in good faith over terms and conditions of employment. Included in the items that an employer must bargain over are retirement and many other forms of benefits. Once the level of benefits to be provided has settled, the employer must offer these benefits for the duration of the labor agreement.

Avoid Additional Mandatory Benefits

The majority of benefits are provided to employees at the option of the employer. Generally speaking, most employers would probably like to continue to have discretionary options to provide or not provide benefits as they see fit. Consequently, benefits may be offered to forestall the threat of legislation requiring additional mandatory benefits.

Discharge Social Responsibility

Employers today recognize that they have an obligation to provide for the welfare and well-being of employees and their families. This elevated social consciousness that began to develop in the 1960s is neither paternalistic nor altruistic; rather, it is an expression of genuine concern on the part of employers for their workers. Better working environments, improved organizational climates, and increased benefits are the avenues many firms use to discharge this sense of concern for employees. Social responsibility suggests that simply providing a job is no longer enough. Employees expect and demand more than this. New and expanded forms of indirect compensation have been the result.

Benefits Do Not Motivate

Although many organizations state that increased employee motivation is one of the objectives of their indirect compensation programs, there is little evidence to support the claim that benefits have any relationship to employee performance or productivity.[5] Research generally suggests that benefits act more as dissatisfiers: Insufficient benefits cause employees to become disenchanted with an organization; sufficient benefits reduce this disenchantment but do not cause employees to exert extra effort to accomplish work.

There are several reasons why benefits do not motivate. First, indirect compensation tends to be taken for granted. Employees view benefits as an entitlement, not as a performance inducement or something to be earned. Second, employees have little comprehension of or concern for the cost of benefits provided. In one study, for example, only 10 percent of the respondents "had a reasonably accurate . . . or inflated perception of the magnitude of employee benefits."[6] Most employees have almost no conception of what it would cost the employee personally if he or she were to have to purchase those same benefits on the open market. Third, employees typically perceive no direct connection between on-the-job performance and benefits, or if they do it is seen as tenuous, with a payoff too distant to be of immediate concern. Profit sharing is a benefit that has often been touted as one with motivational value. In reality, most employees probably perceive that they can have little or no effect on profitability; hence, they may see no relationship between performance and payoff. Management, economic factors, and competition control profitability. Moreover, any reward given in the form of profit sharing comes so far down the road—usually in the form of a distribution to be received upon termination or retirement—that any relationship between high performance and its reward is completely obscured.

In designing an indirect compensation package it is important not to succumb to the notion that employees will be stimulated to higher levels of motivation by what is offered in the form of benefits. It is more realistic, in light of research findings, to view benefits in terms of attracting employees, retaining employees, fulfilling the institution's social responsibility to its workers, and so forth.

For managers and executives, on the other hand, indirect compensation may have a greater motivational impact.[7] Managers can directly affect a firm's earnings, performance can be directly related to results, and the payoff can be significant enough to stimulate increased effort. But organizations should not expect the same result where rank-and-file employees are concerned.

TYPES OF INDIRECT COMPENSATION

Indirect compensation takes many forms, but can be categorized into three major components: (1) benefits required by law, (2) benefits regulated by statute, and (3) benefits provided solely at the option of the employer.[8] Inconsistency arises when, as will be discussed later, attempts are made to subdivide the optional component into clear-cut groupings and assign each form of indirect compensation to one of these groupings.

Legally Required Indirect Compensation

While almost every form of indirect compensation is affected by statutory, administrative, or common law, only four benefits are specifically mandated by statute: Social Security, workers' compensation, unemployment insurance, and family and medical leave.

Social Security

Originally enacted in 1935, and amended many times since, the Social Security Act provides a minimum degree of protection for most U.S. workers and their families. Currently about 95 percent of American workers and self-employed persons are covered and 44.2 million people are on the Social Security rolls. Social Security benefits are designed to replace part, but not all, of lost family income resulting from a worker's retirement, disability, or death. These benefits are funded by required contributions from employers, employees, and self-employed individuals. For the year 2000 there is a payroll tax of 7.65 percent (6.2% Social Security tax and 1.45% Medicare tax) for both employees and employers on the first $72,600 of earnings. For earnings over this amount, employees and employers pay 1.45 percent in Medicare taxes. Self-employed persons pay a tax of 15.3 percent up to $72,600, and then pay 2.9 percent on income over the covered amount. Changes are made every year in Social Security. Since 1975, adjustments in payments to those drawing benefits have been automatic based on changes in the Consumer Price Index.

The amount of retirement benefits available under Social Security depends upon the individual's age at retirement, the number of years the employee has worked in covered employment, average earnings during the period of employment, and the number of eligible dependents at the time benefits begin.

The time at which a person can retire with full benefits depends on the birth year of the individual. As of 1999 the ages for full retirement were as follows:

Birth Year	Full Retirement Age
1937 or before	65
1938–1942	65 plus two months per year after 1937
1943–1954	66
1955–1959	66 plus two months per year after 1954
1960 or after	67

Individuals who retire before the specified full retirement date receive reduced benefits. People who retire at the full retirement age (sixty-five) and continue working may earn as much money as they want without losing any benefits under an amendment to the Social Security Act signed into law by President Clinton in 2000. Workers who retire at seventy receive greater benefits than if they had retired at sixty-five; they also may earn as much as they want and not lose benefits if they continue working. Totally and permanently disabled workers may also be eligible for disability payments under Social Security, depending upon the time spent in covered employment and whether the disability meets the definition established by law. Disability payments continue until age sixty-five, at which time the individual is transferred to the Social Security retirement rolls. In 1999 the average monthly benefit for a disabled worker and family was about $1,217. For a disabled worker alone, it was about $733.

Social Security also provides payments to beneficiaries of deceased workers. These beneficiaries are usually spouse, dependent children, or dependent parents, although under certain conditions a divorced spouse may qualify for payments. The amount of payments is contingent upon the length of time in covered employment, earnings of the worker, age and number of recipients involved, and the health of the recipients.

Through Medicare, Social Security provides a wide range of health care services and benefits to almost everyone sixty-five or older. Individuals over sixty-five are eligible for Medicare whether they receive Social Security benefits or not and whether they are retired or still working.

Because Social Security provisions change every year, the Social Security Administration should be contacted for the latest information whenever questions arise.

Is the Social Security system facing bankruptcy? This is a frequently asked question. As of the year 2000, it is estimated that the Social Security system will be solvent through the year 2030. Because Social Security has become engrained in our society and is also a very political issue, it seems safe to assume that Congress will continue to revise the system to keep it financially sound.

Workers' Compensation

Workers' compensation is funded entirely by contributions from employers and is mandated not by federal law but by statutes in each of the fifty states. Workers' compensation is an insurance program that protects employees from expenses incurred or injuries suffered as a result of work-related accidents or diseases. Coverage is provided either through private insurance carriers or through employer participation in a state fund.

Benefits under workers' compensation vary widely from state to state. Most states provide for lifetime benefits for permanent total disability, but some limit payments to a stipulated time period. Payments are usually tied to the employee's earnings and number of dependents.

To be covered under workers' compensation the injury or disease must typically arise from an accident or condition suffered while in the course of employment. A few states, however, also have laws protecting workers from temporary disabilities arising from nonoccupational injuries or illnesses. Either monetary reimbursement or direct payment of expenses may be made for permanent disability, temporary total disability, loss of use of a body member, medical expenses incurred during treatment, disfigurement, rehabilitation programs, and, in the event of a fatal injury, benefits to surviving dependents.

Unemployment Compensation

Unemployment compensation was instituted in 1935 as part of the Social Security Act; however, unemployment insurance is not a totally federalized program inasmuch as each state is given the latitude, under general guidelines, to develop its own program. As a result, there is variation in the amounts actually paid to unemployed workers in different states.

This benefit is funded almost entirely by the employer. Typically, the employer is taxed at least 6.2 percent of the first $7,000 earned by each employee (employees in Alaska, Alabama, and New Jersey are also taxed). Some states provide for a higher tax rate as well as a higher base earnings level. An experience rating, based on terminations that result in unemployment compensation claims, is also used in calculating the tax that must be paid by a specific employer. In some cases, the state tax rate may actually drop to zero if the employer has had no recent terminations resulting in claims for unemployment compensation.

Approximately 98 percent of the American workforce is covered by unemployment compensation insurance. To collect benefits under this program an employee must meet certain eligibility requirements: (1) be able and available for employment, (2) be actively seeking employment, (3) not have refused suitable employment, (4) not be on strike (except in New York and Rhode Island), (5) not have left his or her previous job voluntarily, (6) not have been terminated for willful or wanton misconduct, and (7) have been previously employed in a covered occupation.

Originally, the Social Security Act provided, under state laws, for payment of up to twenty-six weeks of unemployment compensation benefits. Later legislation now provides for the extension of benefits in times of high unemployment.

Family and Medical Leave

The Family and Medical Leave Act of 1993 was the first piece of legislation signed by President Clinton after taking office. Congress had twice passed similar legislation and President Bush had on each occasion vetoed it.

To be eligible for leave under the FMLA, an employee must have been on the job for at least one year and have worked a minimum of 1,250 hours during the preceding twelve-month period. A company may exempt from FMLA coverage the top 10 percent of its highest paid employees. The act guarantees up to twelve weeks of unpaid leave per year for birth or adoption of a child; caring for an ill child, spouse, or parents; or the employee's own serious health condition. Where practical, employees must give the employer a thirty-day notice of intent to take leave. Employers may require that covered employees use vacation and sick leave first, before the period of unpaid leave begins, provided that vacation and sick leave are compensated at normal company rates. Employers must maintain health insurance benefits during the leave period. In addition, employees are guaranteed the right to return to the same or a comparable job. Employers can require workers to provide medical certification of serious injuries, as well as a second medical opinion.

There are four methods of determining the twelve-month period during which FMLA leave may be taken: any calendar year; any fixed-month leave year, such as a fiscal year; the twelve-month period as measured by the employee's first FMLA leave; or a rolling twelve-month period measured backward from the date an employee uses any FMLA leave. The calculation method selected must be applied consistently and uniformly to all covered employees.

The FMLA applies to private-sector firms that employ fifty workers, including part-time workers, within a seventy-five-mile radius (i.e., the employees do not all have to work at the same job site for an employer to be covered). Public-sector employers as well as the federal government are also covered.

It is estimated that only 5 percent of U.S. employers are affected by the FMLA. Approximately 40 percent of all employees are covered.

Legally Regulated Indirect Compensation

If employers offer health care benefits or pension and retirement plans, there are federal statutes that govern some aspects of these benefits. While not legally mandated, health care and pensions, when offered, are controlled by federal legislation.

Health Care Benefits

The Consolidated Omnibus Budget Reconciliation Act of 1985 and the Health Insurance Portability and Accountability Act of 1996 provide a degree of protection to employees whose employment is terminated, either voluntarily or otherwise.

Under provisions of COBRA, employers with twenty or more employees (churches and the federal government are excluded) must offer extended health care coverage to employees who voluntarily or involuntarily terminate or experience another event that results in a loss of benefits coverage. Coverage must also be offered to widows or divorced spouses of former or current employees and retirees and their spouses. Employers are required to notify eligible employees or others within sixty days after an employee terminates, dies, divorces, or otherwise qualifies for continued health coverage. Individuals electing health care coverage under COBRA must pay the normal premium an employee would pay, plus an additional 2-percent fee to cover the organization's administrative expense.

Under provisions of the HIPAA, the use of preexisting condition exclusions is restricted. Prior to the HIPAA, employees who switched from one company to another often lost their health insurance coverage because of preexisting medical conditions. Employees who change jobs are now covered healthwise regardless of any preexisting condition. Moreover, insurers cannot drop employees from coverage because of health conditions. Insurers must also make individual coverage available to people who, for whatever reason, leave group health insurance plans.

Pension and Retirement Plans

These programs are regulated by the Employee Retirement Income Security Act of 1974. The primary purpose of the ERISA is to protect employees who participate in retirement or pension plans. The ERISA requires that employers (1) communicate the requirements and other features of the plan to employees and report plan information to the federal government, (2) meet certain standards for funding the plan, (3) adhere to fiduciary standards in administering the plan and protect it from the risk of losses, (4) assure employee eligibility after a maximum of one-year of employment and the attainment of age twenty-one, (5) assure that plan participants become fully vested in the plan after five years of employment, and (6) secure insurance to protect private-sector defined-benefit programs against the possibility of the plan terminating prematurely.

Optional Indirect Compensation

Optional indirect compensation includes all of those benefits that are not required by law but may be provided at the discretion of the employer. Describing these benefits as optional or discretionary is not, however, entirely accurate, because tradition, precedent, or competition from other labor market institutions frequently dictates that many of these benefits must be provided if an organization is to experience success in attracting and retaining employees.

It is in the optional area that the greatest number of alternatives exist, the greatest amount of cost is incurred, and the greatest expansion of benefits has occurred. Table 9.1 depicts six major categories of optional indirect compensation and lists some of the benefits that may be offered in each category. Some 104 alternatives are listed, but even more possibilities exist. It is beyond the scope of this text to examine each of the six major categories in depth; however, some of the commonly provided benefits in each category will be described briefly.

Health Care Benefits

Provisions in this area are what employees typically refer to as insurance benefits. Costs of these items may be borne entirely by the employer or, more

Table 9.1

Major Categories of Optional Indirect Compensation

Health Care Benefits	Security Benefits	Retirement Benefits	Payments for Time Not Worked	Employee Services	Other Payments and Provisions
Health Insurance	Group Life Insurance	Pension Plans	Holidays	Financial Counseling	Matching Charitable Contributions
Dental Insurance	Accidental Death and Dismemberment Insurance	401 K Plans	Vacations	Prepaid Legal Services	Flexible Work Schedules
Vision Insurance		Profit-Sharing Plans	Military Leave	Income Tax Preparation	Seniority Awards
Health Maintenance Organizations (HMOs)		TaxSheltered Annuities	Funeral Leave	Tuition Reimbursement	Referral Bonuses
	Short-Term Disability Insurance	Retirement Planning Seminars	Family Leave	Childcare Centers	Casual Days
Preferred Provider Organizations (PPOs)		Employee Stock Ownership Plans (ESOP)	Marriage Leave	Eldercare Assistance	Purchase of Used Equipment
	Long-Term Disability Insurance		Maternity Leave	Credit Union	Professional Memberships
Point of Service Plans (POS)			Paternity Leave	In-House Food Service	Professional Subscriptions
In-House Medical Services	Travel Accident Insurance		Adoption Leave	Discounts on Merchandise or Services	Company Library
	Supplemental Unemployment Insurance		Sick Leave	Free Parking	Gifts
Substance Abuse Treatment			Grievance and Contract Negotiations	Recreational Facilities	Tickets to Entertainment or Sporting Events
Smoking Cessation Programs			Lunch, Rest, and Wash-Up Periods	Social Events	Payment for Unused Sick Leave
Physical Fitness Programs			Personal Leave	Commuting Assistance	Payments in Lieu of Vacation
Wellness Programs			Sabbatical Leave	Uniforms or Clothing Allowances	Severance Pay
Health Fairs			In-House Medical Care	Low Interest or Emergency Loans	Christmas Bonus
Low or NoCost Inoculations			Religious Observances	Educational Seminars or Programs	Contest Awards
Health Screenings			Reporting Time Pay	Company Automobile or Automobile Allowance	Suggestion Awards
Physical Examinations			Miscellaneous Time Off	Umbrella Liability Insurance	Expense Reimbursement
Flexible Spending Accounts			• Election Official	Company Housing	Child Adoption Expenses
			• Witness in Court	Employee Assistance Program	Scholarships for Dependents
			• Voting Time	Career Development Programs	Summer Employment for Dependents
			• Civic Duty	Charter Flights	Attendance Bonuses
			• Blood Donation	Spouse Travel	Telecommuting
			• Educational Activities	Internet Use	
			• Political Activities	On-Site Dry Cleaning and Laundry	
				Tool Reimbursement	
				Relocation Expense Reimbursement	
				Outplacement Services	
				Deferred Compensation	

typically today, shared between employer and employee. The health and security arrangements core traditionally consists of health insurance, group life insurance, pension and retirement plans, and long-term disability insurance.

Health insurance plans provide coverage for a wide range of illnesses or accident-related adversities. Commonly included in these plans are reimbursements to employees or direct payment of expenses connected with hospitalization, surgical procedures, and emergency medical treatment. Many plans also include provisions for payment of expenses related to diagnostic visits to physicians, second opinions on the need for surgery, prescribed medications, outpatient services, and short-term psychiatric counseling.

Most health insurance plans include major medical coverage that compensates for the cost of prolonged illnesses that extend beyond the range of basic health coverage. Major medical coverage usually begins after basic coverage ends. Long-term hospital stays, medical equipment or appliances, private-duty nursing, physical therapy, or long-term institutionalization for psychiatric, alcohol, or drug treatment are the kinds of services and treatments that may be found in major medical coverage. Many plans have a deductible charge that must be paid by the employee before major medical coverage takes effect. There may also be a lifetime dollar maximum that is payable under a plan.

Long-term catastrophic illnesses are, unfortunately, a reality today; consequently, some form of protection against the staggering costs of these events to employees is appropriate.

Security Benefits

This benefit provides financial assistance to dependents upon the death of the employee and thus offers protection against a sudden loss of income to the family. It is common for employers to pay the entire cost of basic insurance provided under group life. Coverage is generally in the range of one to two times the employee's annual salary. Employees may also be given the opportunity to purchase additional insurance by paying the cost, at group rates, of such extended coverage.

Retirement Benefits

These programs are some of the most complex of the core optional indirect compensation components. There are numerous variations in funding methods, there are federal laws with which to comply, and there are tax considerations for both employee and employer that must be addressed.

Most plans do, however, have several common features. They specify (1) an age at which an employee may retire and receive full benefits; (2) an age at which an employee may retire and receive reduced benefits; (3) a basis for determining the amount of benefits an employee will receive; (4) under the Employee Retirement Income Security Act of 1974, a schedule by which employer contributions to the plan become vested (nonforfeitable) to the employee; and (5) procedures whereby benefits will be paid to designated beneficiaries in the event of an employee's death before or after retirement.

Payments for Time Not Worked

From an employee's perspective, one of the most significant and highly desired forms of indirect compensation may be pay for time not worked. The increased value placed on leisure time today coupled with extensive involvement in off-the-job activities have created high demand and preference for this particular form of benefit. In addition to providing opportunities for rest and relaxation without incurring economic loss, time off with pay permits employees to fulfill various personal and civic responsibilities.

Employee Services

One of the most rapidly expanding areas of indirect compensation is employee services. In essence, these benefits are directed toward helping employees enjoy a better lifestyle by providing various forms of assistance and opportunities at no cost or at reduced cost to the employee. These benefits are, in many instances, services that employees would not avail themselves of if they had to purchase these items for themselves; for example, physical fitness programs and financial counseling.

Other Payments and Provisions

This is the catch-all category of optional indirect compensation. It includes payments made directly to employees for various items, reimbursement of sundry expenses incurred, and miscellaneous payments made on behalf of employees. The purposes of these benefits are, generally, to increase employee commitment to the organization and enhance morale.

DESIGNING THE INDIRECT COMPENSATION PACKAGE

There are several important considerations in designing a benefits package that is appropriate for a given organization: the costs involved, the wants and needs of employees, the desirability of creating separate sets of benefits for employees and executives, the need for periodic changes, and the possibility of using a flexible or cafeteria approach to benefits.[9]

Cost Containment

Expenses associated with indirect compensation, fueled by rising costs and expanded levels of benefits, are a matter of concern to many organizations.[10]

In the past it was not unusual for top management to take a relatively passive stance regarding benefits, leaving the determination and administration of them in the hands of compensation specialists. Today more and more top managers are actively involved in the benefits planning process, and the cost of providing benefits is increasingly subject to top-management scrutiny. Accelerating expenditures for indirect compensation, especially in the health care area, are causing organizations to examine costs and implement measures to control expenses. Cost containment is a crucial issue in benefits management. The following are some of the ways that organizations are attempting to control expenditures.

Waiting Periods

Establishing probationary periods before an employee becomes eligible for benefits is not a new idea. Increasingly, however, organizations are subjecting this matter to closer scrutiny. Penetrating questions requiring careful answers are being asked. Should employees be eligible upon employment for particular kinds of benefits or should they have to wait a stipulated period of time before becoming eligible for coverage? Should different probationary periods be required for different types of benefits? There are no easy answers to questions such as these. However, closer examination of waiting periods and development of a sound rationale for their use can aid in controlling the costs of some aspects of indirect compensation.

Cost Sharing

Contributory programs in which the cost of a benefit is shared on some basis between employer and employee is another old approach that is being more widely used.[11] Contributory plans can reduce indirect compensation costs greatly; moreover, they offer other advantages that may be important. First, when an employee is required to pay part of the cost of a benefit the employee's sense of responsibility may be enhanced because, in effect, it becomes his or her benefit. Second, an employee who shares in the cost often becomes more knowledgeable about the benefit—people want to know what they are paying for. Third, cost sharing often increases the employee's appreciation of what the organization is actually providing.

Benefits Management

The whole area of indirect compensation has become so complex and so significant an element of cost that it is necessary to have specialists design, administer, and monitor an organization's program. Large organizations typically have designated benefits managers or benefits administrators. Small organizations cannot afford this degree of specialization. Fortunately, benefits consultants are available to assist organizations, and although they are not inexpensive they can save an organization substantial sums on benefits costs by putting together a well-developed benefits package. It is important to remember that benefits must be managed just as effectively as any other organizational investment.

Alternative Benefits Methods

In their efforts to control indirect compensation costs, organizations are also utilizing alternative methods for providing and funding benefits. One alternative used by some large organizations is self-insurance. Basically this approach entails the establishment of a trust fund from which benefit claims are paid to employees. Instead of paying premiums to an insurer the firm makes contributions to the fund. Cost savings as compared to commercial insurance plans can be substantial.

In health benefits, managed care programs utilizing health maintenance organizations (HMOs), preferred provider organizations (PPOs), and point of service (POSs) plans have become almost universal. HMOs provide medical services to an organization's employees. An HMO has an established network of physicians and hospitals that provide the needed services. An employer contracts with the HMO to provide services for a fixed period on a prepaid basis. Employees using the services of an HMO must utilize physicians who are members of the HMO's network and must have certain services approved in advance. If an employee goes outside the HMO network he or she usually pays for the bulk or all of the treatment. PPOs are health care providers that contract with an employer to provide services at competitive rates. Employees may go to other providers, but if they do so they typically pay the difference in costs. Point of service plans combine the features of HMOs and PPOs. Employees can get treatment in or out of the network, but approval must be obtained for all services.

Managed care programs have accomplished their goal: to reduce health care costs. One study suggests that employers saved $400 per employee annually or 11 percent on their health care costs by using managed care. Another study reported that in California alone, HMOs saved $770 per family per year.[12]

Employee Wants and Needs

Employee wants and needs should play a part in the design of the indirect compensation package, but usually they are not given much consideration. Typically, management decides and employees have no input. There are signs, however, that this is beginning to change. Larger organizations are starting to address the matter of preferences through surveys of employee attitudes and desires relative to benefits. These surveys provide useful information for initiating changes in the benefits package. An interesting finding of preference surveys has been that there is little relationship between the amount an employer spends for a particular benefit and the value the employee attaches to that benefit. This would seem to be a clear indication that employers are not getting maximum advantage from their expenditures on indirect compensation.[13]

It is safe to assume that workers' ages have a bearing on the types of benefits preferred; for example, older workers tend to have a higher preference for pension and retirement plans than do younger workers. Likewise, the number of dependents an employee has affects his or her preference; for example, workers with families are usually more concerned about health and medical coverage than workers without dependents. These two findings are, unfortunately, the only clear-cut relationship between demographic factors and benefits preferences. Wants and needs do influence preferences, but exactly how and to what extent is not certain. Nevertheless, wants and needs should always be assessed in designing or redesigning a benefits package. Periodic surveys for this purpose are recommended.

Different Packages for Different Levels

While employers can obtain tax advantages only for benefits that do not discriminate in favor of highly compensated employees, most organizations use at least a two-tiered system of benefits: one package for executive-level management and one for all other employees.[14] The executive-level package is normally tied in with organizational performance and is far more generous than the benefits provided to employees. It is beyond the scope of this book to explore executive benefits; however, it is important for an organization to design an executive-level package that will assure the highest performance and results from its leaders. In essence, this means that an organization should have at least two benefits packages.

Changing the Package

Periodic changes in legislation—the Older Workers Benefit Protection Act of 1990, the Family and Medical Leave Act of 1993, and the Health Insurance Portability and Accountability Act of 1996 are pertinent examples—necessitate alterations in indirect compensation programs and practices. Moreover, emergence of new benefits, increased costs of continuing to provide certain forms or levels of coverage, and shifts in employee preferences are additional forces that compel periodic modification in benefits.[15] The entire indirect compensation program should be monitored on a continuous basis to determine when changes are needed and what these changes should be. Unfortunately, few guidelines are available to assist in this process. Nevertheless, an important principle to remember about benefits is this: What has once been given cannot be taken away unless it is replaced by something of equal or greater value. In other words, a benefit cannot be abolished without providing an equivalent alternative. To eliminate a benefit without replacing it exposes an organization to risks of increased employee turnover, lower morale, and a decreased competitive stance in the labor market.

This does not mean that the package cannot and should not be modified from time to time. Rather, it suggests that alterations must be made carefully and thoughtfully with a view toward how proposed changes are likely to be perceived by employees. Sudden shifts from noncontributory to contributory funding arrangements, for example, are certain to be perceived negatively. It is much easier to make adjustments to benefits where the employee perceives a gain instead of a loss.

The Cafeteria Approach to Benefits

Under this approach to benefits employees are allowed some latitude in picking and choosing the benefits they want.[16] For example, a young single worker might forego certain health care benefits and opt for additional vacation time, whereas a divorced mother with three children might choose additional health coverage as well as childcare benefits. Workers are allowed to fit benefits more closely to their needs and circumstances with a cafeteria approach.

In a typical cafeteria plan, certain core benefits are provided to all employees. These items might include basic medical coverage, life insurance, short-term disability, and a pension plan. Beyond these basic items employees may choose from a wide variety of options. Each employee is assigned a certain dollar amount and may spend that amount almost any way he or she chooses.

Proponents contend that cafeteria benefits offer several advantages: (1) increased satisfaction with benefits, (2) opportunities for working couples to avoid excessive duplication of benefits, (3) greater understanding of benefits since employees participate in designing their own plans, and (4) opportunities for employers to pass along to employees some of the rising costs of benefits. Possible disadvantages of cafeteria plans include (1) higher costs of administration due to the variations in benefits from worker to worker, (2) increased need for communication of benefits so that employees can make wise decisions, (3) determining when or how often employees may alter their combination of benefits, and (4) the possibility that employees might lose some of the tax-sheltered aspect of certain benefit choices.

CURRENT TRENDS IN BENEFITS

In the changing world of indirect monetary compensation, three broad trends are discernible: a movement toward sharing the costs and risks of benefits, an emphasis on health maintenance, and the offering of lifestyle benefits.[17]

Cost and Risk Sharing

Organizations expect employees to share in the cost and risks of benefits today. In health care, for example, there has been a shift away from insurance plans that reimburse an employee or a health care provider for all or almost all costs of health care services. Managed care (HMOs, PPOs, and POSs), in which treatments and services are evaluated for their necessity, is the order of the day.[18] Insurance plans spell out very carefully what is covered and what is not covered. Employees electing treatment or services that are not covered must pay for these services. Employees using physicians not in the specified network bear the burden of all or most of the costs of using such services.

In pension plans there is a shift away from defined-benefit plans to defined-contribution plans in which employees share the risk of investment but also gain a greater role in determining how funds will be invested. Recognizing that neither Social Security nor company-sponsored retirement plans are likely to be fully sufficient for retirement in the future, employees are expected to contribute to their own retirement programs through such vehicles as 401(k) plans.[19]

Emphasis on Health Maintenance

A second trend in benefits is an emphasis on health maintenance: prevention of health problems rather than treatment when they occur. Many organizations today offer health education information; programs on stress management, smoking cessation, or weight management; low-cost or free health screening and inoculations; health fairs; or fitness centers. Studies generally indicate that corporate wellness programs save organizations three or more dollars in health care costs for every dollar spent on wellness initiatives. With burgeoning health care expenditures that account for approximately 15 percent of the U.S. Gross National Product, the emphasis on wellness programs promises to be around for a long while.[20]

Lifestyle Benefits

Another trend in benefits is the extension of medical benefits to domestic partners of either the opposite sex or the same sex. This trend reflects what is occurring in society, as gays and lesbians are more open about their lifestyles and more heterosexual couples live together before marriage or instead of marrying. Firms that offer domestic partner benefits include Electronic Data Systems, Walt Disney, Levi Strauss, Coors Brewing, IBM, Harley Davidson, Charles Schwab, and Microsoft.[21] Firms such as these have found it necessary to offer domestic partner benefits in order to attract and retain the skilled personnel they need.

Family-friendly benefits are also becoming more common as the nature of the workforce changes. Family relationships of employees in the 1990s were as follows: traditional families, 17 percent; two-worker families, 43 percent; single-parent families, 16 percent; and other families, 25 percent.[22] This increase in the number of nontraditional families in the workplace has focused attention on benefits to accommodate the changing needs of families. Included in these benefits are (1) flexible work schedules; (2) childcare (some organizations operate on-site facilities, while other firms subsidize the expense of daycare for children); (3) eldercare (which promises to become a larger concern in the future as the population of the United States ages); (4) adoption benefits (many organizations are beginning to provide these benefits largely in a sense of fairness to couples who cannot give birth to children); (5) convenience benefits (on-site dry cleaning, banking, auto repair, etc.) that enable employees to accomplish some tasks that cannot be dealt with after normal working hours; and (6) employee assistance programs that help people deal with stress, family problems, substance abuse, and other matters.[23]

THE IMPORTANCE OF COMMUNICATION

Simply having an attractive benefits package is not enough for any organization. Employees must have ample knowledge of all benefits available and the value of those benefits. Unfortunately, this is not normally the case. According to one study, the typical employee was able to recall less than 15 percent of the benefits received from the company. Effective communication is, apparently, the exception rather than the rule.[24]

The four most commonly used communications methods are booklets and brochures, employee newsletters, benefits manuals, and orientation sessions. Undoubtedly, herein lies the problem with benefits communication. As previously indicated, many forms of indirect monetary compensation are extremely complex—for example, health insurance and pension plans—and as a result are difficult to explain, particularly via the written word. Most employees do not take the time to read employee handbooks that explain benefits. Those that do read the booklets are not likely to understand fully what they read because of the way explanations are written and the terminology that is used. If effective communication is to occur, more effective means of getting the message across will have to be used. Some organizations are now using group meetings, videotapes, interactive computer sites, annual refresher sessions, and one-on-one discussion with benefits administrators as more effective ways of explaining various aspects of indirect monetary compensation.

Two communication methods that have proven to be useful and effective in getting the benefits message across are periodic meetings on specific benefits and personal counseling sessions.[25]

Employee meetings generally explore in detail one benefit per session. Significant features of the benefit are presented, procedures for using it are discussed, and questions raised by employees are addressed. Intermittent meetings create greater employee involvement in benefits and demonstrate that the organization considers benefits to be important enough to expend sufficient time to see that they are thoroughly understood. Certainly, this approach involves time and expense, but it seems worthwhile, considering the high cost of benefits.

Personal counseling sessions are also extremely effective in communicating benefits information. In most instances these sessions take place when an employee is planning to use a particular benefit, such as family and medical leave or retirement. In other cases, benefits specialists schedule periods of time in which they will be available to talk individually with employees of a given department about the indirect compensation package. One-on-one counseling is perhaps the best means of communication, but it is also the most expensive and time consuming.

Many employers provide their employees with an annual benefits statement that translates benefits into dollar amounts so that employees can more readily see the value of their benefits. Benefits statements give employees a greater appreciation of the cost of employer-provided benefits. This practice, despite its additional cost, is highly recommended.

NOTES

1. Donald L. Caruth, *Compensation Management for Banks* (Boston: Bankers Publishing, 1986), 152.

2. "Benefits Average 27.5 Percent of Employer Costs," *ACA News*, September 1999, 10.

3. Caruth, *Compensation Management*, 152.

4. Ibid., 152–154; Robert L. Mathis and John H. Jackson, *Human Resource Management*, 8th ed. (Minneapolis–St. Paul: West, 1997), 435.

5. Caruth, *Compensation Management*, 154–155; George T. Milkovich and Jerry M. Newman, *Compensation*, 6th ed. (Boston: Irwin–McGraw-Hill, 1999), 394.

6. Milkovich and Newman, *Compensation*, 398.

7. Paul T. Clausen, "Executive Compensation or Business Value?" *ACA News*, March 1999, 25.

8. Caruth, *Compensation Management*, 155–161.

9. Milkovich and Newman, *Compensation*, 399–409.

10. Wayne F. Cascio, *Managing Human Resources*, 5th ed. (Boston: Irwin–McGraw-Hill, 1998), 443–444.

11. Ibid., 460.

12. Cascio, *Managing Human Resources*, 444–445.

13. Milkovich and Newman, *Compensation*, 408–409.

14. "Different Benefits for Different Employees," *TexasBusinessToday* (1998): 2–3.

15. Caruth, *Compensation Management*, 173–174.

16. Mathis and Jackson, *Human Resource Management*, 456–458.

17. Cascio, *Managing Human Resources*, 460–461.

18. Ibid., 445.

19. Ibid., 446–450.

20. Kenneth Cooper, Lecture at Cooper Institute for Aerobics Research, Dallas, Texas, 24 February 1998.

21. Cascio, *Managing Human Resources*, 460.

22. James T. Bond, "Single Parents in the Wage and Salaried Labor Force," *ACA Journal* (Winter 1998): 66–69.

23. Marcia P. Ellis and Sandra Sullivan, "Flexible Work Arrangements," *ACA Journal* (Winter 1998): 45–48; Nancy Hatch Woodward, "Child Care to the Rescue," *HR Magazine*, August 1999, 82–83; Joy Loverde, "The Growing Need to Be Eldercare Aware," *ACA Journal* (Winter 1998): 77–80; MaryAnne M. Hyland, "Benefits: Current Challenges in Providing Cost-Effective Employee Supports," in *Managing Human Resources in the 21st Century*, ed. Ellen Ernst Kossek and Richard N. Block (Cincinnati: South-Western College Publishing, 2000), 18.17; Michael F. Carter, "Convenience Benefits: The Fourth Wave," *ACA Journal* (Winter 1998): 32–33; Cascio, *Managing Human Resources*, 585–588.

24. Milkovich and Newman, *Compensation*, 410–412.

25. Caruth, *Compensation Management*, 177–178.

10

INCENTIVES: PAY FOR PERFORMANCE

Incentive compensation, broadly defined, is any financial reward given to an employee for accomplishing specific results of a quantitative or qualitative nature. In a much narrower sense, incentive compensation is pay based on output. Incentives provide for variable rewards dependent upon results accomplished, amount of work produced, or measurable performance. At one extreme of the incentive spectrum, compensation is determined solely by the level of output: no output, no compensation. At the other extreme, a base level of compensation is assured and additional financial rewards are given for exceeding stipulated expectations: a guaranteed salary, plus a performance bonus.[1]

Incentive compensation is quite common in some occupations or industries. Salespeople, for example, are traditionally paid on a commission basis that directly links the total amount of compensation to the total amount of sales. In the garment industry, seamstresses are frequently compensated according to the number of units they produce. In other occupations or industries, such as administrative work and information technology, incentive compensation is neither traditional nor common.

Various plans exist for relating output to pay. Incentive compensation may be paid on the basis of individual effort or group effort. Incentive schemes may be used at the employee level of the organization, the top-management level, or any combination of organizational levels. This chapter examines the purposes of incentives, types of incentive plans, requisites for effective use of incentives, and problems associated with the use of incentive payment plans. This examination of incentives will be centered on their use at the employee level of an organization. Many of the considerations addressed, however, also apply to developing incentive pay plans for other organizational levels. Also addressed in this chapter are additional aspects of team-based compensation that may or may not involve the use of traditional incentive pay.

PURPOSE OF INCENTIVES

The purpose of incentives is to increase productivity. By relating compensation to output, an employer is attempting to induce workers to turn out a greater volume of work, thereby lowering the cost of producing a single unit of output.[2]

Productivity can be defined as the ratio of the quantity of output to the quantity of input. Raising the amount of output for the same input will, obviously, increase productivity. All things being equal, it will also lower the cost of producing one unit of work. To accomplish the desired result of increased productivity, all incentive plans focus on two major areas: (1) improving motivation so that employees work at or near their full capacities, and (2) reducing or controlling expenses that directly affect the costs of production.

Improve Motivation

Incentive plans seek to increase motivational levels in several different ways. Even though they are listed separately, each of the ways in which incentives attempt to enhance motivation actually work in concert with each other.

Tie Pay to Performance

In the absence of incentive plans, the link between a particular employee's performance and his or her compensation is often tenuous at best and nonexistent at worst. Employees may simply put in their time and receive their pay. Under such conditions, so the advocates of incentive pay claim, there is little stimulus to be other than nominally productive because greater effort will not necessarily mean greater earnings.

Incentives attempt to tap the wellspring of motivation that exists within each individual by establishing a direct link between effort expended and rewards received: The higher the output, the higher the pay. Tying the level of compensation to the level of performance, it is claimed, causes employees to want to produce more so that they can increase their earnings.

Recognize Differences in Employee Performance

Under conventional compensation systems, significant differences in employee performance may not be recognized or, if they are recognized, may not be rewarded proportionally. Because incentives relate output directly to pay, differences in employee performance can be identified precisely and rewarded accordingly. With an incentive system the high-producing employee will always earn more than an employee who is an average or low producer; consequently, incentives are likely to spur employees to higher performance because employees know their performance will be recognized.

Increase Competition among Employees

One of the cornerstones of our economy and our culture is competition. Competition brings forth the desire to be the best, to excel in one's efforts. The use of incentives is one way that the natural competitiveness of individuals can be channeled productively in the workplace. Incentives put each employee in competition with every other employee, thereby encouraging each individual to want to do his or her best. Often, the top producer is singled out for special recognition by the organization as "Top Producer of the Month" or "Salesperson of the Year." Even without formal organizational recognition, employees may informally bestow this honor on a coworker. Incentives increase productivity, so the theory goes, because employees compete with each other on an organizationally sanctioned basis: output, performance, and end results.

Attract and Retain Productive Employees

From an organizational standpoint, an effective incentive program can help attract and keep highly motivated individuals. An organization with a reputation for paying significant incentives is far more likely to attract a greater number of applicants than a company that does not pay incentives. Moreover, within the total pool of applicants, the percentage of those willing to work hard is almost certain to be higher for the incentive-paying institution than for the nonincentive-paying organization.

Because incentives tie monetary rewards to performance, motivated employees are more inclined to remain with an organization paying incentives, since they can earn more than they could with another organization. Conversely, insufficiently motivated employees are more likely to terminate their employment, thereby affording the institution an opportunity to replace them with workers who are more motivated.

Reduce Absenteeism

Another motivational thrust of incentives is to reduce absenteeism. Because earnings are related to output, time away from the job directly affects a person's level of compensation. Abuses of sick leave, for instance, are less likely to occur when an incentive system is in operation because an employee directly experiences the result of unnecessary time off.

Reduce Idle Time

Incentives tend to reduce idle time—excessive breaks, long lunches, personal business, telephone calls, and chatter—because time spent in a nonproductive fashion is reflected in the quantity of results and the quantity of results directly impacts the level of earnings. Incentives tend to make employees more conscientious in their use of time.

Reduce or Control Costs

Productivity, if expressed in terms of costs, means getting more output for the same dollar expenditure or getting additional output at decreasing unit cost rates. Consequently, one of the aims of incentive systems is to reduce or control costs, particularly labor costs.

Utilize Equipment More Effectively

The equipment used in today's organizations is becoming increasingly expensive. As the cost of equipment goes up, utilization rates become more and more important. Incentives are a means of assuring that equipment is used as fully and effectively as possible. By motivating employees to spend their time wisely in the performance of assigned tasks, incentives tend to keep equipment in operation a greater percentage of the time. If machines malfunction or break down, employees will be likely to report it promptly so that needed repairs can be made as quickly as possible. In the absence of incentives, breakdowns may be viewed as a welcome relief from work.

Relate Increases in Compensation to Increases in Productivity

The pay increase an employee receives frequently bears little or no relationship to changes in the employee's productivity. Consequently, under typical approaches to rewarding employees through annual adjustments in pay, compensation costs may continue to rise without corresponding increases in performance. Incentive systems attempt to correct this situation by relating compensation costs to performance so that in any given period compensation expenses will not exceed increases in productivity. The establishment of a direct relationship between labor costs and output creates a mechanism that controls expenditures.

Avoid Additions to Staff

By eliminating or at least seriously curtailing idle time and below-capacity performance on the part of employees, incentives can help an organization avoid staff increases. Compensating employees on the basis of their performance encourages them to be more productive and to utilize their time better. Avoiding additions to staff through better utilization of current personnel can, therefore, produce a significant savings in labor costs.

Create Uniform Processing Costs

Incentives make it possible to determine in advance—and accurately—the labor costs associated with producing one unit of output. Actual labor costs are not subject to fluctuations from month to month; therefore, an organization can price its goods and services with confidence that per-unit processing costs will remain uniform throughout a given period.

Direct Efforts Toward Achieving Organizational Objectives

A final way that incentives can help reduce or control costs in an organization is by directing the efforts of employees toward accomplishing important organizational objectives. In the course of developing an incentive system, it is necessary to identify precisely what constitutes productive work for a department or section and what constitutes nonproductive work. By cleaning up operations before the introduction of incentives, unnecessary activities, functions, and make-work are eliminated. When the system goes into operation, all effort is focused on accomplishing work that is important. In essence, the use of incentives forces an organization to think through what it wants each work unit to do; the end result is a clear and definite focus on accomplishing those things that contribute to the goals of each work unit as well as the organization as a whole.

TYPES OF INCENTIVE PLANS

Incentive plans fall into two broad categories: individual and group.[3] Individual incentives pay each employee according to his or her specific level of performance. Group incentives reward a section, department, or the entire organization's workforce for the accomplishment of performance objectives. Each of these two broad categories of incentives will be examined in the following sections.

Individual Incentives

The oldest known incentive compensation method is the individual incentive plan, whereby a worker is paid for the number of units produced.[4] Regardless of the specific features of a given plan, three preliminary steps are required to establish a basis for paying incentives to individuals.

The starting point in the development of individual incentives is to determine a standard level of performance. Time studies are commonly used to discover the time that it takes to produce one item or to specify the total number of items that should be produced in one hour. From these figures the standard number of units that should be produced per day or per week is established. This standard level of performance becomes the incentive baseline; production above the baseline will be compensated at whatever incentive rate is set, while production below the standard level will be compensated at another rate, usually an hourly rate.

The second step in formulating individual incentives is to set an appropriate hourly rate for performance that is below the standard level. This rate guarantees the employee a specified level of compensation. Obviously, the guaranteed rate must be at least equal to the minimum hourly wage as specified by the Fair Labor Standards Act. In most cases, because of today's bustling economy, the rate will probably be set much higher than the minimum wage. The average hourly rate that prevailed in the section or department before the introduction of incentives is likely to be the level at which the guaranteed rate is set.

The final step is to determine the monetary rates at which production above the standard level will be compensated. In piecework plans, this will be the amount paid per unit of work produced. In standard hour plans, it will be the amount paid per minute or hour.

As used today in manufacturing or clerical work settings, individual incentives payments usually take one of three forms: (1) straight piecework, (2) differential piecework, or (3) standard hour plans.[5]

Straight Piecework

This is the most widely used type of individual incentive plan. A straight piecework system is relatively simple to develop and is readily understood by employees. Straight piecework pays an employee a fixed amount per unit of output for every item produced above the specified standard level of output.

A simple illustration will illustrate how a plan of this type works. Assume the following: (1) The standard level of output has been set at 250 units per day, (2) the guaranteed rate is $8.00 per hour or $64.00 per day, and (3) all units produced in excess of the standard level will be compensated at a constant rate of $0.15 per unit. Table 10.1 shows the amounts an employee would earn at various levels of production under this plan. By increasing his or her output from 250 units to 350 (an increase of 40%), an employee raises his or her total compensation by 23.4 percent.

While an employee is increasing his or her earnings, the cost of producing items is declining. At a level of 350 units, labor costs are 11.8-percent lower than they are at the standard performance level of 259 units per day. The actual total cost of producing one unit would decrease even more if fixed costs were taken into account because these costs would be spread over a much larger volume of production.

Table 10.1
Straight Piecework Incentive

Units Produced	Units Above Standard	Incentive Unit Rate	Incentive Earnings	Base Rate	Total Earnings	Production Cost per Unit
250	0	0	0	$64.00	$64.00	$0.2560
260	10	$0.15	$1.50	$64.00	$65.50	$0.2519
270	20	$0.15	$3.00	$64.00	$67.00	$0.2481
280	30	$0.15	$4.50	$64.00	$68.50	$0.2446
290	40	$0.15	$6.00	$64.00	$70.00	$0.2414
300	50	$0.15	$7.50	$64.00	$71.50	$0.2383
310	60	$0.15	$9.00	$64.00	$73.00	$0.2355
320	70	$0.15	$10.50	$64.00	$74.50	$0.2328
330	80	$0.15	$12.00	$64.00	$76.00	$0.2279
340	90	$0.15	$13.50	$64.00	$77.50	$0.2279
350	100	$0.15	$15.00	$64.00	$79.00	$0.2257

As this example illustrates, a straight piecework incentive plan may be advantageous to both employees and organizations. Its basic simplicity makes it relatively easy to install, administer, and communicate to workers.

Differential Piecework

Unlike straight piecework that pays a constant rate per item once the standard has been exceeded, a differential plan pays a variable rate per unit. The incentive rate per item may either increase as the number of units produced goes up, or it may decrease.

Table 10.2 illustrates a differential payment plan utilizing increasing rates per unit of output. Theoretically, this payment scheme may be more motivational than a straight piecework plan because of the emphasis it places on incremental increases in payments; the employee not only increases total earnings by turning out more units, he or she also earns progressively more per unit as output is raised. Because employees know that higher output is worth more in both aggregate and incremental terms, they may be psychologically stimulated to produce at the maximum levels of which they are capable.

A differential piecework plan may also use a declining payment schedule, as shown in Table 10.3. Although the worker still earns more at each higher level of production beyond standard, the actual payment per unit decreases. From management's point of view, this arrangement would seem to be preferable because unit production costs decline more rapidly than they do under straight or increasing incentive payment rates. From a motivational standpoint, however, such a payment method is likely to be perceived by employees as unfair. Certainly, it is difficult to explain to workers why they are paid less per unit as their total production increases.

Table 10.2
Differential Piecework: Increasing Rates

Units Produced	#Units Above Standard	Incentive Unit Rate	Incentive Earnings	Base Rate	Total Earnings	Production Cost per Unit
250	0	0	0	$64.00	$64.00	$0.2560
260	10	$0.132	$1.32	$64.00	$65.32	$0.2512
270	20	$0.134	$2.68	$64.00	$66.68	$0.2470
280	30	$0.136	$4.08	$64.00	$68.08	$0.2431
290	40	$0.138	$5.52	$64.00	$69.52	$0.2397
300	50	$0.140	$7.00	$64.00	$71.00	$0.2367
310	60	$0.142	$8.52	$64.00	$72.52	$0.2339
320	70	$0.144	$10.08	$64.00	$74.08	$0.2315
330	80	$0.146	$11.68	$64.00	$75.68	$0.2293
340	90	$0.148	$13.32	$64.00	$77.32	$0.2274
350	100	$0.150	$15.00	$64.00	$79.00	$0.2257

Differential piecework plans are seldom used today. When a plan is utilized, it is likely to be of the increasing rate variety.

Standard Hours

This type of individual incentive plan is quite similar to the piecework plan, except that time allowances are used as the payment basis instead of specified amounts per unit of production. For the sake of illustration, assume that 250 units per day is the standard level of output and $64.00 is the rate of pay for an eight-hour day. The time allowance per unit in this case is 1.92 minutes (8 hours × 60 minutes ÷ 250 units = 1.92 minutes per unit). If an employee turns out 310 units in a day, the employee would be producing at 124 percent of standard (310 items actually produced ÷ 250 units = 124% of standard production). In other words, an employee producing at this rate actually accomplished 9.92 hours of work in an eight-hour day (310 units × 1.92 minutes = 595.2 earned minutes; 595.2 earned minutes ÷ 60 minutes per hour = 9.92 earned hours). Therefore, the employee would receive a bonus of $15.36 for the day's work ($64.00 standard daily rate × 24% = $15.36). The actual pay received for this particular day's work would be $79.36 ($64.00 standard rate + $15.36 bonus for production in excess of standard). The calculations can be greatly simplified by multiplying the daily rate of pay by the level of output attained ($64.00 × 124% = $79.36).

Several advantages are claimed for standard hours over piecework incentive plans: (1) They do not require detailed analysis to establish precise incentive payment rates per unit; (2) standards can be set through historical averages or estimates, thus eliminating the need for extensive time studies; (3) they are easy for employees to understand; and (4) they are simpler to administer than piece rates.[6]

Table 10.3
Differential Piecework: Decreasing Rates

Units Produced	Units Above Standard	Incentive Unit Rate	Incentive Earnings	Base Rate	Total Earnings	Production Cost per Unit
250	0	0	0	$64.00	$64.00	$0.2560
260	10	$0.150	$1.50	$64.00	$65.50	$0.2519
270	20	$0.148	$2.96	$64.00	$66.96	$0.2480
280	30	$0.146	$4.38	$64.00	$68.38	$0.2442
290	40	$0.144	$5.76	$64.00	$69.76	$0.2406
300	50	$0.142	$7.10	$64.00	$71.10	$0.2370
310	60	$0.140	$8.40	$64.00	$72.40	$0.2335
320	70	$0.138	$9.66	$64.00	$73.66	$0.2302
330	80	$0.136	$10.88	$64.00	$74.88	$0.2269
340	90	$0.134	$12.06	$64.00	$76.06	$0.2237
350	100	$0.132	$13.20	$64.00	$77.20	$0.2206

Group Incentives

For a number of years there has been a movement away from individual incentive plans at the employee level toward plans that reward groups of employees. This movement has its origins in the changing nature of work, from emphasis on task specialization to team effort, and from competition among individuals to group cooperation.

Individual incentive plans are based on certain assumptions: (1) Individual employee contributions can be measured, (2) there are sufficient numbers of employees performing identical work to justify the development of a plan, and (3) it is cost effective for an organization to implement and operate an individual incentive plan. Often these conditions cannot be met in the workplace, thereby precluding the use of group incentives.

Increasingly work is organized such that productivity results from collective, not individual effort; it is difficult, if not impossible, to separate each individual's contribution from that of the group to which the employee is assigned. Thus, it is not always practicable to reward a specific employee's output. Frequently, work is accomplished in a series of successive stages and each worker must await completion of the preceding step before he or she can begin his or her processing step. Individual incentives, moreover, are usually costly to develop and administer. Their use where small numbers of people perform the same work may not produce sufficient savings or productivity gains to justify their use.

Group incentives can be designed to reward teamwork on any organizational-unit basis: section, department, division, shift, or total organization. For incentives purposes, a group may be defined somewhat narrowly or quite broadly, depending upon the extent of cooperative effort to be measured. Team-based compensation, which may not necessarily include the use of incentive plans, will be considered more specifically later in this chapter.

Group incentives are typically based on (1) an overall productivity measure such as the end product resulting from the group's efforts, group piecework; (2) a measurement of the group's efficiency as determined by its standard hours produced compared to total personnel hours available, group standard hours; (3) savings in labor costs for the current period as compared to a previous or baseline period, cost savings; or (4) earnings in the present period, profit sharing.

Group Piecework

In principle, a group piecework plan is identical to an individual piecework plan in that payments are made for exceeding specified levels of performance. The only difference is that rewards for output above the stipulated amount accrue to the group as a whole rather than to individual performers. These rewards are then distributed among group members on some predetermined basis. When output standards are not exceeded, each group member is simply compensated at his or her normal rate of pay. As with individual piecework, payments for production above standard may be made on a straight rate, an increasing rate basis, or a declining rate basis.

Incentives earned by groups can be distributed in various ways, but the most commonly used methods are an equal distribution among group members or a weighted distribution based on each member's earnings. Table 10.4 shows a comparison of these two methods of distribution. A weighted distribution of incentive earnings would appear to be more desirable because it rewards employees on a relative basis, which suggests equity and encourages higher performance from higher-paid employees.

Group piecework is appropriate in situations where some members of a work unit are directly involved in producing units—machine operators, for instance—but are supported by other members who facilitate the direct production—expeditors, inspectors, or materials coordinators.

Group Standard Hours

Group incentives based on standard hours are useful in work centers where output is comprised of several items rather than one end product. Time standards are set for each of the various items produced. The total number of each particular unit produced during a given period is multiplied by the standard time for that item to arrive at the number of standard hours produced. The total standard hours for each product are added together to determine the total number of standard hours earned. Total standard hours earned are then divided by total personnel hours available during the period to compute an efficiency index. Table 10.5 illustrates the basic approach for a hypothetical work group. As seen in Table 10.5, the total work group is producing at a rate of 16.2 percent in excess of standard. Under a standard hour incentive plan,

Table 10.4
Group Piecework Payments

	Equal Distribution			Weighted Distribution		
				Percent of Total		
	Daily Base Rate	Incentive Earnings	Total Earnings	Daily Base Rate	Incentive Earnings	Total Earnings
Willson	$64.00	$9.39	$73.39	13.617	$8.95	72.95
Watkins	64.00	9.39	73.39	13.617	8.95	72.95
Tamanovich	66.00	9.39	75.39	14.043	9.23	75.23
Bernstein	66.00	9.39	75.39	14.043	9.23	75.23
Carlberg	68.00	9.39	77.39	14.468	9.51	77.51
Johnson	70.00	9.39	79.39	14.894	9.79	79.79
Moore	72.00	9.39	81.39	15.319	10.07	82.07
Totals	$470.00	$65.73	$535.70	100.00	$65.73	$535.73

Incentive Calculation
Standard Output = 1,750 Items/Day
Incentive Item Rate = $.15
Actual Output = 2,188 Items

2,188	Actual Output
-1,750	Standard Output
438	Items in Excess of Standard
x $.15	Incentive Item Rate
$65.70	Incentive Payment Earned

each group member would receive a bonus amounting to 16.2 percent of his or her base pay (vacations, illnesses, and other allowed time away from the job would, of course, be taken into consideration when computing the actual dollar amount of bonus earned by a specific employee during the period).

Cost Savings

Cost savings plans are generally used on an organizationwide basis, but can also be used on a division or department basis. These plans provide for employer and employees to share any benefits from a reduction in production costs. Historically, cost savings plans (or *gainsharing* plans, as they are sometimes called) have been utilized almost exclusively in manufacturing. They are described here because of their potential application in other situations.

The philosophy underlying cost savings plans is that cost reduction is the responsibility of everyone in the organization. Each employee has the opportunity as well as the obligation to make effective use of the resources available: his or her time, equipment operated, or materials used. The organization, on the other hand, has the obligation to create a work climate that fosters, supports, and encourages employee improvement efforts. Cost reduction,

Table 10.5
Group Incentives Based on Standard Hours

Work Center Activities	Items Processed	Standard Hours Per Item	Standard Hours Earned	Available Hours	Efficiency Index
Cashier's checks	65,360	0.0116	758.2		
Money orders	24,164	0.0117	282.7		
Expense vouchers	8,900	0.0121	107.7		
C.D.s	4,333	0.0135	58.5		
Dividend checks	2,781	0.0044	12.2		
Certified checks	982	0.0045	4.4		
Vacation checks	321	0.0042	1.3		
Customer inquiries	426	0.3332	141.9		
Totals			1,366.9	1,176	116.2
Incentive Bonus = 16.2 percent					

therefore, is a cooperative effort and any resulting savings should be shared between the organization and its employees.

Table 10.6 illustrates the basic mechanics of a cost savings plan. The initial step in developing a plan is to determine the sales value of the organization's output and the ratio of compensation costs to that value. As shown in Table 10.6, the organization has determined that each unit of production has a sales value of $10. During the base period used for the calculations (normally a period of two or more years), the company produced 45 million units that had a sales value of $450 million. Compensation costs during this period were $247.5 million, or 55 percent of the sales value of output. Therefore, 55 percent becomes the allowable compensation ratio to be used in future periods to determine if cost savings have actually been achieved.

Table 10.6
Group Incentives Based on Cost Savings

I. Base Period	
Sales value of output (SVO)	$450,000,000
($10.00 per item x 45,000,000 items)	
Total compensation costs	$247,500,000
Allowable compensation ratio (ACR)	55%
($247,500,000 ÷ $450,000,000)	
II. Current Period	
SVO	$37,500,000
(3,750,000 units x $10.00 per unit)	
ACR	$20,625,00
($37,500,000 x 55%)	
Actual compensation expense	18,333,333
Savings	2,291,667
Less: company portion (30%)	687,500
Cost savings bonus	$1,604,167

In the second portion of Table 10.6 the determination of the cost savings bonus during an actual operating period is illustrated. Total compensation costs in the month illustrated were $2,291,667 below the allowable amount. This is the amount of labor costs that have been saved and are available for distribution between the organization and the employees. In the example shown, the company retains 30 percent of the savings and the rest is distributed among employees. Each employee typically receives a bonus amounting to the percentage of distributed cost savings relative to total compensation costs for the period. In this case the bonus would be 8.75 percent ($1,604,167 cost savings bonus ÷ $18,333,333 actual compensation expense).

For the sake of simplicity, this example of a cost savings plan has been predicated on a single type of output. The approach can also be used where multiple outputs are produced. The sales value of each product or service would simply be accumulated to determine the total value of all outputs.

Profit Sharing

It is often difficult to determine whether profit sharing is a type of incentive plan or merely another form of indirect compensation.[7] Many organizations tout profit sharing as an incentive program, but use it as a vehicle for funding retirement plans, hence the term *profit sharing retirement plan*. When used to fund retirement benefits, profit sharing loses its value as a stimulator of short-term performance because the payoff is so far in the future that employees cannot readily link increased effort in the present to a far removed reward.

Some organizations make cash distributions to employees as soon as profits are determined, either quarterly or annually, thus using profits as short-run rewards for increased productivity. The following discussion will consider profit sharing as a form of incentive only when profits are actually distributed to employees in cash or cash equivalents immediately after the period in which profits are earned.

The first formal definition of profit sharing was put forth by the International Cooperative Congress in Paris in 1899. "Profit sharing is an agreement freely entered into by which the employees receive a share, fixed in advance, of the profits."[8] This simple definition is still valid today. The purpose of profit sharing is to motivate employees to be more productive. By emphasizing profits, it is hoped that employees will not only become more conscious of using their time effectively, but will also become more conscious of costs in general. Concomitantly, profit sharing seeks to foster a greater spirit of cooperation between employees and the organization that works to the mutual benefit of both.

Two issues to be addressed in using profit sharing as an incentive are the basis on which profits will be distributed between company and employees and the basis for allocating the profits to individual employees. The percentage of profits that the company will distribute to employees may be determined in several ways: (1) a percentage of profits before provision for federal income tax, (2) a percentage of profits after deduction of taxes, (3) a percentage of profits after taxes and deduction of dividends to stockholders, or (4) a percentage of the total amount declared as a dividend. Most cash-distribution plans are based on a pretax formula. The actual percentages used by organizations vary and the percentage rate is typically revised periodically.

Allocations of profits to employees are customarily made on the basis of an employee's base pay. Eligibility requirements used by the organization affect the amount a specific employee might receive. (The Employee Retirement Income Security Act as well as the Internal Revenue Code regulates profit sharing plans. An organization contemplating the use of such a plan should seek legal advice concerning conformance to statutory requirements before implementation of a plan.)

Cash distribution profit sharing plans are used primarily by small firms. In a small organization, profit sharing represents a simple form of incentive plan because elaborate unit-cost accounting and work measurement are not required for its usage. Moreover, employees in a small firm can have a greater impact or influence on profits than they could have in a large company. A current-distribution profit-sharing plan, consequently, provides a means for a small organization to capitalize on incentives without incurring a great deal of development and administrative cost.

PROBLEMS WITH INCENTIVES

Incentives, although becoming increasingly popular in some circles, are not without their problems. Because an awareness of potential difficulties in the development, implementation, and administration of pay-for-performance arrangements can aid in designing effective plans, attention will now be turned to examining the problems associated with the use of incentives. Some of the problems described pertain directly to either individual or group incentives, while others relate to all plans.[9]

Restriction of Output

A basic assumption of incentive plans is that employees, because they are rewarded on the basis of output, will produce as much as they are capable of producing. Research, unfortunately, does not bear this out. Findings over a number of years suggest that employees, acting as a group, set certain production limits that they will not allow an individual to exceed. These restrictions are set informally and enforced through social pressure. "Rate-busters" quickly find themselves ostracized by the work group.

Restriction of output occurs for two reasons. First, employees may believe that if they earn too much money under an incentive arrangement management will cut the piece rate or adjust the standard. In other words, employees are suspicious of management's intentions. Consequently, employees seek to protect themselves against the threat of management action by establishing informal levels of output that each worker is expected to abide by. The result is that incentive plans often do not produce the productivity gains initially forecast by management. Second, employees are a social group. Primary functions of any social group, whether family, sorority, or club, are the establishment of its own values, protection of weaker members of the group, and control of the group's more iconoclastic members. Individual incentives pit group member against group member, thus threatening the solidarity of the group. Group response is likely to be output restrictions that preserve the unity of the group, even at the expense of individual members.

Money as a Motivator

As indicated in Chapter 3, money itself is no longer considered to be a good general motivator. (Undoubtedly, there are still many individuals who exhibit a strong money motivation, but for people as a whole, money has lost much of its importance as an effective stimulus.) In the late 1880s and early 1900s, when the prototypes of pay-for-performance systems were being developed, it was assumed that employee behavior in the workplace was motivated solely by money. Incentive plans still assume that money is a primary motivator. In the absence of strong money motivation, incentive plans may not accomplish significant improvements in productivity, especially if other on-the-job psychological factors, as discussed in Chapter 3, are ignored.

Compensation Inequities

Compensation inequity problems may arise from two sources: (1) those workers who are not paid incentives, and (2) disagreements about the fairness of payments or time standards. Where individual incentives are used it is not always possible to cover all employees in a work unit. If some workers are on incentives and some are not, conflicts are likely to arise because the nonincentive employees, whose contributions may be just as valuable, feel they are not compensated fairly in relation to employees on incentives. In some cases, they may be right. Less-skilled workers on an incentive plan may actually earn more than workers of a higher skill level who are not on incentives. Perceived inequities as well as actual inequities can arise unless great care is taken to structure the incentive plan or to find ways to reward those not covered by incentives. Group plans, of course, alleviate this problem.

The piece rates or time standards used in an individual incentive plan are typically matters of contention to employees. Common complaints are that the rates are too low or the standards are too high, thus making it difficult for employees to earn the amounts they feel should be earned through the exertion of extra effort. In other words, employees often see incentives as inequitable because the rates or standards do not permit them to earn what they feel they are entitled to. Extensive communications may be required to deal with this problem.

Fluctuations in Earnings

Because almost any type of operation is subject to variations in activity levels, earnings of employees on an incentive plan may fluctuate from one pay period to another. If total earnings depend on incentives, fluctuations in earnings can be a source of real frustration to workers.

Deterioration in Quality

Emphasis on quantity of output may cause quality levels to suffer. For example, if an incentive program in a sales department is based entirely on the acquisition of new customers, servicing existing accounts may be neglected in order to get as many new accounts as possible. Or, if an incentive program in a consumer loan department of a bank is based on the number of new loans booked, there will probably be a tendency to book some loans that are marginal at best. The solution to the quality problem is to assure an adequate balance between numbers of items produced and the quality of those items.

Administration Expense

Incentive plans are not generally noted for their ease of administration. Depending upon the type of plan used and the complexity of computing payments, costs of administering incentives can be significant. Additional records may have to be kept by employees or supervisors; verifications may have to be made by disinterested third parties; and supplemental entries may have to be made to payroll records. Automated accounting systems help, but incentives always add to overhead expense.

Opposition to Changes

Changes in methods, procedures, and equipment are apt to be resisted vigorously when an incentive plan is in operation. Changes mean that workers will have to learn new ways of performing their jobs. During the period when relearning is taking place, incentive earnings will, in all probability, decrease; consequently, workers are likely to be highly negative or openly resistant to any changes that affect work processes.

Connotation of Factory Approach

When used in nonmanufacturing situations, incentives often suffer from the stigma of their factory origination. Clerical workers, even those performing routine, repetitive work, normally feel that their activities are different from what is done in the manufacturing area. The introduction of incentives into an office environment may have negative connotations to workers: an assembly-line approach, a management attempt to speed up operations, or a depersonalization of the individual employee.

Suspicions of Management's Purposes

Many employees feel that management is not altruistic by nature. The implementation of an incentive plan may arouse suspicions about why management is introducing such a plan. Is the purpose to reduce employment levels? To make employees work harder? To avoid paying merit increases? To fatten the corporate coffers? If a climate of distrust has existed prior to incentives, the introduction of a plan will tend to increase the amount of distrust.

Improper Management Practices

Arbitrary management actions can kill any incentive plan. Unnecessarily adjusting time standards, reducing piece rates, or breaking up sales territories because salespeople are "making too much money" are examples of inappropriate practices. While theoretically supporting the concept that the more a worker produces, the more a worker should earn, management sometimes appears taken aback by the actual amount an employee earns when producing at a high rate under an incentive plan. If this occurs, the temptation may be to reduce the amount employees can earn.

Developing Accurate Standards

Accurate time standards are absolutely essential for any type of individual piecework incentive plan. The use of sophisticated work-measurement techniques is required to set standards that are valid. Once set, these standards must be checked periodically to assure their continued accuracy. Inaccurate standards establish performance levels that are too high or too low; improper performance levels result in over- or underpayment of employees.

Inaccurate Reporting

An accurate production reporting system, one that lends itself to periodic audits, is a requirement for an incentive plan. If manual counting of output is used, reporting inaccuracies may occur accidentally or deliberately. Where bundles of work are used as the basis for determining output (a common practice for paperwork processing), employees have been known to reduce the number of items in each bundle in order to increase the total number of bundles that they have produced. In one instance, where a municipality was using the total weight of garbage collected by individual sanitation crews as a basis for awarding incentive bonuses, it was discovered that crews were adding rocks and other heavy items to the garbage to increase their incentive pay! Adequate safeguards must be built into the reporting system to eliminate the possibility of inaccurate or erroneous reporting.

Rewards for Methods Improvement

The best source of ideas for improving work methods and procedures has always been those employees who are performing the work. Under an incentive plan, however, employees may not be motivated to suggest improvements because improvements will result in a new standard or a new piece rate. Employees may feel that reporting suggestions for improvements may produce a negative reward: lower earnings. Consequently, one of the problems associated with the use of incentive systems is devising an approach that encourages the submission of new ideas by rewarding employees appropriately. A suggestion system with very liberal rewards for improvement ideas is one way of handling this problem.

Short-Term Focus

A major criticism of American industry in general is its focus on short-term rather than long-term results. This is reflected in the emphasis on this month's results, this quarter's profits, and this year's sales growth. Quite often, however, actions taken in the short run to improve a situation can have a negative effect in the future unless there is a sufficient integration of short-term actions with long-run objectives. Incentive plans usually have a focus of immediacy: Increase productivity *now*, raise employee motivation *now*. Normally, incentives will do just that. The risk involved is that by attempting a quick fix through incentives, the organization may not be dealing with underlying problems that require permanent solutions, such as more effective employee selection, better training, or elimination of boring jobs. Furthermore, by adopting an incentive program an organization is locking itself into a compensation scheme that cannot be abandoned in the future without highly negative effects on employee morale.

This examination of problems associated with incentives should not be interpreted as a condemnation of incentives or pay-for-performance schemes. Incentives have a place in business and industry. An intelligent decision concerning their appropriateness in a given situation or a specific firm can only be made after considering both their positive and negative features.

REQUIREMENTS FOR EFFECTIVE USE OF INCENTIVES

Incentives are not a panacea for an organization's productivity problems, nor are they universally applicable to all types of work or organizations. Effective use of incentives hinges upon a number of factors.[10] The nature of the work itself is a major consideration, but control systems and human responses to incentives are important too. There are many requirements that must be met for optimal utilization of pay-for-performance plans. Each of these requirements should be viewed as an issue, problem, or area of concern to be addressed before an incentive system is implemented.

Direct Relationship Between Effort and Output

Because incentive payments are predicated on output, one of the first requirements of an incentive system is the existence of a direct relationship between employee effort expended and resulting output. By exerting more effort an employee must be able to increase his or her output. Ideally, the relationship between additional effort and additional output should be one to one; for example, by increasing effort 25 percent the employee should be able to raise his or her production by 25 percent. While such a direct relationship may not, in fact, exist, the closer effort and output are related, the greater the chance that incentives will be perceived as fair by employees. Where the relationship is marginal, employees are unlikely to exert greater effort because the additional expenditure of energy produces limited results that may not be worth the effort required.

Readily Identified Units of Output

The end product of employee effort, either on an individual or a group basis, must be a unit of output that is readily and easily identified; for example, loans processed, sales calls made, automobiles sold, or wiring harnesses completed. Where units of output are not readily identifiable, as in the case of a security guard or a custodian, the use of incentives may be precluded altogether.

Even, Continuous Flow of Work

Because incentives tie earnings to work produced, there must be an even, continuous supply of work for the employee. A sporadic workflow reduces the potential of increasing earnings through the steady application of effort. Morale and motivation to exert increased effort can be damaged if availability of work to process is subject to wide fluctuations. Incentives work best where there is a constant supply of units to be handled.

Standards of Performance

It is axiomatic that if payment is to be based on output, there must be accurate and precise output expectations expressed either in terms of time per unit, units per period of time, or quality levels. Standards establish "par for the course" or production norms; bettering par or beating the norm results in incentive payments. Effective use of incentives requires that the work lend itself to the setting of standards of some type. If work standards cannot be set, the use of an incentive plan is not advisable.

Quality Standards

Incentives typically emphasize quantity of work. However, quality must also be emphasized. If not, the result is likely to be increased output of an inferior nature. In many areas of clerical or accounting work, quality expectations are built into the nature of processing operations: The work balances at the end of the period or it does not balance. In other administrative areas, such as customer service, quality standards are not always explicitly identified or stated. In these areas it is extremely important that quality expectations be clarified before using incentives. Calling on potential customers or interfacing with retail purchasers are activities where the quality of service is as important as the number of calls made or the dollar amount of sales made. In activities where quality of performance is the overriding consideration, incentives that emphasize the volume of work should not be used.

Measurement Systems

A measurement system is necessary to capture the number of units produced or hours earned and actual hours if a standard hour form of incentive plan is used. In the case of individual incentives, the system must be capable of identifying output or other data by specific employees. Measurements should not rely upon manual counting or recording by employees themselves unless the data are subject to independent verification.

Opportunity for Cost Reduction

Because one of the basic goals of incentive plans is to reduce costs, it is necessary to know prior to implementation that the plan will actually produce a reduction in costs by increasing output per employee or by enabling more volume to be handled without adding to staff. In calculating the costs savings brought about by incentives it is important not to overlook the additional overhead expenses that implementation and administration of the plan will necessitate. Setting standards, collecting measurements, and calculating incentive earnings are just a few of the additional expenses incurred with incentive plans. Gains in productivity must be significant enough to offset both the direct and indirect costs involved with an incentive plan. Where opportunities for reducing costs are marginal, incentives may not be appropriate.

A Good Unit-Cost System

A good unit-cost system is necessary so that processing costs can be carefully monitored and evaluated; it affords a degree of control by providing a basis for tracking costs over time. A unit-cost system permits an organization to determine if incentives are actually producing the results they are supposed to produce.

Sufficient Financial Inducement

To be effective motivators, incentives must offer employees sufficient financial rewards to compensate for the extra effort or energy expenditure required to gain that reward. In other words, the potential gain must be great enough to offset the effort necessary to produce more. There must be perceived equity between the amount to be earned and the energy expenditure needed to earn that amount. For instance, if an employee has to work 25-percent harder to increase his or her earnings by 5 percent, the financial inducement is likely to be perceived as totally insufficient because too much effort is required to gain a meager financial reward. Incentives work best when there is a high degree of correlation between additional effort expended and additional earnings.

Reasonable Time Spans for Payment

A reward, according to psychological theory, is more effective if it comes soon after the behavior that has earned it rather than at some later point in time. This is true for incentives: The shorter the time span between earning an incentive and receiving the payment, the better. Weekly, semimonthly, or monthly payouts for employees on individual incentives are preferable because the immediacy of the payoff reinforces the behavior that produced the reward. The longer the payoff is delayed, the less connection employees see between behavior and reward.

Relatively Stable Technology

Technology is the process by which inputs are converted to outputs. Where the conversion process is subject to rapid changes in equipment, procedures, or forms, the use of incentives is severely limited. Changes in technology necessitate changes in standards and incentive-payment formulas. Moreover, they necessitate relearning by employees. Some relative degree of stability in operations over a period of time enhances the potential of effectively using incentive plans.

Selective Application

Incentives are useful for some types of work; they are applicable to some organizational departments; they perform well at some organizational levels. One of the keys to effective use of incentives is knowing when and where to apply them. Incentives should not be imposed on types of work or organizational areas where there is doubt about their applicability. Neither should they be used at a higher organizational level simply because they are being used at a lower level. Incentives will not succeed at one firm just because they have been used successfully at another firm. A selective, situational application of incentives is required.

Management Control System

Because incentive systems are complex propositions, a management control system is a requisite for assuring that they function smoothly. Scheduling workflow, evaluating results, monitoring standards, and auditing reported data are a few of the activities the control system must address. A control system keeps the program on track and provides feedback indicating where and when changes are needed.

Communication to Employees

Extensive communication to employees is required prior to the implementation of an incentive program. What, when, how, why, who, and where relative to the program must be thoroughly communicated to allay any employee apprehensions or misunderstandings. Once the program is operational, continuous feedback is required to assure continued employee cooperation. Periodic reports on results, earnings paid in incentives, anticipated revisions, and so forth are essential.

Grievance Procedure

No incentive plan yet devised has been completely free of gripes, complaints, or dissatisfactions. Disputes over incentives may arise because employees feel that payments are too low, standards are too difficult to meet, workflow is irregular, or equipment breaks down too frequently. Effective use of incentives requires that a formal mechanism be established to address any complaints. A grievance procedure provides an outlet for employee dissatisfaction as well as reassurance that management will investigate problems with the program.

Employee Support

An essential requirement for any incentive program is unqualified support from those who will be paid under such a plan. Employees must believe in the payment method, the fairness of the standards, and all other plan elements. No plan can succeed without the active support of its participants.

Supervisory Support

Inasmuch as employee attitudes often reflect the attitude of their immediate supervisor, support from first-line management is necessary for successful use of incentives. Not only must supervisors believe in the plan, they must actively demonstrate their support by eliminating bottlenecks in workflow, expediting requests for equipment repairs, and encouraging employees to put forth their best efforts. Without active supervisory involvement, incentives are unlikely to be totally effective.

Top-Management Commitment

Management commitment is vital to the success of any pay-for-performance program. There must be a commitment to the cost and time needed to implement and administer the program; there must be a commitment to maintaining the integrity of the program. Management must resist the temptation to adjust payment rates or standards simply because employees are "making too much money" under incentives. Management must be willing to stick with the program when productivity gains are not as great as originally anticipated. Management must view the use of incentives as a long-term effort, not a quick fix. Lacking sufficient commitment from top management, a firm is ill-advised to undertake the implementation of incentive payment plans.

Implementation of programs designed to reward employees on the basis of their output or performance should not be taken lightly. Careful study and thoughtful assessment must precede implementation.

DO INCENTIVES REALLY WORK?

Do pay-for-performance plans really work? Do they actually increase productivity and reduce costs? Evidence seems to suggest that, where judiciously applied, employee incentive plans do work.[11] Individual incentive plans have been successfully applied to a broad spectrum of activities in manufacturing as well as administrative operations. Group incentive plans have also been used to good effect in varying environments.

Certainly, pay-for-performance arrangements are a compensation alternative that should be explored as a means of reducing costs and increasing productivity. They are not, as this chapter has indicated, a panacea for resolving compensation issues and improving employee performance.

TEAM-BASED COMPENSATION

Closely allied to the concept of group incentives is the concept of team-based pay. Over the last decade or so there has been a great interest in configuring work groups into teams and designing compensation plans that would reward interdependent team effort rather than individual effort.[12] While team-based compensation plans contain some elements of group incentive systems, they also speak to other types of rewards for teams, such as opportunities for problem solving, autonomy, and cross-functional training, rewards that are psychological in nature rather than financial. This section examines the use of teams in organizations, schemes for compensating teams, and the difficulties involved in developing team pay plans that are equitable and motivational in nature.

WHAT IS A TEAM?

While the word "team" means different things to different people and organizations, it may be best described as "a small number of people with complementary skills who are committed to a common purpose, performance goals, and approach for which they hold themselves mutually accountable."[13]

The size of the team is dependent on its overall purpose, specific performance goals, common approach, skills, and accountability. Occasionally a large number of people may be considered a team. However, groups of much over twenty-five are likely to break into subteams rather than function as a single unit.[14] The larger the number of team members, the greater the difficulty they will have interacting and agreeing on courses of action to be taken. Where large numbers of members are involved, for example, the team is likely to experience difficulty in determining simple issues such as convenient meeting locations and times. If communication breaks down, the team will be more likely to revert to hierarchy, structure, policies, and procedures. Consequently, the team will stop performing as a team.

At the core of the definition of teams is the concept that teams and performance are connected. Unfortunately, too many teams are not successful because they fail to pay sufficient attention to the company's performance standards or the goals of the team. Whether the team is a work group, a department, or a division within the organization, the concept of teams should remain the same.

Requirements for Team-Based Compensation

A team-based compensation system can be an effective compensation plan for some companies. In order to be truly beneficial, it requires (1) complete support from all levels of management, (2) a reward system that equitably rewards team members for performance as a team, and (3) recognition that rewards do not have to be in the form of money but can be expressed as psychological satisfactions. Whatever forms rewards take, they must, obviously, be perceived by all team members as fair.[15]

The first condition necessary for a successful team-based compensation plan is often the most difficult one for managers to accept. Management must learn to give the team sufficient autonomy. As an effective team culture develops, power must shift from managers or supervisors to the team. As this occurs, managers may feel that they are losing control because they no longer know which employee did what on the team. However, to support the team process, it is necessary to give the team autonomy. True commitment to the team process on the part of management begins by allowing the team to determine how it will accomplish its objectives and to suggest how rewards and recognition will be distributed.

When teams are implemented in the workplace, initially there may be a great deal of uncertainty. This period of uncertainty may last anywhere from eighteen to twenty-four months. During this period productivity may be lowered. If so, it is important to remember that compensation levels must not be affected during this start-up period. Lost productivity must be viewed as a cost of implementing the team concept. It is essential that all team members and organizational leaders give and communicate full and consistent support for the team process.

During the initial transition period managers will need to make sure that members of a team are working together, rather than competing against each other. This can often be accomplished by emphasizing and communicating the mission or purpose of the team. Teams will not be successful unless team roles and goals are fully clarified. Managers can help teams stay on track by promoting training opportunities and defining appropriate performance goals and measures.

The team's performance goals must always relate directly to the purpose of the team. Without this ingredient the team may become confused, pull apart, and revert to mediocre performance behaviors. Sufficient direction from management must be communicated so as to define the boundaries and scope of team authority.

It is sometimes claimed that the success of a team depends on two factors: communication and reward. That is, team members must want to share information and it must be worth their while to work as a team. Consequently, it is important that team members be given a role in distributing rewards. Members of a team can best determine what is a sufficient reward to motivate and encourage teamwork.

With the implementation of team compensation there is always the question of how to share financial gains with the members of the team. The solution ultimately rests with a simple question: What will enable the team to perform better? The answer to this question may vary from organization to organization.

Some companies are discovering that compensating team members individually for outstanding team performance is more effective than compensating the team as a whole. An individual team member's compensation may vary according to individual contributions to the overall team effort. At the same time, management must openly recognize the team as a group and reward the group's efforts.

Time and effort must be invested in designing an effective team compensation plan. It must be remembered that implementing a change in a current compensation system is never an easy task. A great deal of forethought is required to effectively communicate any significant changes in a compensation plan. If changes are not communicated correctly and with sensitivity, employee motivation can be lost, at least initially. Inasmuch as compensation plans are meant to enhance motivation, it is wise to invest sufficient effort in communicating upcoming changes. Also, any change must be communicated long before the change is actually made. Time must be allowed for feedback and for employees to get accustomed to the change in pay plans.

Today organizations probably no longer need to prove to employees that teams can have a positive impact on the company's bottom line of productivity and quality.[16] A quick glance back to the advent of quality circles in the early 1980s and the mushrooming of quality teams in the late 1980s and 1990s provides an example of the benefits of teams and employee participation. In the 1980s teams were implemented to work on special projects. Teams were assigned the goal of discovering ways to cut costs, developing new products, reviewing production processes; they essentially worked on all kinds of problem-identification or problem-solving activities.

Team-based compensation systems enable employers to offer additional rewards to indirect labor (workers who provide essential services to line workers), who are normally paid only their base pay. These systems also encourage cooperation rather than competition among employees. Thus, they produce a positive impact on both the organization and individual performances of employees.

Team-based compensation systems also have their disadvantages: (1) Employees may fear that employers will reduce the number of employees if the teams produce too much, (2) competition between teams may hurt the company as a whole, (3) individual employees may have difficulty identifying their individual contributions to the team as a whole, and (4) employees may have difficulty seeing how their individual performance affects their incentive pay.

Determining Base Pay

Employees will generally accept team-based compensation if it is communicated correctly and signals cooperation both within and across groups. It may, in fact, increase the participation of employees in the decision-making processes of the organization. However, fairness in dealing with teams does not mean equal pay for all team members. Companies that merely give dollars to reward team performance are finding that this does not always work.

It has been said that organizations of the 1990s were trying to manage with compensation tools of the 1950s and 1960s.[17] In solving team-pay issues it is important to remember that work performed and behaviors required in a team environment do not fit traditional compensation approaches, including group incentive systems. Rewarding team performance requires that managers go beyond traditional concepts of rewarding individuals.

Many team compensation systems emphasize that risk taking is necessary for teams. Teams must be willing to take the necessary risks associated with an assignment in order to move the organization forward. Rewarding strictly according to results may punish a team's effort.

Some advocates of team-based compensation recommend rewarding behaviors and activities rather than rewarding team members based on results achieved by the team. It is not uncommon for teams to be put into positions of risk in order to increase organizational performance. Teams are often assigned the task of improving or making suggestions that challenge those in authority or question past organizational practices. If the results of team effort fail to succeed, an organization should refrain from punishing team members. Punishment will only lead to disenchantment with the entire idea of teams.

Recognizing high performers in a team environment is not an easy task.[18] To take a group of individual contributors and pay them as a team may be counterproductive. Employees should be compensated on a team basis only if their performance is truly interlocked and interdependent.

Many companies view team compensation as a means of encouraging individual behavior that facilitates the group's progress toward its goal. It is recommended that managers look at all elements of team play when considering the distribution of rewards. Did individuals display participative or nonparticipative behaviors, such as listening to other team members, participating in team activities, and facilitating group efforts? A team may be unsuccessful simply because of lack of team play by certain members of the team. A lack of teamwork by individual team members should be corrected as soon as it is detected.

The Role of Performance Appraisal in a Team Environment

Recent research indicates that problems with performance appraisal can be reduced through the use of good performance-measurement techniques.[19] Organizations with meaningful performance standards will encourage team effectiveness. Standards assist the team in tailoring team goals and understanding how the achievement of these goals contributes to the organization's goals.

Performance-appraisal systems must be designed to effectively reward the behaviors the organization most wants to create and maintain. Compensation should be addressed after the institution decides on specific goals and desired performance. In short, an organization's performance-appraisal system and performance ethic provides the essential tools and direction for a team's effort.

Increasing Base Pay

Team performance requires individual team members to continually develop skills necessary to express themselves within the context of cooperation, rather than for individual gain. Ideally, "team compensation is not a payoff but a means of nurturing behavior that benefits the group."[20] Team members must have the necessary mix of skills necessary to do jobs as assigned. These skills might include technical or functional expertise, problem-solving and decision-making skills, and interpersonal skills.

A team cannot be an effective team without an appropriate combination of skills of team members. These skills are essential in order to achieve team goals and objectives. As members develop stronger team-based skills, base pay must reflect the development level of individual members.

A performance-appraisal rating of an individual's teamwork and team-participation behaviors should be reflected in any reward given. Increases in base pay, awards of stock ownership, gainsharing bonuses, profit sharing, or promotional advancements must reflect the increased performance in team behaviors displayed in the team.

Recognition Rewards

Monetary compensation alone will not guarantee high levels of team performance. Other types of rewards must also be used.[21] Studies indicate that employees find personal recognition more motivating than money. Maslow's hierarchy of needs and Herzberg's motivation–hygiene theory, as discussed in Chapter 3, also supports this finding.

Management theorists in general agree that money is not all that employees, either as individuals or members of a team, desire in a working relationship. When rewarding teams there are a number of other nonmonetary ways that may be used to reward team effort: Plaques, trophies, gifts, family vacation trips, meals, and communications of appreciation during organizational meetings or through companywide bulletins represent a few of these ways. Whatever means of appreciation are used, they must be sincere expressions of management recognition. Time spent investigating individual wants, needs, and backgrounds of team members may also help in selecting the most meaningful form of recognition.

The timing of rewards is also important. To be effective (as discussed earlier in this chapter), rewards must be given as soon as possible after the behavior that earned them. If rewards are given months after the behavior that earned them, a team may see little or no connection between behavior and reward; consequently, any chance to reinforce positive team behavior may be lost. For greatest psychological impact, the team should be informed of any rewards it is to receive before public recognition is given. To do otherwise may detract from the impact of the reward.

Incentive Compensation

It is no secret that paychecks are significant communication devices. Pay often sends a loud and clear message to employees that can be interpreted as a sign of appreciation. Employees, as team performers or individual contributors, have a need to feel appreciated and generally never outgrow the desire to feel valued by an employer.[22]

In general, people will perform or behave according to how they are measured and paid. Employees do not desire to be mediocre. Therefore, it is important to continue to search for effective reward alternatives that will encourage employee productivity. This search should ultimately supply an answer to the question of how to create a motivating and psychologically fulfilling work environment for employees. However, if employees are going to work together as teams, they must also be paid as teams. If they are not, chances are they will not work together effectively. To ensure that team members work together, the organization must make certain that they are working toward common goals. Some form of assessment of team performance, recognition, shared reward, or team incentive helps assure effective performance.

Team incentives provide an opportunity for each member of the team to receive a bonus. Normally the bonus is based on the output of the team as a whole toward the achievement of established goals (see the discussion of group incentives earlier in this chapter). Incentives are most appropriate when jobs are highly interrelated. Organizations may need to be more creative than they have in the past in using team performance appraisal and team incentives in dealing with highly interrelated jobs.[23]

Which is better, group or individual incentive plans? To answer this question things such as type of task, organizational commitment to teams, and type of work environment must be examined. Compensation experts tend to agree that individual incentive plans have better potential to encourage productivity, pointing out that team incentive plans suffer from what is called the *free-rider* syndrome. Many companies report that they are not satisfied with their team compensation plans.[24] The causes of this dissatisfaction include (1) difficulties in determining what constitutes a team, (2) the size of the team, (3) the complexity of designing pay plans that equitably compensate teams and team members, (4) difficulties in assuring that team performance measures are actually under the control of the team, and (5) difficulties in communicating the pay plan to team members.

Research suggests that the communication step is extremely important.[25] Management must communicate all elements of team-based compensation: guidelines, objectives, policies, procedures, and so forth. These things must be thoroughly communicated prior to implementation of the plan. Employees may not always openly welcome something new. However, if the reasons for the change are carefully communicated in advance and employees are given the opportunity to voice their opinions, employees will typically accept changes the organization desires to make.

NOTES

1. Donald L. Caruth, *Compensation Management for Banks* (Boston: Bankers Publishing, 1986), 179.

2. Ibid., 180–184.

3. Ibid., 184–194.

4. Ibid., 185.

5. Ibid.

6. Ibid., 188.

7. Ibid., 193.

8. J. D. Dunn and Frank M. Rachel, *Wage and Salary Administration: Total Compensation Systems* (New York: McGraw-Hill, 1971), 261.

9. Caruth, *Compensation Management*, 195–200.

10. Ibid., 200–205.

11. Wayne F. Cascio, *Managing Human Resources*, 5th ed. (Boston: Irwin–McGraw-Hill, 1998), 405.

12. Richard B. McKenzie and Dwight R. Lee, *Managing Through Incentives* (New York: Oxford University Press, 1998), 3–21.

13. Steven E. Gross, *Compensation for Teams* (New York: AMACOM, 1995), 23.

14. Ibid., 24.

15. Ibid., 189–209.

16. Ibid., 5.

17. Perry Pascarella, "Compensating Teams," *Across the Board*, February 1997, 16.

18. Gross, *Compensation for Teams*, 130.

19. Ibid., 86–107.

20. Pascarella, "Compensating Teams," 16.

21. Gross, *Compensation for Teams*, 129–146.

22. Ibid., 147–169.

23. McKenzie and Lee, *Managing Through Incentives*, 84–92.

24. Pascarella, "Compensating Teams," 16–22.

25. Gross, *Compensation for Teams*, 66.

11

PERFORMANCE APPRAISAL SYSTEMS

Job pricing, as discussed in Chapter 8, establishes the range of pay for jobs in an organization. Performance appraisal is the vehicle that permits an employee to progress from one specific salary to another within the established pay range. Even where step increases—based essentially on seniority—are used, performance appraisal is necessary to assure that an employee is performing the job adequately enough to move to the next higher pay step. (In a step increase system, performance appraisal is usually more of a formality, except where appraisal is used to justify withholding a step increase.) In merit pay systems performance appraisal is absolutely essential for determining the level of performance that has been demonstrated and the amount of pay increase that has been earned.

PERFORMANCE APPRAISAL DEFINED

Performance appraisal may be defined as "an on-going, systematic evaluation of how well an individual is carrying out the duties and responsibilities of his or her current job. Additionally, it typically includes an assessment of the individual's need or potential for further development."[1] Four key terms in this definition merit further consideration because they indicate the nature of an effective approach to assessing employee performance. These terms are (1) ongoing, (2) systematic, (3) evaluation, and (4) development.

Performance appraisal is an ongoing activity, not something that is done once a year when a supervisor or manager completes an employee evaluation form.[2] Monitoring and assessing the efforts expended and results produced by employees must be done, if it is to be accomplished effectively, on daily, weekly, and monthly bases. The culmination of this continuous process is the completion of a written report or form. The completion of the formal document, however, is not performance appraisal. Rather, it is a recapitulation of the many individual evaluations of how an employee has carried out the duties and responsibilities of his or her job over the entire period covered by the report. In fact, if it were not for the continuous evaluations made of performance, the formal report could not be completed accurately.

Performance appraisal is, or should be, systematic in nature. It should be a logical, objective assessment of how well an employee has performed a job. Effective performance appraisal depends upon well-defined standards of accomplishment that are measured in accordance with a systematic approach that eliminates—or severely reduces—subjectivity. Job standards are the yardsticks by which job accomplishments are measured; a consistent methodology for comparing accomplishments with standards establishes the system necessary for accurate, effective performance appraisal.

Performance appraisal is an evaluation. To evaluate means to determine the amount of—in this case, the amount of work actually accomplished. Measurements are critical to evaluation. Without measurements and standards, there can be no evaluation. There can only be guesses, subjective opinions, and estimations.

Finally, performance appraisal, if it is to be fully effective as a compensation management tool, must include a development aspect. The focus of development is twofold: identifying current needs for employee growth and improvement on the present job and identifying employee potential for promotion to positions of higher responsibility. The developmental aspect of performance appraisal looks at what the employee has done and seeks to determine what he or she needs to be able to perform the job better or be promoted to higher-level positions.

USES OF PERFORMANCE APPRAISAL

Unfortunately, most managers—and employees—have a very restricted view of performance appraisal, visualizing it as merely the means whereby increases in compensation are awarded. But performance appraisal, used to its fullest extent, is much more than a compensation device. It can be used as a mechanism for

- Providing feedback to employees on how well they are accomplishing job duties and responsibilities.
- Identifying individuals whose present performance and future potential warrant promotion to positions of greater responsibility.

- Identifying individuals whose inability to perform on the present job indicates the need for demotion to a position of lesser responsibility, lateral transfer, or termination.
- Identifying the need for training of individual employees or work units.
- Verifying the effectiveness of the selection process. (If new hires consistently perform below expectations, inappropriate selection criteria are possibly being used.)
- Determining the need for disciplinary action because of low output, poor quality of work, or frequent infraction of company rules, procedures, or policies.
- Determining the extent of an employee's progress in performing job duties.
- Identifying employees who have potential that may be significantly increased through additional training or other developmental activities.
- Increasing communication between supervisors and employees relative to job performance.
- Providing a basis for determining which employees should be granted pay increases and which should not.[3]

If used fully, performance appraisal can be a major motivational tool as well as a compensation mechanism. By providing feedback on actual results achieved and progress made, performance appraisal often serves as a stimulus to higher performance; by identifying improvement needs, it provides an employee with a sense of direction; by increasing communication between supervisor and employee, performance appraisal leads to greater job satisfaction and commitment to the organization. From an institutional standpoint, performance appraisal can be a vital aid in training and development, employee selection, human resource planning, and personnel actions.

PERFORMANCE APPRAISAL METHODS

Over the years several different methods of formally appraising performance have been developed. The eight most commonly used approaches found in organizations today are (1) rating scales, (2) ranking, (3) checklists, (4) behaviorally anchored rating scales (BARS), (5) work standards, (6) essays, (7) management by objectives (MBO), and (8) 360° performance appraisal.

Rating Scales

The single most widely used method of appraising the performance of nonexempt employees is some form of rating scale. Perhaps as many as 50 percent of all organizations utilizing performance-evaluation systems use this approach.[4] This method is so popular because it is simple and quick to use.

With rating scales, employees are evaluated according to a set of predetermined factors, such as quantity of work, quality of work, absenteeism, or the like. Each evaluation factor is ranked from the lowest level of performance to the highest in as many as fifteen categories. Most rating scales use five categories. In some instances, definitions of the evaluation factors are printed on the evaluation form itself; in other instances, only the factor title is shown.

To complete a performance appraisal using a rating scale, the evaluator simply checks the degree of each factor that is most descriptive of the employee's performance during the period covered by the appraisal. Figure 11.1 shows a fairly typical rating scale. Often, numerical values are assigned to each degree of each factor so that the evaluator can quickly compute a numerical average performance rating for the person being evaluated.

Many rating-scale forms also include a comments section below each factor so that the appraiser can provide written justification for the factor degree assigned. Other rating-scale forms provide a comments section at the end of the form, allowing the evaluator to make general comments supporting the overall appraisal.

Advantages

There are several advantages to rating scales as a method of performance appraisal: (1) They are easy to use, (2) they do not take much time to complete, (3) a set of standardized factors can be developed to cover all jobs in an organization, and (4) when numerical values are assigned to factor degrees, an average performance rating can be calculated quickly.[5]

Disadvantages

Although rating scales are probably the oldest approach to performance appraisal still in use, they have significant disadvantages: (1) Factors and degrees are often vaguely defined, if they are defined at all; (2) lack of factor and degree definitions may produce highly subjective evaluations by supervisors; (3) there is usually no factual basis for the evaluation; (4) frequently the factors contain items that are, at best, tangentially related to the job; (5) central tendency errors are likely to occur because it may be difficult for the appraiser to factually justify a rating above or below acceptable performance; and (6) the courts have usually taken a jaundiced view of rating scales because the factors used often include personality traits that have the potential for discrimination.[6]

Ranking

The simplest approach to performance appraisal is the ranking method. In its most elementary form, ranking entails placing all employees into a specific order based on their overall performance, from the highest or best performer to the lowest or worst performer. In a group of seven employees, for example, the best performer would be designated as a one, the next best performer a two, and so on. To determine the rankings, evaluators frequently use

Figure 11.1
Typical Rating Scale

Performance Factors	Below Minimum (unacceptable)	Below Expectations (marginal)	Meets Expectations (normal)	Exceeds Expectations	Clearly Outstanding
Judgment					
Initiative					
Creativeness					
Problem Solving					
Thoroughness & Accuracy					
Quantity					
Communication					
Job Knowledge Improvement					
Working With Others					
Leadership Ability					
Advancement Potential					
Adaptability					
Absenteeism/Punctuality					
Attitude					

an alternation ranking procedure: The evaluator first selects the best performer and then identifies the worst performer; next, the second-best performer is selected and the second-worst performer is identified. This alternation is continued until all employees have been assigned a rank order.

As typically used, ranking involves no specific criteria or performance guidelines; it relies entirely upon the appraiser's (or evaluator's) judgment for determining the order of employee performance.

Advantages

Ranking, it is claimed, has several advantages as a performance appraisal method: (1) It is inexpensive, (2) it is easy to use, (3) it eliminates the problem of central-tendency error because it forces the appraiser to place employees into a ranking based on overall performance, (4) it does not require extensive training of evaluators, and (5) since employees and supervisors naturally tend to rank individuals in some order of performance anyway, it legitimatizes an already existing informal procedure.[7]

Disadvantages

Unfortunately, no simple approach to dealing with a complex process is without its shortcomings. The disadvantages to ranking are (1) there are usually no objective criteria for determining an employee's position in the rank order; (2) it may be difficult to explain to an employee his or her ranking, since most employees consider themselves to be above average in performance; (3) ranking may produce morale problems among employees who are not rated at or near the top of the list; (4) performance comparisons across departmental lines are impossible, since a lower-ranking employee in one unit may actually be superior in performance to a higher-ranked employee in another work group; (5) ranking forces a distribution of performance that may not fit a work group because it is possible that all employees may be superior or all may be inferior; and (6) ranking does not provide the evaluator with useful information for counseling employees about their performance.[8]

Checklists

Performance appraisal checklists provide the evaluator with a series of statements, phrases, or adjectives that describe employee performance. These statements may be subdivided into specific factors such as quantity of work, quality of work, and so forth, with the descriptors listed under each category. Occasionally, the phrases or adjectives are simply listed without categorization. The appraiser marks the statement or adjective considered to be most descriptive of the employee's performance during the period covered by the appraisal. Figure 11.2 shows a typical checklist.

Figure 11.2
Typical Performance Appraisal Checklist

QUALITY OF WORK (Disregard Quantity)

___Extremely neat and accurate.
___Good accurate worker. Makes few mistakes.
___Adequate but some improvement would be desirable.
___Barely up to minimum standards. Often inaccurate.
___Below minimum standards. Complete checking required.

QUANTITY OF WORK (Disregard Quality)

___Outstanding volume.
___Well above average volume.
___Adequate volume.
___Barely up to minimum standards.
___Below minimum standards. Needs much improvement.

JOB KNOWLEDGE (Technical)

___Expert. Has superior knowledge.
___Well-rounded knowledge. Seldom needs assistance.
___Possesses acceptable knowledge.
___Knowledge is adequate to perform minimum job requirements.
___Very limited knowledge. Needs frequent assistance.

RESPONSIBILITY (Ability to Plan and Direct Work)

___Plans and carries out own work in superior manner. Self-sustaining.
___Plans and carries out work well. Requires little supervision.
___Requires occasional work direction.
___Carries out only the most tasks without follow-up.
___Always waits to be directed.

There are two variations to the straight checklist method. One variation is the forced-choice technique. In this approach the appraiser reviews a series of statements about an employee's performance and indicates which statement is most descriptive or least descriptive of that individual's performance. Figure 11.3 is an example of a forced-choice checklist. After the checklist is completed, the evaluator reviews all of the behaviors checked and composes a written description of the employee's performance.

Figure 11.3
Forced-Choice Checklist

Most Descriptive   Least Descriptive

☐	☐	Seldom makes mistakes
☐	☐	Fails to follow through on assignments completely
☐	☐	Always meets deadlines
☐	☐	Constantly seeks help on routine assignments
☐	☐	Does not plan ahead
☐	☐	Grasps instructions quickly
☐	☐	Seldom wastes time
☐	☐	Communicates well
☐	☐	Leader in group activities
☐	☐	Spends too much time on trivial matters
☐	☐	Patient with others
☐	☐	Industrious worker

Another variation of the checklist is the weighted checklist. It is very similar to the forced-choice method, except that weights have been assigned to each possible response. Normally the weights, developed by the human resource department, are not known to the evaluator. This approach, it is believed, tends to reduce bias on the part of the person conducting the appraisal.

Advantages

Proponents of checklists claim that this method offers the following advantages: (1) The evaluation is not as vague as in the ranking or rating scales approaches because actual job behaviors are described in the checklists, (2) evaluator objectivity is greater than with rating scales or ranking because appraisers have to evaluate specific job performance behaviors, (3) the evaluator tends to act more as a recorder of observed behaviors than as a judge, and (4) checklists are typically developed for groups of similar jobs so that evaluation factors are more job specific than the general ones used in rating scales.[9]

Disadvantages

The shortcomings of checklists include (1) the time and expense of developing statements for various job groups that are actually reflective of job performance; (2) appraisers often have difficulty interpreting the statements because some items appear to be virtually identical; (3) when the weighted checklist is used, the appraiser has no knowledge of the assigned weights and may give an employee a different evaluation than intended; (4) factual data to support the assigned evaluation are usually absent; (5) lacking knowledge of which items are the most heavily weighted, the appraiser may be at a disadvantage in counseling the employee relative to his or her job performance; and (6) there is little evidence to indicate that checklists are an improvement over other appraisal methods.[10]

Behaviorally Anchored Rating Scales

Behaviorally anchored rating scales are basically a more detailed and refined version of the traditional rating scale. The implementation of BARS begins with a detailed job analysis and a precise identification of specific effective and ineffective job behaviors—a job analysis that goes beyond the ones discussed in Chapter 5. Once each performance factor has been identified, descriptive statements for each level of performance for each job factor are then arranged on a scale in rank order. Typically, the scale provides for seven descriptive statements for each performance factor, although sometimes points along the scale will not have a behaviorally descriptive statement attached to them. Figure 11.4 provides an example of a behaviorally anchored rating scale for the performance factor "customer relations" in a payments cashier's job.

BARS was developed to overcome weakness in other performance appraisal methods by addressing specific job behaviors and performance expectations. Where research has been conducted on the effectiveness of BARS as compared to other methods, such as rating, the results appear to be mixed.[11] It does not appear, though, that this approach has fulfilled earlier expectations about its improved effectiveness as a performance appraisal technique.

Advantages

Proponents of BARS claim several advantages for this method: (1) It is job based inasmuch as each job must be carefully studied to identify specific

Figure 11.4
Behaviorally Anchored Rating Scale

Job: Payments Cashier

Factor: Customer Relations (includes all those behaviors the cashier demonstrates when dealing with the customers).

☐ 7 Clearly Outstanding Performance	Carefully explains company services to customers and attempts to cross-sell services whenever possible.
☐ 6 Excellent Performance	Answers all questions knowledgeably and occasionally attempts to cross-sell one or two services.
☐ 5 Good Performance	Answers most customer inquiries knowledgeably and courteously.
☐ 4 Neither Good nor Bad Performance	Is friendly toward customers and answers some questions correctly.
☐ 3 Slightly Poor Performance	Answers questions by referring customers to another department.
☐ 2 Poor Performance	Responds to customers inquiries grudgingly and lacks adequate knowledge of company services.
☐ 1 Very Poor Performance	Indifferent to customers needs.

behaviors that will be used to assess performance, (2) it is more objective than other methods because specific behavioral statements rather than vague descriptions of performance are used, (3) its validity is superior to methods that rely on worker traits or personality factors that may not be job related, and (4) it provides for an easier communication of job expectations to employees, since these expectations are specifically identified in advance.[12]

Disadvantages

As a performance appraisal device, BARS has the following disadvantages: (1) It is expensive and time consuming to develop, since each job must be studied in detail; (2) its development normally requires professional expertise because of the extensive job analysis entailed; (3) there are usually little or no backup data collected to support the evaluator's assessment of performance; (4) problems of evaluator bias are not eliminated because judgment still plays a significant part in the evaluation; and (5) there is no clear-cut evidence that this method, although more detailed and expensive, is superior to other commonly used approaches.[13]

Work Standards

The work standards approach to performance appraisal is one in which each employee's output is compared to a predetermined level of output of acceptable quality. Standards, established through work measurement techniques such as time study, work sampling, or predetermined time systems, reflect the amount of work that a qualified employee working at a normal rate of speed under normal conditions could produce within a specified period of time.[14] This method is most commonly used in manufacturing, where output is readily quantifiable, but is also sometimes found in clerical and other nonmanufacturing environments.

Advantages

Where work standards can be used, they offer distinct advantages: (1) They are objective, quantifiable criteria for determining performance; (2) they provide for the easy identification of high as well as low performers; (3) they establish a definitive basis for relating merit pay increases to performance; and (4) they set expectations that can readily be communicated to employees.[15]

Disadvantages

Some of the drawbacks to work standards include the following: (1) The standards used to measure output must be very accurate,[16] (2) standards cannot be applied to jobs where there is no readily quantifiable output, (3) this approach typically does not provide developmental data that can be used for counseling employees, (4) workers must be convinced that the standards are fair, and (5) any changes made in the standards may have an adverse impact on employee morale.

Essays

Free-form essays are another performance appraisal method. In their simplest form, the evaluator merely writes a brief narrative describing the employee's performance, usually elaborating on strengths as well as indicating areas where the individual needs to make improvement. This method tends to focus on extremes in an employee's behavior rather than routine day-to-day performance because the appraiser more easily remembers extremes. Evaluations of this type, obviously, depend quite heavily upon the writing ability of the evaluator. However, some managers believe that this approach is perhaps the best approach to performance appraisal.[17] There are no constraints on the subjects that can be covered in an essay appraisal. Essays, however, are most often used in conjunction with other appraisal methods rather than as the sole method. They are also more common for managerial than for operative-level jobs.

Advantages

The advantages claimed for the essay approach include (1) the thoughtful attention an appraiser must give to writing a report that is truly reflective of an employee's performance, (2) the wide latitude given to the evaluator to cover items that may not be included in a set of predetermined evaluation factors, (3) the attention that must be given to citing specific examples of demonstrated performance in order to compose an accurate narrative, and (4) the kind of information provided to the employee may help the individual improve his or her performance.[18]

Disadvantages

Essays have several inherent drawbacks when used as the only means of performance appraisal. Among these are (1) the quality of the evaluation is more often than not a function of the appraiser's ability to write well rather than of the employee's ability to perform a job successfully; (2) the method can be very time consuming if it is given the attention it deserves; (3) inasmuch as essays require time, appraisers may be inclined to perform them perfunctorily if several employees are being appraised at once; (4) the evaluator tends to concentrate more on behavioral extremes than examples of day-to-day performance; and (5) comparisons of employee performance across departmental lines is difficult because appraisers do not all cover the same aspects of performance nor possess the same writing skills.[19]

Management by Objectives

As an approach to performance appraisal, MBO is a results-centered technique that does not attempt to evaluate traits or personality characteristics; its focus is entirely on actual achievements measured in terms of expected achievements set by employees themselves. With MBO the focus of the appraisal process shifts from evaluation of the worker's personal attributes or tangentially related job factors to actual job accomplishments. The appraiser's role changes from that of performance judge to one of counselor, mentor, coach, and performance facilitator. The employee's involvement in the appraisal function becomes one of active participator rather than passive bystander.

In an MBO appraisal system, the employee and his or her supervisor mutually set goals that the employee will achieve during the next evaluation period. These goals then become the standards by which the employee's performance will be measured. While goals are normally set in terms of quantitative terms that lend themselves to clear-cut measurement, qualitative goals that are not as easily measurable are often used too. At the conclusion of the appraisal period the employee and the supervisor meet to discuss the extent to which stated goals have been achieved and review further actions that may be necessary to accomplish goals that were not met in the current appraisal period. In this review session, goals for the next period are also normally established. With MBO, the supervisor keeps communication channels open and attempts to assist in any way possible to see that the employee actually achieves the goals that have been set.

Advantages

MBO has been touted as a performance appraisal system for over fifty years. Among the advantages claimed for it are (1) it increases the employee's involvement in setting performance objectives and concomitantly increases the motivation required to reach those objectives; (2) it offers an objective, factual basis for measuring accomplishments; (3) it emphasizes results, not traits or personality characteristics; (4) it is entirely job centered; (5) it establishes the appraiser as a facilitator of performance rather than as a critic of performance; (6) it assures the organization that all employees are working toward a common purpose; and (7) it supports the psychological concept that people will exercise self-direction and self-control in the accomplishment of organizational aims that they have participated in setting.[20]

Disadvantages

While the advantages of management by objectives as a performance appraisal system are real, it also has disadvantages that are just as real. For example, (1) MBO is incompatible with certain managerial styles—it will not work under authoritarian conditions; (2) it is an organizational philosophy and cannot operate at one organizational level without operating at all levels; (3) installing a truly effective MBO approach is time consuming and requires an installation period of at least five years before it can permeate the entire organization; (4) MBO cannot be implemented at all organizational levels simultaneously, nor can it be implemented from the bottom up—it must begin at the very top of the organization and work its way down; (5) it requires a total and sizable commitment of management support, interest, and time if it is to succeed; (6) it does not lend itself to all types of jobs—individuals performing routine, repetitive, or machine-paced jobs are better appraised by another method; and (7) employees require extensive training before they normally will respond in a positive fashion to MBO.[21]

360° Performance Appraisal

360° performance appraisal is a multirater appraisal system in which an employee is evaluated by some combination of subordinates, peers, superiors, external customers, internal customers, or others with whom the employee has contact. The basic premise of 360° appraisal is that a complete assessment of an individual's performance can only be obtained by gathering information from all those who have a relevant view of how the person being appraised has actually performed. The necessary performance information is gathered through surveys, either paper and pencil or online. Frequently the appraisee has input as to who will be selected to provide appraisal information. Proponents of this approach claim that it provides inclusive information about all aspects of an individual's job performance.

Advantages

Among the advantages claimed for 360° appraisal are (1) it provides complete performance information, (2) it provides multiple perspectives on performance, (3) it formalizes communication between employees and their internal and external customers, and (4) studies suggest that performance improvement and behavior change may occur as a result of the complete information it provides.[22]

Disadvantages

Theoretically, 360° appraisal would seem to be a sound idea. There are, however, some distinct disadvantages associated with its use. Some of the major disadvantages are that (1) raters typically receive no training in using the system; (2) employees, where they have the option of selecting raters, may choose raters who will give them a good rather than an honest appraisal; (3) time and cost demands are higher than in traditional appraisal systems; (4) more administrative support is required in this approach as compared to others; (5) there is no evidence to suggest that 360° is actually an improvement over other performance appraisal systems; and (6) facilitators may be required to help managers interpret the results.

This brief discussion of performance appraisal methods demonstrates that there is no perfect approach to assessing employee job performance for the purpose of awarding merits increases or other uses. In selecting an approach an organization must take into consideration the uses that will be made of the results, the organization's philosophy and climate, the types of jobs being evaluated, and the time and expense that will be required to furnish the organization with an effective system.

PROBLEMS IN PERFORMANCE APPRAISAL

Many of the problems in performance appraisal occur not so much from the method used (although some methods are more susceptible to problems than others) but from the way it is used. Often problems occur because appraisers are largely untrained in how to evaluate employee performance. Even when appraisers are trained, they frequently find it difficult to accurately and effectively assess the accomplishments of their subordinates. Some of the most common problems encountered in performance appraisal are described in the following sections.

Perfunctoriness

For many appraisers, performance appraisal is a task they find difficult and unpleasant. Some view it as too time consuming; some see it as an unnecessary administrative function the human resource department requires; others do not relish the thought of having to explain or discuss an evaluation with an employee. Therefore, it is not unusual to find the appraisal handled very superficially. The form is completed without much thought; any discussion with the employee is cursory. While it is important to both employee and employer, performance appraisal is often handled as if it is not important.

Lack of Objectivity

An obvious weakness of many performance appraisal systems is their lack of objectivity. Rating scales, for example, commonly use personality traits or characteristics such as attitude, loyalty, appearance, resourcefulness, and personal conduct that are not only difficult to measure, but are also open to completely subjective interpretation. In addition, these and similar factors may have little or nothing to do with job performance. While some element of subjectivity probably exists in even the best of systems, a definite attempt must always be made to ensure that objective factors—quantifiable, measurable, and job related—are stressed in the appraisal method used. Lack of objective criteria places the evaluator and the employer in an untenable position if an employee challenges the performance appraisal system.

Central Tendency

Perhaps one of the most common errors in appraising performance is central tendency: rating all employees as average or at the middle value of a numerical scale. This problem may occur for three reasons. First, it is the most expedient way for managers to do appraisals, especially when many employees have to be evaluated at the same time. Second, rating scales have a built-in tendency that forces ratings toward the center rather than toward the outer limits. Third, evaluating an employee as average relieves the appraiser of having to explain or justify high or low evaluations. Appraisers committing central tendency errors are seeking to avoid controversy, criticism, or lengthy discussions.

Halo and Horns Effects

A halo effect refers to the tendency to rate an employee high on all aspects of performance, even though actual performance has not been uniformly high, because the evaluator places an extraordinary importance on one factor on which performance has been high. For example, if an evaluator places great importance on quantity of work produced, the employee who turns out the most items will tend to receive a higher rating on quality of work than is justified by the actual quality level. Likewise, other factors will receive a higher rating than can be factually supported.

The horns effect is the opposite of the halo effect. Poor performance on one highly valued aspect of performance leads to lower than deserved ratings on all other performance factors.

Leniency and Strictness

Leniency, sometimes referred to as *evaluation inflation*, is the giving of undeserved high ratings. Research on performance appraisal suggests that where the evaluators are required to discuss evaluations with employees there is a tendency to overrate actual performance.[23] In many instances, the evaluator simply gives the employee the benefit of the doubt about performance. In one study it was discovered that more than 50 percent of the employees in a particular organization were rated in the most favorable category possible.[24] Leniency obviously eliminates the necessity to discuss any unpleasant aspects of performance with the employee. The problem of overrating is more apt to occur when subjective appraisal factors are used.

Strictness refers to the problem of being unduly critical of an employee's work performance. Unfortunately, supervisors sometimes use performance reviews as an opportunity to enumerate all of an individual's deficiencies, weaknesses, and developmental needs—ostensibly, of course, for the employee's own good. When performance appraisal is used in this manner, the result is likely to be a much lower than warranted evaluation.

Personal Biases

An evaluator's personal feelings about the person being appraised can significantly affect the result of a performance appraisal. Appearance, mode of dress, hairstyles, mannerisms, and a host of other factors may cause an evaluator to like or dislike particular employees and produce negatively or positively skewed appraisals. Individuals of particular religious affiliations, ethnic groups, sex, age, or disability status, although protected by law, do not always receive fair evaluations because of personal biases of the supervisor conducting the appraisal. Personal biases are often subconscious prejudices that are difficult to eliminate or control.

Recent Behavior Bias

This type of bias occurs when the appraiser takes into account only the latest performance of the employee and fails to consider the performance that has occurred over the entire evaluation period. Since the normal appraisal period is one year, it is difficult in the absence of detailed documentation to remember what has happened in the earlier part of the period; thus, the appraiser tends to focus on the most recent and easiest to remember aspects of performance.

Employees also contribute to this problem. Employees are very aware of when they are scheduled for a performance review, and while their actions may not be intentional, their behavior and productivity tend to improve shortly before the scheduled evaluation. Consequently, the appraiser's memory of recent behavior is even more positively reinforced.

Guessing

In the absence of quantitative, objective performance measures, evaluators may resort to guessing about what an employee has or has not done during the appraisal period. Lacking sufficient documentation relative to accomplishments, appraisers may simply make assumptions about an individual's performance. Often these guesses are incorrect.

Use Bias

The way in which performance appraisal is used by an organization may introduce another form of bias into the process. If the primary purpose of the evaluation is for awarding merit pay increases, appraisers may display a tendency to rate poor performers as average so as not to deny them raises. In times of high inflation, supervisors may also tend to overrate performance so that employees receive raises that are more commensurate with inflation rates.[25]

On the other hand, where the emphasis of performance appraisal is on helping the employee to develop and improve job skills, evaluators may tend to be more stringent in their performance assessments because they are concerned with helping employees to develop their talents more fully.

Lack of Appraiser Training

Many organizations offer little or no training in how to evaluate performance and conduct performance appraisal interviews. It often seems that firms believe promotion to a supervisory or management position automatically gives an individual the ability to perform all managerial functions without the benefit of formalized training. Most of the aforementioned performance appraisal problems could be eliminated through proper training, training that begins with promotion to a supervisory position and training that is reinforced through at least annual updating sessions.

Lack of Documentation

A major problem with most appraisal systems is that they do not require continuous documentation of employee performance. When documentation does exist, it is often inadequate to support an accurate assessment of employee accomplishments. Nonexistent or inadequate documentation leads supervisors to commit many of the performance appraisal errors described.

CHARACTERISTICS OF AN EFFECTIVE APPRAISAL SYSTEM

It is highly unlikely that any performance appraisal system will be totally free from criticism or immune to legal challenge. However, systems that possess certain characteristics are more likely to be defensible legally and to produce useful results for an organization, its managers, and its employees. The following are twelve characteristics that an effective performance appraisal system should possess.

Formalized

The first requirement for an effective performance appraisal system is that it be formalized. There should be definite policies, procedures, and instructions for its use. Written guidance should be furnished to all appraisers, either as part of the organization's personnel policy handbook or in a separate document. General information about the system should be given to all employees in an employee handbook or in a separate memorandum if there is no handbook.

Formalizing the system forces an organization to think through all facets of performance appraisal and to clarify what it wants the system to achieve and how it will achieve it. Reducing the system to writing can eliminate many potential problems.

Job Related

All factors used to evaluate performance must stem from the jobs that are being appraised. Only appraisal factors that account for success or lack of success in performing a job should be used. These factors must be susceptible to standardized definition and uniform interpretation.

Developing job-related performance factors may necessitate creating different sets of factors for different groups of jobs. Because jobs are dissimilar in their content and expected results, it is difficult to develop a single set of performance appraisal factors that will adequately cover every job in an organization.

Standards and Measurements

Standards are expectations, norms, desired results, or anticipated levels of job accomplishment that express the organization's concept of acceptable performance. To set standards an organization must carefully examine each of its jobs and determine reasonable expectations that are acceptable to both the institution and the employees performing the jobs. This is not an easy task, but it is one that must be accomplished if performance is to be meaningfully evaluated.

Once standards have been set, some method of measuring actual results must be developed. In many cases, measurements are difficult to establish because the jobs do not lend themselves to easy or meaningful quantification. Yet comparisons with an established standard must be based on measurements. Even an imperfect measurement is better than no measurement at all.

Establishing standards and measurements is difficult and challenging, as suggested in a previous chapter. It is a necessary task, however, if job performance is to be accurately evaluated and merit increases awarded effectively.

Valid

Any test is valid if it measures what it purports to measure. In performance appraisal, the system employed or the method used is valid if it measures what it is designed to measure: actual job performance.

Establishing the validity of performance appraisal actually begins with job analysis, the process wherein job performance factors are clearly identified. These factors may include such items as quantity of work, quality of work, meeting deadlines, and adhering to prescribed procedures. The factors must be quantifiable and specifically defined so as to reflect expected outcomes.

In performance appraisal, there should be a reasonably high relationship between the evaluation an employee receives on a particular performance factor and the actual results the individual achieves measured by that factor. Employees who consistently produce high volumes of output should consistently receive higher ratings on this performance factor than employees whose output is lower.

Reliable

Reliability, statistically speaking, refers to the ability of any test or measure to yield consistent results. A performance appraisal system that does not consistently measure work performance accurately cannot be considered effective. Assume, for example, that an employee's actual work performance on a particular job factor or a whole series of factors is considerably above expectation for three evaluation periods, but that the individual received an average rating on the job factor or factors for the first period, a high rating for the second period, and a below-average rating for the third period. A performance appraisal system producing such results could not be considered a reliable one because there is an absence of consistency. In a reliable performance appraisal system, high performance consistently receives a high rating, and low performance consistently receives a low rating.

If definitive standards and measurements are not used, reliability problems often arise in performance appraisal because supervisors lack objective criteria for evaluating performance. Thus, they may commit performance evaluation errors that produce inconsistent, unreliable results.

Open Communication

All employees have a strong psychological need to know how well they are performing. An effective performance appraisal system ensures that feedback is provided on a continuous basis—not in an annual written evaluation, but in the form of daily, weekly, and monthly comments from a supervisor. The annual evaluation and its accompanying interview or performance discussion must be devoid of surprises. While the interview presents an excellent opportunity for both parties to exchange ideas in depth, it is not a substitute for day-to-day communication about performance.

Trained Appraisers

Essential to the effectiveness of performance appraisal is thorough training—as well as updating and retraining—of all individuals in the organization who conduct evaluations. Classroom training is especially important when a new or revised system is being installed; it is also essential for all new managers and supervisors. An organization must not assume that because performance appraisal information is contained in a supervisory handbook or is included in the company personnel policy manual supervisors will automatically learn how to conduct effective appraisals.

Easy to Use

A performance appraisal system does not have to be complex to be effective. In fact, the simpler and easier a system is, the more readily it can be understood by evaluators, and the more likely it is to be used in the manner intended. If the system is firmly based on standards and measurements, it will not only be easier to use but also more valid and reliable than many other performance appraisal approaches.

Employee Access to Results

Employees should be allowed to examine their job performance records. First, secrecy breeds suspicion about the fairness of both appraisal systems and compensation systems. Perceived equity has been mentioned several times as a consideration in compensation matters. Secrecy in any portion of the compensation plan will only undermine employees' perceptions of equity. Second, concern about the fairness of the system could lead to lawsuits. Third, fairness in dealing with employees suggests that they have an implicit right to certain information that directly affects them on their jobs. Fourth, permitting employees to review their performance records builds a safeguard into the system because employees have the opportunity to detect errors. Finally, since one of the purported goals of performance appraisal is employee development, employees must have access to performance records so they can try to improve their job performance.

Review Mechanism

To eliminate any problems of bias, discrimination, or favoritism, a performance appraisal system should contain a review mechanism. The next higher level of management—usually the evaluator's immediate supervisor—should automatically review each evaluation of an employee. The purpose of this review is not to have the superior perform a second appraisal. Rather, it is to audit the evaluation for fairness, consistency, and accuracy, and to make certain that the evaluator has objectively carried out the appraisal task. While review by the immediate superior increases the time that must be devoted to the performance appraisal process, it protects both the employee and the organization by ensuring fairness and consistency in employee evaluations.

Appeal Procedure

An accepted principle of American jurisprudence is the right of due process. Unfortunately, in a number of organizations there is no procedure whereby an employee can appeal what he or she considers to be an unfair or inaccurate performance appraisal or an inadequate merit increase. The employee is simply stuck with the immediate supervisor's evaluation. In such situations the employee has few options other than living with the unfavorable review and insufficient increase or leaving the organization for employment elsewhere. There have even been instances where employees whose performance was acceptable for years were summarily discharged on the basis of one bad performance appraisal. Now that an employer's right to fire at will is being challenged more and more in the courts—often successfully—the need for a clearly delineated appeal procedure in the performance appraisal system seems clear. (It should be noted that organizations having to deal with unions have long had well-established appeal mechanisms in the form of grievance procedures.)

The number of steps that should be contained in an appeal procedure depends on the size of the organization. At a minimum, there should be two steps: an appeal to the next higher level of management and an appeal to the level above that. In larger organizations the human resource department would be included at some point in the process, possibly the third or fourth step. The procedures by which an employee can appeal an unfavorable review should be clearly spelled out in the formalized policies and procedures of the performance appraisal system and in the employee handbook.

An appeal process serves three purposes: It protects the employee, it protects the organization, and it helps ensure that supervisors do a more conscientious job of evaluation, since they know that their appraisals are subject to scrutiny and interpretation by others in the organization.

THE PERFORMANCE APPRAISAL INTERVIEW

Once the appraisal forms have been completed and the necessary documentation prepared, the evaluator faces what is often the most difficult of all performance appraisal tasks: the appraisal interview.[26] Many evaluators consider the interview or performance discussion an unpleasant task, particularly if the employee has not performed up to standard. Others view the discussion as simply an organizational requirement that should be disposed of as quickly as possible. A more realistic perspective of the interview, however, would suggest that it is an opportunity for both evaluator and evaluatee: an opportunity for the evaluator to coach, counsel, and assist the employee to improve his or her performance; and an opportunity for the evaluatee to recognize his or her areas of strength and potential growth and development possibilities. Conducted properly, the performance appraisal interview can increase organizational effectiveness.

Preparing for the Interview

An effective performance appraisal interview is not something that just happens; it must be carefully planned. To prepare for the interview, the evaluator must clarify in his or her own mind and outline the following:

- The favorable aspects of performance that will be covered in the discussion.
- The areas of performance deficiencies or areas where improvement is needed.
- The anticipated reaction of the employee to both areas of strength and areas of improvement.
- The employee's likely emotional or personal reaction to the performance discussion.
- The specific facts to present during the discussion and the order in which they will be presented.
- The specific suggestions and assistance that will be offered to the employee.

- The amount of merit increase to be awarded and a discussion of how this amount was determined to be appropriate.
- The follow-up action that will be taken to ensure that improvements in performance take place.[27]

Guidelines for Conducting the Interview

Performance appraisal interviews are not easy tasks to accomplish. They have to be well planned and carefully thought out. If handled improperly, they can create poor morale, misunderstanding, or even outright hostility on the part of employees. Some suggestions for conducting an effective performance interview include the following:

- Prepare the employee. Notify the individual far enough in advance that he or she can come to the interview prepared to meaningfully discuss performance.
- Establish the proper climate. Create an atmosphere that suggests the discussion is important.
- Compare actual performance to standards or expectations. Use specific examples. Avoid vague generalities about performance.
- Bite the bullet. If performance has been unsatisfactory, address the subject directly. Don't try to evade the issue by attempting to cover up poor performance with insignificant items of good performance.
- Comment on improvement. Recognize areas where the individual has improved and express appreciation for the improvement.
- Avoid sitting in judgment. The rightful role of the evaluator is coach, counselor, and facilitator, not judge.
- Listen and ask questions. Give the employee ample opportunity to discuss areas that he or she thinks are important.
- Explain the amount of merit increase and the justification for it. Have sufficient documentation to substantiate the reason for the amount of increase.
- Ask what you can do to help the employee improve. Offer whatever assistance you can to facilitate performance and growth.
- Work with the employee to establish new performance goals. Make this a joint effort so the employee becomes more committed to actually achieving the goals.
- Allow sufficient time. Never rush the interview. Make certain the discussion will not be interrupted.[28]

Keeping these points in mind when discussing a performance appraisal will help ensure that the discussion achieves its objectives.

OTHER PERFORMANCE APPRAISAL CONSIDERATIONS

Three final considerations that must be taken into account in designing and operating an effective performance appraisal system are assigning the responsibility for conducting the appraisal, determining the length of time to be covered by the appraisal period, and establishing the point in time at which the appraisal will occur.[29]

Responsibility for Appraisal

Typically, the compensation department or the human resource department designs and administers the performance appraisal program. Responsibility for actually conducting the appraisals, however, is assigned to others within the organization. Several possibilities exist for fulfilling this responsibility.

Immediate Supervisor

The most logical choice for conducting a performance appraisal is the employee's immediate supervisor because this individual is in the best position to know the most about the employee's degree of performance. The immediate supervisor is also the most common choice in organizations. One study disclosed that 96 percent of the firms surveyed assign the responsibility for appraisal to the immediate supervisor.[30] Three reasons favor the supervisor's handling of the appraisal: (1) He or she normally observes the employee's performance on a day-to-day basis, (2) assigning the responsibility to someone else seriously erodes the supervisor's authority as manager of a work unit, and (3) one of the primary functions of any supervisor is training and development of his or her people, a function that is inextricably tied to performance appraisal.

Subordinates

Can a supervisor or manager be effectively evaluated by his or her subordinates? The conclusion reached by a limited number of firms is that they can. Subordinates are in a unique position to view the overall effectiveness of their managers; they can sometimes recognize strengths or weaknesses not seen by others. Managers who advocate this approach suggest that evaluations by subordinates will make supervisors more conscientious in carrying out their responsibilities. On the negative side, ratings by subordinates may cause a supervisor to become excessively concerned with popularity rather than effective performance of the work unit.

Peers

Evaluation by one's peers may be feasible in limited instances. Where employees must work closely together as a team, it is possible that coworkers would know more about an individual's work performance than the unit supervisor. The fact that evaluation is seldom performed by peers would seem to suggest that this approach is not considered a viable alternative by the vast majority of organizations.

Team Appraisal

This form of evaluation occurs when two or more supervisors who are familiar with an employee's performance jointly appraise his or her performance. In many instances an employee actually works for two or more supervisors; in other cases, the employee works for one supervisor but interfaces across organizational lines with several supervisors or managers. Under these conditions a collective appraisal would probably be more accurate and objective than one by a supervisor who has not had sufficient opportunity to observe the employee's work in all areas. Perhaps the biggest disadvantage to this approach is that it undermines supervisory authority and responsibility.

Self-Appraisal

Another appraisal possibility is to have each employee evaluate his or her own performance. If individuals truly understand the objectives they are expected to reach and the standards by which their accomplishments will be measured, they may well be in the best position of all to appraise their performance.[31] Moreover, since all development is essentially self-development, appraisal by employees themselves may lead to greater levels of motivation.

Combinations

Often some combination of these approaches is used. The combination used most frequently is some form of self-appraisal and appraisal by the supervisor. With this approach, the employee is asked to complete an evaluation form and the supervisor does likewise. Then the two parties meet to discuss their separate appraisals, resolve any discrepancies, and complete a mutually agreed-upon evaluation. This approach works well because it involves the employee in the process and reemphasizes the joint responsibility for effective performance.

The Appraisal Period

Annual is usually a word that is attached to formalized performance appraisal and is probably a fairly good indicator of how often appraisals are conducted. But is an annual appraisal enough? There are two schools of thought on this matter. One maintains that performance feedback should be given on a more frequent basis, especially if the primary purpose of the appraisal is employee development. The other school of thought maintains that if the system is operating effectively, feedback will be provided on a daily, weekly, and monthly basis and that there is no need for a formal appraisal more than once a year.

In the case of new employees, exceptions should be made to the annual review. Good management practice suggests that a new employee should be given a formal evaluation at the end of his or her probationary period, the juncture at which the organization makes the decision as to whether the individual will be retained. A review at this point can also relieve anxiety on the part of employees who pass the probationary period because they know that they are performing at an acceptable level.

When to Appraise

Assuming that formal evaluations will occur annually, there is still the question of precisely when the evaluations will take place. There are two approaches to solving this problem: evaluate all employees on a fixed date or evaluate each employee on the anniversary date of his or her employment. The latter approach appears to be the most feasible. Conducting a performance appraisal properly and discussing it thoroughly with the employee is time consuming. For a supervisor to have to evaluate all employees on a fixed date leads to rushing through the process and not accomplishing it effectively. Consequently, the recommended approach is the employment anniversary date method, since the supervisor will have fewer evaluations to conduct at any specific time and can give each one the thorough attention it deserves.

NOTES

1. Donald L. Caruth, *Compensation Management for Banks* (Boston: Bankers Publishing, 1986), 206.

2. Donald L. Caruth, Bill Middlebrook, and Frank Rachel, "Performance Appraisals: Much More Than a Once a Year Task," *Supervisory Management*, September 1982, 28–36.

3. Caruth, *Compensation Management*, 208.

4. Ibid., 212.

5. Ibid.

6. Ibid.

7. Ibid., 216.

8. Ibid.

9. Ibid., 214.

10. Ibid., 215.

11. Stephen J. Carroll and Craig E. Schneier, *Performance Appraisal and Review Systems: The Identification, Measurement, and Development of Performance in Organizations* (Glenview, Ill.: Scott, Foresman, 1982), 117.

12. Caruth, *Compensation Management*, 216, 218.

13. Ibid., 215.

14. Donald L. Caruth, *Work Measurement in Banking,* 2d ed. (Boston: Bankers Publishing, 1984), 206.

15. Ibid., 28.

16. Ibid., 76.

17. R. Wayne Mondy and Robert M. Noe III, *Personnel: The Management of Human Resources*, 6th ed. (Upper Saddle River, N.J.: Prentice Hall, 1996), 336.

18. Caruth, *Compensation Management*, 218.

19. Ibid., 218–219.

20. Ibid., 219.

21. Ibid., 220.

22. Susan E. Jackson and Randall S. Schuker, *Managing Human Resources*, 7th ed. (Cincinnati, Ohio: South-Western College Publishing, 2000), 466.

23. Hubert S. Field and William H. Holley, "Subordinates' Characteristics, Supervisors' Ratings, and Decisions to Discuss Appraisal Results," *Academy of Management Journal* (1977): 315–321.

24. William H. Holley, Hubert S. Field, and Nona J. Barnett, "Analyzing Performance Appraisal Systems: An Empirical Study," *Personnel Journal* (1976): 458.

25. Caruth, *Compensation Management*, 211.

26. Caruth, Middlebrook, and Rachel, "Performance Appraisals," 32.

27. Donald L. Caruth and Gail D. Handlogten, *Management 2000* (Rockwall, Tex.: Spinnaker, 1996), 7.

28. Ibid., 78–79.

29. Ibid.

30. Margaret A. Bogerty, "How to Prepare Your Performance Reviews," *S.A.M. Journal* (1982): 12.

31. Caruth, *Compensation Management*, 235.

12

COMPENSATION OF
SPECIAL GROUPS

This book has described compensation systems as if they were identical for all jobs in every organization. In reality compensation systems are similar for most but not all jobs in an organization. There are special groups in every organization whose compensation may not be determined in the same manner as the majority of an organization's jobs.[1] Typically, these groups have particular compensation needs over and above those of employees in general. This chapter examines three of these special groups: sales personnel, executives, and international employees.

EXECUTIVE COMPENSATION

No area in compensation has received as much attention in the last few years as executive compensation. Much of this attention has focused on the size of monetary rewards earned by top executives (chief executive officers) of American corporations. In 1996 the average salary of CEOs was $2.3 million per year. When incentives, stock options, and other benefits are added to base pay, the average total compensation package rises to $5.8 million.[2] A 1998 survey reported that total compensation for CEOs of multibillion-dollar U.S. industrial and service companies had reached a record high of $7.6 million per year.[3]

The sheer numbers involved in executive compensation tend to assure that it is a subject that will be discussed and written about. Adding additional fuel to the compensation discussion fire is the fact that in 1999 the average CEO was paid some 467 times the pay received by the average factory worker.[4]

The question often asked is, "Are CEOs worth what they are being paid?" Evidence tends to suggest that they are.[5] Executive pay is subject to the same forces that drive compensation for other organizational employees: the labor market, job responsibilities, required skills, and so forth. In addition, there are other driving forces: the spread between CEO pay and that of the next lower management level, the personal influence a CEO can exert on his or her own level of compensation, organizational performance attributable to actions of the CEO, and the attitude of the organization's board of directors. In short, an executive's compensation is subject to market forces on the one hand and may be the result of political or manipulative factors on the other hand.

Components of Executive Compensation

Executive compensation plans generally consist of five basic elements: (1) base salary, (2) short-term incentives, (3) long-term incentives, (4) indirect monetary compensation (benefits), and (5) perquisites.[6] Over time the emphasis placed on each of these components has fluctuated, largely because of tax considerations. Currently, base salary plays a smaller role in executive compensation than short- and long-term incentives.

Base Salary

According to one survey, only 27 percent of a CEO's total compensation package consists of base salary.[7] While salary has been decreasing as a percentage of the total package, it is still an important consideration. Executives' salaries are typically determined by the board of directors of an organization or by a special compensation committee created for that purpose. Where a committee is used, it is normally a subcommittee created by and composed of members of the board of directors. Methods used to set executive compensation levels vary greatly from organization to organization. Some committees examine compensation data from competing organizations to set executive pay rates. Others may use a form of benchmarking to arrive at an equitable pay level. The actual salary level established usually depends upon the following factors: organization size, company stage of development (e.g., start-up versus mature), industry type (e.g., high tech, retail, manufacturing, etc.), financial resources available, and the organization's pay philosophy.[8]

Short-Term Incentives

A second component of executive compensation is an annual bonus awarded for achieving certain short-term goals related to sales, profits, or other similar factors.[9] The criteria for these bonuses and the amount of payment are normally decided by the executive compensation committee or the board of directors. Evidence suggests that use of short-term bonuses is fairly widespread among American corporations.

Long-Term Incentives

Concerns with short-run decisions and results that may not be in the best interest of organizations have led many organizations to turn to long-term incentives. Long-term incentives have five purposes: (1) to tie executive interests to shareholder interests; (2) to encourage executives to engage in long-term planning for organizations; (3) to assist the organization in attracting, holding, and motivating capable high-level executives; (4) to reward executives for long-term financial success of the organization; and (5) to take advantage of tax considerations benefiting both the executive and the organization.[10]

The six most commonly used long-term incentives are stock options, nonqualified stock options, phantom stock plans, stock appreciation rights, restricted stock plans, and performance-based stock plans.[11]

A stock option gives an executive the right to purchase stock at a stipulated price over a fixed period of time in accordance with Internal Revenue Service regulations. Nonqualified stock options do not conform to IRS requirements and do not receive favorable tax treatment. Phantom stock plans are rights given to an executive, but no stock is actually held and no voting rights attach to the shares. Once employment terms or conditions are met, the executive receives cash, shares of stock, or some combination of cash and shares. Stock appreciation rights are linked to increases in the price per share of a company's stock. After meeting the appreciation goals, the executive may receive stock or cash. Restricted stock plans provide an outright grant of stock to an executive at a reduced price. The shares, however, do not transfer to the executive or cannot be sold before a specified date. Performance-based plans provide an executive with a predetermined number of shares when predetermined performance goals are achieved within a stipulated timeframe.

Indirect Monetary Compensation

Executives typically receive a higher level of benefits than other organizational employees because many benefits—life insurance, disability coverage, and so on—are directly linked to compensation levels. But executives may also receive benefits over and above those directly linked to pay. There are, however, certain ERISA and tax-code regulations that limit what organizations may do for executives.

One particular benefit that large organizations often provide high-level executives is a *golden parachute*. A golden parachute is a financial settlement with a key executive whose employment is terminated because of merger, acquisition, or liquidation of the firm.[12] It typically includes severance pay, stock options, and bonuses. The purpose is to allow an executive to maintain an appropriate lifestyle until he or she can find other employment.

Perquisites

Perquisites or *perks*, as they are generally called, are those nice-to-have extras that make life easier for an executive or allow an executive to conduct business more effectively for the organization.[13] Common perks include

- Luxury office
- Club membership
- Physical exam
- Company car
- Chauffeur
- Company plane
- Financial counseling
- First-class air travel
- Spousal travel
- Spousal club membership
- Mobile car phone
- Special parking
- Estate planning
- Income tax preparation
- Bodyguard

Increasingly, perks have come to be viewed as taxable items. Consequently, organizations designing executive compensation plans are well advised to ascertain the taxation status of perks before incorporating them into a compensation package.

SALES PERSONNEL

Payment of an organization's salespeople has long been an issue marked by trial and error.[14] Many companies have struggled for years to discover just the right formula or approach for compensating salespeople, typically using some form of combination of base pay and performance incentive. Theorists are wont to point out that sales compensation is an ideal forum for using incentives because of four factors: (1) Most salespeople are not subject, as are production workers, to close supervision because salespeople may spend most of their time away from the organization; (2) salespeople often see themselves as independent employees who view incentives as recognition for their efforts; (3) commissions are one of the most direct ways of relating performance to reward; and (4) because sales tasks consist of several activities, an organization can choose to reward the behavior it wants to reward.

In reality, there are four basic sales personnel compensation arrangements: (1) straight salary, (2) straight commission, (3) salary plus commission, and (4) salary plus performance bonus.

Straight Salary

A straight salary compensation plan does not involve any form, obviously, of incentive payment. Salespeople are simply paid a flat hourly, weekly, or monthly rate. This approach is often used when salespeople are essentially order takers, sales are the result of a group effort, or customer service is critical.

Advantages

Straight salary offers a number of advantages: (1) Sales personnel have a steady and predetermined income level, (2) sales personnel can be more easily directed to perform nonsales tasks without loss of income, (3) teamwork is more likely to occur among sales personnel, (4) customer service is more likely to be encouraged, and (5) inequities in time required to make a sale are likely to be reduced.

Disadvantages

Several disadvantages are associated with straight salary plans: (1) Sales personnel may exert little or no extra effort in making sales, (2) the proper mix of products may not be marketed because salespeople may focus on types of sales that are easier to make, (3) straight salary may impede an organization's ability to attract top-notch salespeople, and (4) a straight salary plan may negatively affect motivation inasmuch as everyone makes the same relative salary.

Straight Commission

A straight commission compensation plan rewards sales personnel on the basis of how much they sell of an organization's products or services.[15] The commission is usually stipulated as a percentage of the person's total sales for the period specified. Organizations using such compensation arrangements typically allow sales personnel to draw against future sales commissions. The theory behind draws against future commissions is that sales are often seasonal or cyclical and salespeople should not be punished by wide swings in earnings. A draw thus enables a salesperson to smooth out his or her income so that it is more consistent from period to period.

Advantages

Straight commission compensation plans offer some significant advantages: (1) An organization is likely to attract results-oriented sales personnel who value a high earnings potential and the freedom of action that may come with it, (2) an organization is able to share its risks and rewards with its salespeople, (3) straight commission plans tend to quickly eliminate incompetent sales personnel, and (4) commission plans encourage aggressive selling, which may be needed in highly competitive industries.

Disadvantages

The disadvantages of a commission-only approach to sales compensation include the following: (1) A commission-only approach encourages salespeople to think of themselves as free agents rather than company employees, thereby creating a greater than usual sense of disloyalty to the organization; (2) dramatic overpayments or underpayments to sales personnel unless the commission percentage is determined with great accuracy—something that may be difficult to do; (3) salespeople may experience severe fluctuations in earnings from period to period due to variations in sales volumes; (4) salespeople may be tempted to seek out easy sales rather than cultivate more potentially profitable long-run customers; and (5) it may be difficult to open up new territories because of the reluctance of salespeople to perform the necessary missionary sales work.

Salary Plus Commission

A salary plus commission plan provides a salesperson with a guaranteed level of income plus an opportunity to exceed this income level by either selling in excess of a specified sales volume or receiving a commission on all sales.[16] The typical salary plus commission plan allocates 60 to 80 percent of pay to salary.

Advantages

Salary plus commission provides the following advantages as an approach to sale compensation: (1) It assures sales personnel a guaranteed income, (2) an opportunity is offered to make additional compensation, (3) it establishes a relationship between performance and reward, (4) a salesperson's income does not fluctuate as drastically as it does under a straight commission plan, and (5) it allows an organization to attract more salespeople than is usually possible under a straight commission plan.

Disadvantages

Disadvantages of salary plus commission are as follows: (1) Salespeople may not be as aggressive in making sales as they would under a straight commission approach, (2) mediocre salespeople are not as quickly eliminated as they would be under a straight commission plan, (3) it is sometimes difficult to establish the points at which commissions kick in, and (4) determining the salary rate requires a knowledge of what competing labor market organizations are paying similar salespeople.

Salary Plus Performance Bonus

Under this sales compensation arrangement a salesperson receives a specified salary and at the end of the sales period (month, quarter, or year) receives an additional amount for achieving specified goals.[17] These goals can include anything the organization wishes to emphasize: for example, number of sales calls, training of new salespeople, account servicing, or quality of sales made. A performance bonus may either supplement or replace commission. Bonus plans are common in technical sales, where a salesperson may spend a large amount of time on nonselling activities or in situations where a great deal of time and effort is expended in consummating a sale.

Advantages

Among the advantages claimed for this approach are (1) the organization can emphasize what it deems important in the sales area, (2) sales emphases can be changed from year to year, (3) sales personnel are encouraged to pay attention to both selling and nonselling activities, (4) rewards are based on accomplishment of objectives, and (5) greater teamwork is encouraged between sales and service personnel.

Disadvantages

The performance bonus approach has the following disadvantages: (1) Bonus objectives may be expressed in subjective terms, (2) there may be no clear-cut formula for calculating bonus achievement, (3) sales personnel must fully support the established objectives or they may not exert additional effort to accomplish these goals, and (4) when used in combination with salary and commission it may be difficult to integrate all three compensation components effectively.

Factors Affecting Sales Compensation Approach

Selection of a particular methodology for compensating sales personnel is influenced by three major factors: (1) the organization's strategy, (2) compensation practices of competitors, and (3) products or services being sold by the organization.

Organizational Strategy

It is imperative that any sales compensation system adopted directly support the strategic thrusts of the organization. For example, where increasing sales volumes are the organization's goals, some form of sales commission plan should be utilized. On the other hand, where there is an emphasis on customer service, some form of salary payment plan should be used. An organization's strategy indicates the types of behavior the organization is seeking; therefore, its sales compensation scheme must reward these behaviors. Failure to do so will only result in counterproductive behavior by the sales force.

Practices of Competitors

A major factor shaping, or in some cases dictating, the form of sales compensation used is the type of plan used by competing organizations.[18] By the nature of the profession, salespeople frequently cross the paths of each other and are thereby afforded the opportunity to discuss pay plans of their organizations. An organization whose pay system is out of sync with the market may find that turnover of its sales force is unreasonably high. Competing organizations are, consequently, forced to use compensation systems that are similar to their direct competitors.

Products or Services Sold

Some products or services require a great deal of time and effort before a sale can be consummated: for example, large-scale computer systems, commercial aircraft, or commercial real estate. Other products or services—used automobiles, lawn mowers, and nails—require shorter selling periods. In the former case, straight salary or salary plus a small commission are typically required. In the latter case, a small salary plus a larger commission or a straight commission plan may be needed. Where products tend to sell themselves, different compensation approaches are called for than in situations where technical expertise and extensive salesmanship are necessary to sell a product or service.

Other Considerations in Sales Compensation

Compensation experts often recommend consideration of a three-step plan for designing a sales compensation plan. First, the design process should be broadened to focus on all elements of sales compensation: payout mechanics, pay levels, payout frequency, performance measures and weights, pay mix (percent fixed versus variable), and incentive form (commission versus bonus).[19]

Second, organizational strategy, job roles, and competitive pay levels should be used to drive the design process. An organization must consider more than the affordability and business economics of the plan.

Third, sales rewards must be tied to organizational goal setting. Linking rewards to goals communicates how the salespeople will be paid and, more important, what they are expected to achieve.

It is important to bear in mind that sales compensation is only one part of an effective sales management foundation. No matter how good the compensation plan is, it will not make up for organizational deficiencies in definition of the sales role, communication efforts, training and development opportunities, sales staff selection processes, or other areas.

Essentially, compensation should be always a by-product of a company's sales strategy. The specific approach used should be defined by such things as variances in local markets, product strengths or weaknesses, and the competitive posture of the organization's products and services.

There are some definite cautions in designing sales compensation plans. First, compensation plans cannot be expected to take the place of effectively managing a sales team. Commissions can easily be overrated as motivational tools. Moreover, motivation is often overrated in comparison to competence. Good management of the sales representatives should improve both competence and motivation of sales personnel. Good management is often considerably more important than compensation.

No compensation plan can make salespeople more competent, or should be expected to do so. Managers often make the incorrect assumption salespeople know what to do and simply need some type of incentive to do more of it. Motivation without competence is, however, nothing more than good intentions. A manager's job is to work with the sales team. Managers must evaluate and teach. A manager who does not invest a majority of his or her time with the salespeople is not an effective sales manager.

Second, where there is a traditional sales route, sales commission should not be driving force behind the route structure. Frequently managers are interested in being fair with all salespeople and attempt to provide all sales personnel with equal earnings opportunities. Consequently, managers often adjust sales routes for income purposes, failing thereby to consider the impact of this adjustment on the effectiveness of salespeople.

Routes that are designed around compensation or earning potential may overlook such key issues as travel time, overlapping territories, the number of stops, skill fit for the account, and time required to do an effective job. Operational inefficiencies may result from such actions: excessive deliveries one day, too few another day, or overlapping deliveries due to overlapping territories.

Third, compensation and job requirements must not be misaligned; for example, paying commissions on sales when the sales job is basically inventory replenishment or merchandise restocking. The pay system must fit the sales job or the sales team may begin to feel they are being treated unfairly. This may have an adverse impact on motivation and productivity levels.

Fourth, any compensation plan that is implemented should be one that can be managed effectively and as easily as possible. Sales compensation plans require time and precise performance tracking. If internal supporting systems are weak, administration of the plan will take excessive time and effort to manage effectively.

One way of determining if a plan is too complicated is to ask sales personnel to provide feedback concerning the plan. Management should listen carefully to this feedback and make adjustments as required. If sales personnel have difficulty explaining or understanding the plan, it is obvious that adjustments must be made.

Some sales compensation plans place emphasis on payment for goal attainment. These plans can be very effective if they remain simple and are sufficiently explained to those affected. However, such plans can do more harm than good if managers are not skilled in setting goals and measuring results. Poor goal setting can result in goals too high to be attained; if so, demotivation may occur. Goals that are set too low may result in such unfortunate organizational results as higher costs, poor productivity levels, and failure to achieve overall sales objectives.

Fifth, commissions should not be relied upon to drive long-term market-share development. While commissions can be effective, they may also provide little incentive for development of new markets or the introduction of new products. A new product, for example, generally requires a high level of intense up-front sales time. As a result, the new product is often not afforded the requisite sales effort because the sales time required is too excessive for the amount of compensation received. It is easy and convenient for sales personnel to continue spending their time selling established product lines and earning sufficient income levels.

Any sales compensation plan must clearly specify all payment options, such as whether full or partial payment is contingent on the customer's paying in full. Or how will the organization handle future commissions in the event of a termination of the salesperson: Are commissions contingent on continued employment? All payment details must be specified in advance and put in writing to make sure that all possibilities are covered.

Draws against commissions sound simple, but they can be confusing. In most states, unless there is a written agreement stating otherwise, a draw is considered a salary. How draws or advances are to be handled must be clearly specified in the sales compensation plan.

Experienced sales managers know that the highest earning salesperson is not always the best employee. The compensation plan must specify that what a salesperson earns is not necessarily related to overall job performance. Clarifying this issue up front helps to protect an organization. Otherwise it may be difficult to terminate for poor performance, such as inappropriate behavior toward customers or coworkers, a salesperson who is highly paid.

INTERNATIONAL COMPENSATION

Increasingly today, globalization is a reality for organizations of almost any size. Only the smallest companies seem unaffected by the disappearance of global boundaries among organizations, markets, and people. Globalization has increased awareness of and concern for creating internationally equitable compensation systems in many companies. The complex nature of international compensation dictates that it receives special attention from organizations operating in a multinational environment.[20] It is crucial that organizations understand the kind of employees employed by international firms, the elements that comprise an international compensation system, and the special problems associated with returning Americans on overseas assignments to their home corporations.

Categories of International Employees

Organizations operating in an international arena employ three types of employees: expatriates, local-country nationals (LCNs), and third-country nationals (TCNs).[21]

Expatriates

An expatriate, sometimes referred to as an *expat*, is a citizen of the country in which the organization's headquarters is domiciled. For example, an American working for a U.S. subsidiary or branch located in Thailand is an expatriate. An organization may elect to send a domestic employee or manager to an overseas assignment for any number of reasons: to broaden an employee's or manager's perspectives relative to international operations, to start or staff new ventures, to train local employees, to utilize specific expertise possessed by the employee, to protect the organization's interests, to help develop the employee or manager, to assist in the transfer of technology or skills, or to market products. Evidence suggests that American firms use expatriates to a much lesser extent than Japanese firms.

Local-Country Nationals

Local-country nationals are citizens of the country in which the subsidiary or branch of the U.S. company is located. For example, a Mexican working for a U.S. company in its Cabo San Lucas branch is an LCN. There are several advantages to using LCNs: They may cost less than expats, they are fluent in the host country's language, they are familiar with cultural norms, and they may also work better with local customers.

Third-Country Nationals

A third-country national is neither a citizen of the organization's country of origin nor a citizen of the country where the organization's foreign facility is located. For example, a German working for a U.S. company in its Turkish branch is a third-country national. TCNs are often used because they often cost less than expatriates, may be fluent in several languages, and have previous international experience.

Because organizations operating in a global environment use the three classes of employees previously described, international compensation systems are subject to a great deal of complexity. It is beyond the scope of this book to delve into the intricacies of compensating LCNs or TCNs; therefore, only systems for rewarding expatriates will be described.

Components of International Compensation

Compensation for employees of U.S. organizations operating in an international environment consists of four components: base salary, indirect monetary compensation (benefits), equalization benefits, and incentives.[22]

Base Salary

Two alternatives exist for determining base salary for an expatriate: (1) adhering to the established policies and procedures of the parent company's country, including formal job evaluation; or (2) following the policies and practices of the country in which the expatriate works. Since many international assignments are for short durations, usually three to five years, it may be wise to keep base salary aligned with salaries in the home country. Doing so makes the transition back to the United States less complicated, since major salary changes do not have to be made.

Indirect Monetary Compensation (Benefits)

The benefits package for expatriates is generally the same as the one provided in the home country. However, an organization must be aware that specific countries require benefits that may not be offered in the home country. For example, in France employers are required by law to provide every employee with twenty-five days of vacation. Although an American working for an American company in France is not legally entitled to such a vacation, the organization may want to follow this practice to avoid morale problems with expatriates. Other countries have retirement, disability, and termination laws that are different from the United States.

Equalization Benefits

These benefits are intended to keep expatriates in the same financial condition they were in before accepting an overseas assignment and to reduce any negative aspects of living in a foreign country. A limited selection of the benefits available includes the following:

- Housing allowance
- Educational allowance for children
- Foreign service premium
- Assignment completion bonus
- Emergency leave
- Home leave
- Language training
- Domestic staff
- Club membership
- Spousal employment
- Cultural training for family[23]

This list only scratches the surface of the equalization benefits that can be offered in terms of financial allowances, social adjustment assistance, and transitional support for the expatriate's family.

Incentives

Expatriates may receive a variety of incentives ranging from cash bonuses of various kinds to stock options and performance-related payments. The incentives used by organizations are generally similar to those previously discussed in executive compensation.

Crafting an effective international compensation plan requires careful consideration of the various types of compensation, as well as the specifics of the assignment and employee involved.

The Problem of the Repatriate

While some may regard an overseas assignment as glamorous, others may also view it as hindering career progression.[24] Organizations must be sensitive to those employees it is considering sending on overseas assignments. The organization must provide as much information as possible about returning from an international assignment. This repatriation policy must be well thought out and incorporated into a repatriation plan.[25]

In addition, organizations must provide information about career-path opportunities for employees accepting overseas assignments. The organization must do as much as possible to let employees working abroad know that they will not be forgotten and will be reassimilated into the organization upon their return to the home country.[26] Failure to have a sound repatriation policy and plan will make it difficult to get sufficient numbers of employees to accept international assignments.

NOTES

1. George T. Milkovich and Jerry M. Newman, *Compensation*, 6th ed. (Boston: Irwin–McGraw-Hill, 1999), 452.

2. Ibid., 455.

3. "CEO Pay Continues to Rise Due to Stock Options, Strong Market," *ACA News*, April 1999, 11.

4. "Numbers," *Time*, 24 April 2000, 25.

5. Robert L. Mathis and John H. Jackson, *Human Resource Management*, 8th ed. (Minneapolis–St. Paul: West, 1994), 427.

6. Milkovich and Newman, *Compensation*, 458.

7. Ibid., 459.

8. Ibid., 455–462.

9. Ibid., 460.

10. Ibid.

11. Ibid., 461.

12. Donald L. Caruth and Steven Austin Stovall, *Taking Care of Business: The Dictionary of Contemporary Business Terms* (Lincolnwood, Ill.: NTC, 1997), 141.

13. Milkovich and Newman, *Compensation*, 461–462.

14. Ibid., 466–469.

15. Mathis and Jackson, *Human Resource Management*, 414.

16. Ibid.

17. Ibid., 415.

18. Milkovich and Newman, *Compensation*, 468.

19. Ibid., 467.

20. Ibid., 489–492.

21. Wayne F. Cascio, *Managing Human Resources*, 5th ed. (Boston: Irwin–McGraw-Hill, 1998), 644.

22. Milkovich and Newman, *Compensation*, 498–503.

23. Ibid., 516.

24. "Overseas Assignments Can Hinder Career, Expert Says," *Dallas Morning News*, 2 January 2000, 7L.

25. Noel J. Shumsky, "Repatriation: Effectively Bringing Expatriates Home," *ACA News*, September 1999, 39–42.

26. Brian Renwick, "Today's Expatriates—Yesterday's Terms?" *ACA News*, September 1999, 44–47.

13

COMPENSATION ADMINISTRATION

Compensation administration encompasses all of those decisions made and tasks undertaken before, during, and after implementation to assure smooth day-to-day functioning of a compensation system in an organization. Administration begins with the construction of a sound foundation for the compensation program and continues through the resolution of problems that must be addressed on an ongoing basis to keep the program operating effectively.[1]

Key areas and issues where administrative decisions are required have been examined throughout this book. Since these items have been previously explored, many important aspects of program management have already been considered. There are, however, some areas and issues that are worthy of further emphasis and explanation. In addition, there are other items of concern that have yet to be investigated. This chapter will stress some previously introduced points as well as address issues that have not been considered. Specifically, this chapter examines the role of compensation policies and procedures, the importance of communications, functional location and staffing of the program, and other decisions that must be made.

POLICIES AND PROCEDURES

Policies are commonly defined as general guides to action. As such, they provide direction in decision making and express organizational intent. A procedure is a series of steps for achieving a particular objective. Policies and procedures are, obviously, interrelated. Policy establishes the general course of action or direction and procedure specifies the sequential steps necessary for fulfilling policy. Policy is typically concerned with what and why and procedure is concerned with how.

As indicated in earlier chapters, many compensation policies must be formulated before or during the development and implementation of a compensation program. As the administration phase of the program begins, the task at hand is to assure that adequate policies for all aspects of the compensation system have been formulated and reduced to writing.

Policy Areas

An effective compensation program requires policy guidance from management in a great number of areas.[2] At a minimum, each of the following areas must be addressed through organizational policies.

- *General salary policy* expresses the purpose of the compensation program and the competitive stance the organization intends to take relative to the marketplace.
- *Base compensation* addresses salary classes, rate ranges, minimum and maximum starting salaries, salary ceilings, and any exceptions to stipulated rates that will be permitted and the conditions under which exceptions will be allowed.
- *Premium pay* specifies overtime pay, holiday pay, shift differentials, and so forth.
- *Merit increases* describe the type of performance appraisal system in use, specifies how increases in pay will be determined, and indicates the periodicity of increases.
- *Promotions* define what constitutes a promotion, indicates the basis for promotions, and specifies when promotional adjustments in salary are to be made.
- *Transfers* specify whether transfer will affect pay, and if so, to what extent.
- *Job descriptions* identify the format to be used, indicate why job descriptions are necessary, identify the conditions under which job descriptions are to be revised, and so forth.
- *Job evaluation* states the purpose of the system, the method to be used, the composition of the job evaluation committee, and how jobs to be reevaluated are handled.
- *Salary surveys* include the purpose, frequency, composition, and usage of surveys.
- *Incentive compensation* policies set forth management intent relative to incentives, methods of payment, handling of revisions to standards, and so forth.
- *Salary-level adjustment* policies state the conditions for adjustments in the salary structure, the handling of cost-of-living adjustments, and so forth.
- *Benefits* policies explain the full range and scope offered, qualification requirements, employee–employer cost sharing, and all other significant features.

Once formulated, compensation policies should be included in an organization's human resource policy manual. The development of compensation policies will, on occasion, necessitate the reexamination and reformulation of other personnel policies. In any event, the policies of the compensation program should be compared with all other human resource guidelines and practices to assure congruence and mutual support.

Policy Revisions

Policies must always be viewed as working documents that guide decision making, not as commandments cast in concrete or edicts etched in stone. Periodically it is necessary to revise compensation policies because of changes occurring in the general economy, organizational profitability, labor-supply demands, and organizational workforce composition, or because the organization begins to outgrow its original compensation system. A sound practice is to review all compensation policies on an annual basis to determine if revision is in order. An annual review process helps assure that policies remain up to date.

Procedure Areas

Every policy area, with the exception perhaps of the general policy on the purpose of the compensation system, will have its own set of accompanying procedures. These procedures should be well thought out and kept as simple as possible so that they can be easily understood and followed by those who will use them.

Procedure Revisions

Inasmuch as procedures are constantly in use, they will be subject to a greater need for periodic revision than policies. The need for revision is often signaled by complaints from supervisors or employees, excessive time spent in explaining specific steps to take on certain actions, forms or reports that are difficult to complete, or the like. When these kinds of situations arise, procedures must be examined as soon as possible to determine what alterations need to be made. Procedures should also be reviewed on an annual basis to make certain they are current and effective.

Compensation Communication

No area in human resource management is as sensitive in an organization or as important to its employees as compensation. Consequently, the communication of compensation information is an important issue to both the organization and its employees.[3] Employees have an almost insatiable need to know concerning those things that affect them or their job situation directly or indirectly, and compensation is the most obvious and largest element of impact.

This employee need to know includes not only basic information—the specific rate for a job, when paychecks are distributed, how much is withheld for insurance, and so on—but also general information, such as how salaries are set, how jobs are evaluated, why certain benefits are provided and others are not, and so forth. If the organization does not satisfy the needs of its employees for compensation information through formal communication channels, employees will satisfy their information needs through their own informal communication system: the grapevine. The quality of information transmitted through the grapevine varies considerably; sometimes it is very accurate, sometimes it is totally incorrect. To develop trust in its compensation system and to create perceived equity in pay matters, an organization must make a concerted effort to communicate sufficient information to its employees to satisfy their need to know relative to compensation.

Initial Communication

The implementation of an organization's first formalized compensation program will require a great deal of communication. A formalized approach to pay where none has existed before may be greeted by employees with suspicion. The paramount question in the minds of employees is likely to be, "Why?" When most organizations attempt to answer this question, they usually do it from the organization's perspective, emphasizing the benefits that the institution stands to gain. Certainly, it is important to provide this organizational perspective to employees, but communications of this type alone do not go far enough. One of the fundamental principles of psychology is that all behavior is self-centered behavior. What this means in terms of compensation communication is that each employee wants to know, "What's in it for me?" In other words, any explanation of the necessity for a formalized pay system must contain an emphasis on how the system will benefit each individual employee. To the extent that employees perceive advantages accruing to them individually, they will tend to accept and support the system. If so, the organization will gain the benefits it desires too.

The initial communication concerning the implementation of a compensation system is usually best made in the form of a letter to all employees. Ideally, this communiqué is sent out over the chief executive officer's signature. Why the program is being initiated, when implementation will begin, and other key points should be explained. Since all facets of the program cannot be addressed in a single bulletin, a series of subsequent informational updates should be issued periodically to keep employees apprised of the implementation process. An excellent approach for handling areas of employee concern is to include with each update a form on which employees can submit, anonymously, their questions or concerns about the compensation program. These questions can then be answered in later bulletins. By providing a format for addressing employee concerns in an open fashion, management has the opportunity to clear up misunderstandings and allay suspicions relative to the program.

Ongoing Communication

All too often, once a compensation program has been installed, the need for communication is overlooked. It is not unusual to find organizations adjusting their salary levels, revising job evaluation procedures, or altering the performance appraisal system without informing employees. Thorough communication to employees is important not only at the initiation of a program, but also throughout its life. Whenever any changes are made, employees must be informed of those changes and informed as to why those changes are being made. Suppressing compensation information creates dissatisfaction and perceptions of inequity among employees, a point that has been stressed at several points throughout this book. It is imperative that organizations make a conscientious effort to provide more and better information about compensation to their employees. To accomplish this, it is recommended that a series of compensation updates be issued periodically to keep employees informed of changes and to address specific issues, problems, or questions that arise.[4]

The one area in which communication occurs more frequently is benefits. Changes in package components, increasing costs, and legislative requirements are the factors largely responsible for stimulating information flow in this area. But even here, communication may occur spasmodically in many organizations. An excellent communication practice that some organizations use is the issuance of an annual benefits statement. This report informs each employee of the current status of his or her benefits. Each particular benefit for which the employee is eligible is listed on the statement, as is the amount of benefit that accrued during the year and the total amount of benefit currently available. Often the cost to the organization of providing each specific benefit to the employee is also shown. Although somewhat expensive to implement and operate, this approach keeps employees fully informed about the indirect monetary aspects of their compensation. Where an annual benefits statement is not feasible because of the cost involved or the size of the organization, it is recommended that explanations of benefits be included in the series of compensation updates.

Handbooks

Employee handbooks are essential for almost every organization. These publications familiarize an employee with those things that relate to his or her employment relationship with the institution. Topics such as work hours, pay periods, salary increases, promotions, vacation, life insurance, health benefits, profit sharing, retirement, and so on are normally covered. Figure 13.1 shows the table of contents for a typical handbook.

Figure 13.1
Contents of a Typical Employee Handbook

FOREWORD
EMPLOYMENT STATEMENT
SECTION A: EMPLOYMENT

I.	Employee Classification
II.	Employment/Reemployment
III.	References
IV.	Employee Referral Award Program
V.	Inter & Intra Company Transfers
VI.	Job Posting
VII.	Applicant Procedures
VIII.	Temporary Employment
IX.	Nepotism

SECTION B: TERMINATION OF EMPLOYMENT

I.	Voluntary Terminations
II.	Voluntary Termination Final Pay Procedures
III.	Pretermination Counseling
IV.	Involuntary Terminations
V.	Exit Procedures
VI.	Involuntary Termination Final Pay Procedures
VII.	Elimination of Positions
VIII.	Consolidated Omnibus Budget and Reconciliation Act (COBRA)

SECTION C: EMPLOYEE COUNSELING

I.	Grievance Procedures
II.	Corrective Action
III.	Sexual Harassment
IV.	Substance Abuse

SECTION D: ATTENDANCE AND PUNCTUALITY

I.	Tardiness
II.	Attendance
III.	Hours of Work and Recordkeeping
IV.	Time Sheets
V.	Overtime

While handbooks are essential as specific, formalized means of communication, one of the biggest problems associated with their use is the failure of employees to read them carefully. Consequently, even when an organization has a handbook, it is necessary to provide additional compensation communication on a periodic basis.

A recommended companion to the employee manual is the supervisor's handbook. While the contents of this handbook parallel that of the employee manual, the emphasis is usually on procedures, policies, and problems so that supervisors can answer employee questions and deal with particular concerns that may arise on the job. This handbook provides supervisors with sufficient information to answer most compensation system–related questions satisfactorily.

Figure 13.1 (*continued*)

VI.	Sick Leave
VII.	Leave of Absence
VIII.	Personal Leave
IX.	Civic Duty
X.	Occupational Injury
XI.	Vacation
XII.	Holidays

SECTION E: MISCELLANEOUS

I.	Education Financial Assistance
II.	Accidents
III.	Confidentiality
IV.	Conflict of Interest
V.	Hospitalization/Demise
VI.	Telephone Use
VII.	Immigration Reform and Control Act (I-9 Forms)
VIII.	Employee Records
IX.	Solicitation
X.	Personal Grooming and Dress Code
XI.	Press Relations
XII.	Company Property and Personal Property
XIII.	Crises/Workplace Violence
XIV.	Reimbursements
XV.	Smoking Policy
XVI.	Notary Policy

SECTION F: HUMAN RESOURCE FORMS

I.	Absence Report Recruitment & Prescreening Summary
II.	Supervisor's Checklist for Effective Discipline
III.	Employment Termination
IV.	Employee Termination
V.	Request for Personnel (2 pages)
VI.	Application (4 pages)
VII.	Voluntary Applicant Information

FUNCTIONAL LOCATION OF COMPENSATION ADMINISTRATION

Every organization has a compensation function, but not every organization is large enough to designate this function as a distinct, specialized activity.[5] In small companies compensation responsibilities and other human resource management activities are usually assigned, for coordination purposes, to a manager whose primary responsibilities are in other functional areas. Typically, the assignment is made to an administrative manager, such as the chief accountant, because compensation and benefits are seen as accounting activities. If an organization is large enough to have a human resource manager, responsibility for the overall compensation program may be assigned to this functional area, while the payroll function—the actual paying of employees—may be assigned to accounting. Either of these arrangements is logical and acceptable. The important thing is that a particular individual within the company is responsible for overseeing and coordinating the entire compensation function.

Frequently the payroll function of compensation administration is outsourced to a firm that specializes in payroll processing. Many organizations find this to be an arrangement that is cost effective as well as efficient.[6]

When an organization becomes large enough to have a human resource professional, the compensation function and all other human resource management activities then become the responsibility of this person. As a company continues to grow and the human resource function expands and becomes more important, it is likely that the human resource professional will report to a senior executive, preferably the president.

Organization of the compensation function is an evolutionary matter that depends on the number of jobs within an organization and the number of people it employs. The function should always, however, be assigned in accordance with other human resource functions so that coordination between recruiting, selecting, training, compensating, and promoting can be accomplished effectively.

There are no clear-cut guidelines that mark the point in time when an organization needs a full-time person whose only job duties are in compensation. The determination has to be made on an organization-by-organization basis. When an institution has enough work in performing job analyses and job evaluations, conducting salary surveys, and managing the benefits program to justify a person for this responsibility, then, and only then, should it add a compensation specialist to its staff.

SELECTED ISSUES AND PROBLEMS

In managing a compensation program there are many issues and problems to be dealt with. The key to resolving most of the difficulties that may arise is the construction of a sound, logically based system and the development of a series of carefully designed policies to guide management action. Designing a sound system and developing good policies require management to think through problem situations in advance and formulate approaches for resolving problems before they actually occur.[7]

A compensation system is a dynamic thing. As an organization grows and changes, the system must also grow and change. Policies that were once adequate may have to be revised. Unanticipated problems may necessitate the need for system revisions. Action taken to solve one problem may produce another problem at a later date. Close watch over the compensation program is required to keep it running smoothly and producing the desired organizational effect.

There are a few selected issues and problems that may demand consideration at some point during the life of a compensation program. These issues are examined in the following sections.

Pay Secrecy

For a variety of reasons, most organizations tend to keep their pay rates secret. While employees may be informed about the pay range for their particular job, they are not usually provided with information on the pay ranges of other jobs in the organization. If the organization's compensation plan is illogical or inconsistent, pay secrecy may indeed be appropriate, since only a well-designed system can stand careful scrutiny or full disclosure.[8]

Assuming that the compensation system is sound, is pay secrecy advisable? The available research clearly indicates that it is not. Secrecy in pay matters tends to spawn dissatisfaction, distrust, and perceived inequities, and may suggest to employees that there is, in fact, something to hide. Openness in compensation matters tends to suggest just the opposite: The system is fair and well designed.

Just how open should an organization be about pay? A good answer to this question may well be, "Just as open as possible." Thus, it is probably sound practice for an organization to publish a schedule of salary grades and ranges for each grade. This information can be included readily in the employee handbook. With these kinds of data available, an employee will know how far he or she can progress salarywise in his or her current job. Moreover, employees will understand in terms of dollars and cents the potential that exists in other jobs to which they may be promoted.

While the number of salary classes and their ranges should be made known to all employees, specific salaries of specific individuals should never be revealed. In other words, the pay system itself should be a matter of public knowledge within the company, but the exact salaries of individuals should not. The salaries of individual employees are sometimes influenced by factors or conditions about which other employees have no knowledge. For example, to secure a highly qualified systems analyst or information technology specialist, an organization may have to pay more than the normal starting salary, especially in a tight labor market. Revealing the specific starting salary of the employee in this case would certainly tend to create dissatisfaction among other employees in the same job class who are making less money. These employees may not be aware of labor supply and demand factors that necessitate the higher salary of the individual in question.

Many companies still have policies that prohibit employees from discussing their salaries with other employees. Because such policies are no longer legally enforceable there is really no justification for having them. According to the courts, policies forbidding employee discussions about pay are an infringement of the constitutionally guaranteed right to free speech. Any employee discharged for violating such a policy is entitled to legal recourse against the organization.

Pay Compression

Pay compression occurs when pay differentials between unequal jobs become small or nonexistent or when individuals of differing job tenure are compensated at about the same rate of pay.[9] Pay compression is created by (1) adjusting pay rates in lower job classes without adjusting rates in higher job classes, (2) raising job-class pay rates or granting pay increases on a flat dollar rather than a percentage basis, or (3) hiring new employees at rates comparable to those of employees who have been in a particular job for several years.

Pay compression can be a very serious problem that affects employee morale and work behavior. Organizations should be aware of the causes of pay compression and take appropriate action to preclude this problem from occurring or correcting it if it has already occurred.

By necessity, most organizations are familiar with labor market rates for entry-level jobs. When entry-level rates begin to lag market rates, a company may be tempted to raise starting salaries for these jobs in order to attract sufficient personnel. But, if rates for entry-level jobs are raised without elevating the rates of all other job classes, pay compression will occur, especially between the entry-level class and the next higher one. This is an extremely common problem where there is no formal compensation program in an organization; however, it can also be found in institutions that have formal programs. Raising rates for beginning jobs is simple; adjusting rates for all job classes requires more analysis and effort. To prevent pay compression that arises from this cause, an organization should not increase rates for entry-level classes without carefully studying the entire rate structure. Piecemeal adjustments, although expedient, can have serious long-run ramifications.

The second cause of pay compression is handling adjustments to classes or pay increases on a dollar basis rather than a percentage basis. When a pay structure is created, the differences in rates between job classes are based on the establishment of relative differences between classes. Subsequent adjustments to pay rates based on percentages maintain the original relationship between classes. Adjustments made on a dollar basis—without consideration of the percentage adjustment to each class—will cause erosion of the original relationships between classes and produce pay compression. Likewise, merit increases predicted on a dollar-increase amount will tend, over time, to have the same effect. For example, an average increase of $100 per month in job class 1 and job class 2 will eventually erase the difference between the two classes. Adjustments in pay, either to the structure or to individual salaries, should always be based on percentages in order to eliminate pay compression between classes or individual jobs.

A final cause of pay compression is elevating hiring rates without adjusting the salary rates of job incumbents. Shortages of personnel with certain skills—systems analysts, information technology specialists, and electronic engineers are common contemporary examples—compel institutions to adjust their starting salaries if they expect to be able to hire the numbers of qualified people they need. In many cases it is not unusual to find a new hire making more than an employee who has been in the job for some time. Often, merit increases fail to match increases in starting salaries for new hires, so eventually the employee with several years service in a job is making little, if any, more than the person just placed on the payroll. Such a situation can be devastating as far as employee morale is concerned. Pay compression of this sort deserves serious consideration by management. When starting salaries are elevated it may be necessary to adjust rates of current employees in order to maintain an equitable relationship between new hires and experienced employees.

The Internally Equitable, Externally Inequitable Job

Job evaluation establishes a relationship of internal equity between the jobs in an organization. A problem may arise when a job that has internal equity, as established through job evaluation, is actually compensated in the marketplace at a much higher rate than the one set for the class in which the job falls internally. This particular problem normally occurs because of labor supply and demand factors operative in the marketplace.[10]

The first step in correcting this problem is to verify that the job evaluation is accurate. Reevaluation may reveal that certain job factors were not correctly assessed originally. A second look at the job may increase the evaluation points and elevate the job to a class where internal equity is congruent with external equity.

If reevaluation does not correct the situation, two other courses of action are open: (1) remove the job from the salary structure and compensate it on the basis of market rates as an exception to the system, or (2) leave the job within the evaluation system and compensate it on a red circle basis congruent with market rates. Either of these two approaches has a risk attached to it; namely, distortion of the established system of internal equity. If only one or two jobs are involved, however, the risk is probably not great enough to create any real problems; but when the number of exceptions to the system increases to three, four, or more, a different solution is required to protect the integrity of the overall salary structure. This different solution may well be the creation of a separate evaluation system and salary structure for the jobs involved.

The problem of internal versus external equity is usually associated with professional jobs. When a company is small, an evaluation system and salary structure can be constructed to cover all jobs without too much difficulty.

Growth brings changes in the nature of certain jobs and thus necessitates the creation of separate salary structures for different types of jobs.

Cost-of-Living Adjustments

While cost-of-living adjustments are normally addressed in the development of compensation policies, their actual application sometimes raises problems.[11] There are several key questions that have to be dealt with in the application of cost-of-living adjustments: Should adjustments be made automatically on an annual basis? Should adjustments be one to one for increases in living costs or should they be based on some percentage of living cost increases? Should only increases above a certain level be considered or should all cost-of-living increases be considered? To what extent do such adjustments increase employee expectations of receiving a certain percentage of salary increase whether it is warranted or not?

Much of the difficulty in handling cost-of-living adjustments can be eliminated by carefully developing a policy that addresses this issue. A policy that states that the need for adjustments will be evaluated annually and that any such adjustments to salaries will be made when deemed necessary would appear to be operationally sound. Such a policy gives management some flexibility in dealing with the problem; it commits management to an annual examination of need, but does not obligate management to make adjustments every year. Automatic cost-of-living adjustments tend to create entitlement in the minds of employees, the expectation that increases will be forthcoming each year even when circumstances do not warrant increases. A general policy gives management latitude to decide if an adjustment is necessary and, if so, the amount of adjustment that should be made.

When adjustments are needed most organizations do not normally give them on a one-to-one basis; that is, a 10-percent increase in cost of living does not result in a 10-percent across-the-board salary increase. An accepted approach seems to be to adjust salaries by a given percentage of the increase in living costs. In practice, these percentages vary considerably, but something between 60 to 80 percent of the cost-of-living increase would appear to be a reasonable adjustment.

The use of a threshold or floor simplifies the matter of determining the need for making any adjustment at all. For example, management policy might state that cost-of-living increases below 6 percent will not result in any adjustments to the salary structure; increases above 6 percent may result in adjustment. Again, management creates some flexibility for handling the situation by creating a general policy rather than a specific one.

In making adjustments to salaries based on cost of living, it is important that these adjustments be clearly identified so they won't be confused with merit increases. Merit increases should be based solely on merit; cost-of-living increases should be based solely on external economic factors.

Job Posting and Bidding

Job posting allows employees to be informed of and apply for other positions in the organization. Announcements of job openings are placed on bulletin boards in conspicuous places such as the employee cafeteria, posted on company e-mail sites, or listed on telephone hotlines. Employees who consider themselves qualified may place a bid for a particular opening, whether it is a promotional opportunity or simply a transfer.[12]

Job posting and bidding works hand in hand with a formal compensation program because it encourages promotion from within. Posting and bidding emphasizes upward mobility and serves as a motivational stimulus. It suggests that the organization is interested in its employees and wants them to have the first chance at any openings that may advance their careers.

In the absence of a posting and bidding system, employees, even in very small organizations, often do not know of upcoming job vacancies until someone is hired from outside to fill the vacancy. Morale and motivation typically suffer when this occurs. Although filling openings from inside creates additional openings to be filled, the motivational advantages of internal promotions usually far out weigh any training problems that may be created. It is suggested that this system be implemented whenever a formal compensation plan is developed.

Comparable Worth

The basic premise of comparable worth issue is that jobs traditionally held by males are compensated at a higher rate than those traditionally held by women, even though both sets of jobs make an equal contribution to organizational results. Comparable worth would suggest that dissimilar jobs such as secretary and sanitation worker be compared under some form of job evaluation plan and pay rates for both jobs be determined on their worth to the organization.[13]

Proponents of comparable worth point to statistics indicating that, as a whole, women earn 75 cents for every dollar a man earns as proof of the need to address male–female pay differentials in terms of organizational contributions.[14] Opponents of comparable worth point to the Equal Pay Act of 1963, which proscribes pay differentials where jobs require equal skill, effort, responsibility, and are performed under similar working conditions. They also contend that gender differences in compensation are explained by factors such as education, job experience, career interruption, career aspiration, and occupational attainment.

What does the issue of comparable worth mean to organizations? First, organizations must assure that whatever means of job evaluation is used is applied fairly and without discrimination. Second, organizations must commit to vigorous enforcement of equal employment opportunity laws. Third, organizations should encourage women to train for and enter nontraditional jobs. And finally, organizations should focus on creating family-friendly environments that encourage women to work for these organizations.

As this book has shown, compensation management is neither an arcane science nor an overly complex undertaking.[15] Implementing a sound pay system is largely a matter of logical thinking and hard work. Managers who understand what is involved in installing and maintaining equitable compensation systems will find themselves better prepared to deal with compensation specialists. At the same time, managers who are knowledgeable in compensation will find themselves better prepared to deal with employees' compensation questions and problems. The goal of this book is to create managers who understand compensation systems and therefore can ask the right questions of compensation professionals. Hopefully, this goal has been achieved.

NOTES

1. Donald L. Caruth, *Compensation Management for Banks* (Boston: Bankers Publishing, 1986), 238.

2. Ibid., 239–241.

3. Ibid., 241–244.

4. Ibid., 242.

5. Ibid., 245–246.

6. George T. Milkovich and Jerry M. Newman, *Compensation*, 6th ed. (Boston: Irwin–McGraw-Hill, 1999), 575.

7. Caruth, *Compensation Management*, 246–247.

8. Wayne F. Cascio, *Managing Human Resources*, 5th ed. (Boston: Irwin–McGraw-Hill, 1998), 403.

9. Ibid., 404–405; Caruth, *Compensation Management*, 247–248.

10. Caruth, *Compensation Management*, 248–249.

11. Ibid., 249–250.

12. Donald L. Caruth and Gail D. Handlogten, *Staffing the Contemporary Organization*, 2d ed. (Westport, Conn.: Quorum Books, 1997), 272; Caruth, *Compensation Management*, 250–251.

13. Milkovich and Newman, *Compensation*, 556–557.

14. R. Wayne Mondy and Robert M. Noe, *Human Resource Management*, 6th ed. (Upper Saddle River, N.J.: Prentice Hall, 1996), 386

15. Caruth, *Compensation Management*, 251.

APPENDIX:
COMPENSATION WEB SITES

Thanks to the Internet, a great deal of information on compensation, benefits, and related matters is now readily available and accessible. There are, in fact, so many compensation-related Web sites that it would be impossible to even attempt to list them all. The following is a selected sample of forty-one Web sites that the reader may find helpful. These sites will, as happens in all Internet research, lead the reader to yet other Web sites of interest.

Site	Address	What the Site Provides
A Predictable, Secure Pension for Life	www.pbgc.com	Information on defined benefit pensions
AARP Webplace "Explore Health"	www.aarp.org	The latest information from AARP on Medicare, managed care, health insurance options, health legislation, and more
Administration on Aging	www.aoa.dhha.gov/aoa	Information on aging and employment
American Association for Retired Persons	www.aarp.org	Information on aging
American Compensation Association	www.acaonline.org	Association information and member services

Site	Address	What the Site Provides
American Society on Aging	www.asaging.org	Information on aging
Arthur Anderson Human Capital Services	www.arthuranderson.com/hcs	Human capital challenges
Axiom Partners Payroll Network, Inc. "Time & Attendance Software"	www.axiomoanners.com	Software and online information
Benefits Link.com	www.benefitslink.com/index.shtml	Benefits information and services
BenefitsReview.com	www.benefitsreview.com	An online benefits communication tool designed to allow access to health and welfare information
Committee for Economic Development	www.ced.org	Information on aging and employment
Compensation Link.com	www.compensationlink.com	Compensation information and services
Deloitte & Touche LLP	www.us.deloitte.com	A tax, audit, and investment consulting firm
Department of Labor, Bureau of Labor Statistics	www.stats.bls.gov/ecthome.htm	Compensation information and employment and related activity
Economic Research Institute's Platform Library	www.erieri.com	Software and online information
Employee Benefits Research Institute	www.ebri.org	Information on aging and employment
Employment Cost Index	www.bls.gov; www.stats.bls.gov/ecthome.htm	Information from the U.S. Department of Labor's Bureau of Labor Statistics on ECI measures and changes in compensation costs
Employment of Older Workers	www.ezsis.org/portal/Oworkers.htm	Information on aging
Entero Market Support Solution	www.dmwworldwide.com	Software and online information
Fifty And Overboard	www.50andoverboard.com	Information on aging
Government Institutes Online Store	www.govinst.com	Software and online information
Greenthumb	www.greenthumb.org	Information on aging
Hewitt Associates LLC	www.hewitt.com	A benefits consulting firm
HR Answers, Inc.	www.salarysource.com	Software and online information
HR Library.com	www.HRLIBRARY.com	A central location for all human resource information and resources

Site	Address	What the Site Provides
Institute for Human Development, Life Course on Aging	www.library.utorono.ca/ agining/deptubs.html	Information on aging and employment
Kaiser Family Foundation	www.kff.org	Information about Medicare program
MaturityWorks!	www.maturityworks.org	Information on aging
Michele Brown, McGladre & Pullen LLP	www.mcgladrey.com	Accounting and consulting services
Office of Compensation Levels and Trends	www.ocltinfor@bls.gov	Information about compensation, surveys, and employment cost index
Older Women's League	www.aoa.dhls.org	Information on aging
PaineWebber	www.painewebber.com	Corporate stock benefit services
SalariesReview	www.salariesreview.com	An online salary communication tool designed to allow access to salary information
SHRM Diversity	www.shrm.org/diversity	Information on aging and diversity
Society for Human Resource Management	www.shrm.org	Resources and human resource information
The Hay Group	www.haygroup.com	A compensation and benefits consulting firm
The Medicare Web Site	www.medicare.gov	General information about Medicare as well as up-to-date information about private health plans
The National Insurance for Quality Assurance (NCQA)	www.ncqua.org/Pages/ Main/consumers.htm	Information on accredited HMOs
U. S. Census Bureau	www.census.gov	Information on aging and employment
Watson Wyatt Worldwide	www.watsonwyatt.com	Compensation information and company services
William M. Mercer, Inc.	www.mercer.com	Compensation information and company services

SELECTED BIBLIOGRAPHY

The following bibliography has been compiled for readers who desire to pursue a study of compensation management further. The references cited will help the reader acquire more detailed and technical information, as well as gain a better understanding of compensation problems and their solutions. Included are classic reference works in the field and contemporary texts. The bibliography is representative rather than exhaustive. Journal articles have been omitted in order to reduce the length of the reference list and make it more manageable for the working manager.

Belcher, David W., and Thomas J. Atchison. *Compensation Administration*. 4th ed. Homewood, Ill.: Richard D. Irwin, 1987.

Bemis, Stephen E., Ann Holt Belenky, and Dee Ann Soder. *Job Analysis: An Effective Management Tool*. Washington, D.C.: Bureau of National Affairs, 1983.

Bennett-Alexander, Dawn D., and Laura B. Pincus. *Employment Law for Business*. 2d ed. Boston: Irwin–McGraw-Hill, 1998.

Bereman, Nancy A., and Mark L. Lengnick-Hall. *Compensation Decision Making: A Computer-Based Approach*. Fort Worth: Dryden Press, 1994.

Burgess, Leonard R. *Compensation Administration*. 2d ed. Columbus, Ohio: Merrill, 1984.

Carroll, Stephen J., and Craig E. Schneier. *Performance Appraisal and Review Systems: The Identification, Measurement, and Development of Performance in Organizations*. Glenview, Ill.: Scott, Foresman, 1982.

Caruth, Donald L. *Compensation Management for Banks*. Boston: Bankers Publishing, 1986.

Caruth, Donald L., and Gail D. Handlogten. *Staffing the Contemporary Organization*. 2d ed. Westport, Conn.: Quorum Books, 1997.

Caruth, Donald L., and Steven Austin Stovall. *Taking Care of Business: The Dictionary of Contemporary Business Terms*. Lincolnwood, Ill.: NTC, 1997.

Cascio, Wayne. *Costing Human Resources: The Financial Impact of Behavior in Organizations*. 3d ed. Boston: PWS–Kent, 1991.

Cihon, Patrick J., and James Ottavio Castagnera. *Employment and Labor Law*. 2d ed. Cincinnati: West Educational Publishing, 1999.

Colt, Stockton B., Jr. (ed.). *The Sales Compensation Handbook*. 2d ed. New York: AMACOM, 1998.

Dunn, J. D., and Frank M. Rachel. *Wage and Salary Administration: Total Compensation Systems*. New York: McGraw-Hill, 1971.

Evans, James. *Law on the Net*. 2d ed. Berkeley, Calif.: Nolo Press, 1997.

Gael, Sidney. *Job Analysis: A Guide to Assessing Work Activities*. San Francisco: Jossey-Bass, 1983.

Gross, Steven E. *Compensation for Teams*. New York: AMACOM, 1995.

Henderson, Richard. *Compensation Management: Rewarding Performance*. 5th ed. Englewood Cliffs, N.J.: Prentice Hall, 1989.

Hills, Frederick S., Thomas J. Bergmann, and Vida G. Scarpello. *Compensation Decision Making*. 2d ed. Fort Worth: Dryden Press, 1994.

Latham, Gary P., and Kenneth N. Wexley. *Increasing Productivity Through Performance Appraisal*. 2d ed. Reading, Mass.: Addison-Wesley, 1994.

Lenesis, Peter M. *Workers' Compensation*. Westport, Conn.: Quorum Books, 1998.

Lepsinger, Richard, and Anntoine D. Lucia. *The Art and Science of 360° Feedback*. San Francisco: Jossey-Bass, 1999.

Marosy, John Paul. *A Manager's Guide to Elder Care and Work*. Westport, Conn.: Quorum Books, 1998.

Maslow, Abraham H. *Maslow on Management*. New York: John Wiley & Sons, 1998.

McKenzie, Richard B., and Dwight R. Lee. *Managing Through Incentives*. New York: Oxford University Press, 1998.

Milkovich, George T., and Jerry M. Newman. *Compensation*. 6th ed. Burr Ridge, Ill.: Irwin–McGraw-Hill, 1999.

Nelson, Bob. *1001 Ways to Reward Employees*. New York: Workman, 1994.

Sibson, Robert E. *Compensation*. 5th ed. New York: AMACOM, 1990.

Twomey, David P. *Equal Employment Opportunity Law*. 2d ed. Cincinnati: South-Western Publishing, 1990.

Twomey, David P. *Labor and Employment Law*. 10th ed. Cincinnati: West Educational Publishing, 1998.

Steingold, Fred S. *The Employer's Legal Handbook*. Berkeley, Calif.: Nolo Press, 1994.

U.S. Department of Labor, Manpower Administration. *Handbook for Analyzing Jobs*. Washington, D.C.: U.S. Government Printing Office, 1972.

Wallace, Marc J., Jr., and Charles H. Fay. *Compensation Theory and Practice*. Boston: Kent, 1983.

INDEX

Compensation administration: communications, 247-251; definition, 245; departmental location 251-252; employee handbooks, 249-251; issues and problems in, 252-258; ongoing process, 19; policy areas, 246-246; policy revisions, 247; procedures areas, 247; procedure revisions, 247; program development, 19; role in recruitment, 4

Compensation programs: benefits, 3-8; purpose, 1-2; role of indirect monetary compensation, 16-17

Compensation surveys: analyzing nonsalary data, 117-118; analyzing salary data, 114-117; confidentiality, 112-113; cover letters, 113; definition, 101; key jobs, 109-110; methods, 110-111; National Compensation Survey (NCS), 118; number of organizations to include, 106-107; Occupation Employment Statistics Survey (OES), 118; possible labor markets, 104-105; proprietary surveys; 120-121; purpose, 14-15, 102-103; relevant labor market, 104; response rates, 112-113; requested information, 108-109; summary of results, 112; survey design, 105-106; types of jobs to include, 109; types of organizations to include, 108-108

Competency-based pay. *See* Job pricing

Consolidated Omnibus Budget Reconciliation Act (COBRA) of 1985, 29, 160

Consumer Price Index, 157

Coors Brewing Company, 169

Copeland Act of 1934, 22

Cost control, 5

Cost of living, 9, 256

Cost savings plans. *See* Incentive compensation

Davis–Bacon Act of 1931, 21-22

Department of Labor Job Analysis Schedule. *See* Job analysis

Dictionary of Occupational Titles, 54, 63

Differential piecework plan. *See* Incentive compensation

Direct market pricing. *See* Job pricing

Disabilities, 26-27, 28-30

Disability insurance, 3, 162

Distributive justice, 43

Electronic Data Systems Company, 169

El Paso, Texas, 9

Employee handbooks. *See* Compensation communications

Employee Retirement Income Security Act (ERISA) of 1974, 27-28, 32, 161, 163-164, 186, 233

Equal benefit principle, 30-31

Equal Employment Act of 1972, 24

Equal Employment Opportunity Commission (EEOC), 25, 56

Equal Pay Act of 1963, 5, 12, 23-24

ERISA. *See* Employee Retirement Income Security Act (ERISA) of 1974

Essential job function. *See* Job analysis

Expectancy Theory. *See* Motivation

Executive compensation: average compensation package, 231; base salary, 232; components of, 232-234; golden parachute, 233-234; indirect monetary compensation, 233-234; long-term incentives, 233; nonqualified stock options, 233; performance-based stock plans, 233; perquisites, 234; phantom stock plans, 233; restricted stock plans, 233; short-term incentives, 232-233; stock appreciation rights, 233; stock options, 233

Exempt employees, 23

Expatriates. *See* International compensation

External equity, 6

Evaluation inflation, 218

Fair Labor Standards Act (FLSA) of 1938, as Amended, 11-12, 23, 27, 32, 178

Family and Medical Leave Act of 1993, 32, 159-160, 167

Family-friendly organization, 51

Minimum wage: federal, 21; original wage, 23; Tucson, Arizona, 21

Morale: definition, 7; effect of job posting and bidding, 257; role of compensation in improving, 7

Motivation: defintion, 35-36; esteem needs, 35-36; expectancy, 41; expectancy theory, 41-43; hierarchy of needs theory, 37, 200; money and, 45-48; motivating work environment, 48-50; motivation-hygiene theory, 38-41, 200; physiological needs, 37; role of compensation in, 4-5; safety needs, 37; self-actualization needs, 38; social needs, 37; theories of, 36-43; valence, 41-42

Motivation-Hygiene Theory. See Motivation)

Multiple pay structures, 148

National Compensation Survey. See Compensation surveys

National Labor Relations Act of 1935, 22-23, 155

National Labor Relations Board, 23

New York City, 9

Nonexempt employees, 23

Nonqualified stock options. See Executive compensation

Occupation Employment Statistics Survey (OES). See Compensation surveys

OFCCP. See Office of Federal Contract Compliance Programs

Office of Federal Contract Compliance Programs (OFCCP), 27

Older Workers Benefit Protection Act of 1990, 30-31, 167

Organizational culture, 50

Overtime pay, 23

PAQ. See Job analysis, Position Analysis Questionnaire

PAS. See Job analysis, Position Analysis Schedule

Pay compression, 254-255

Pay discrimination, 23-24

Pay secrecy, 253-254

Pension plans. See Retirement plans

Perceived equity, 6, 43

Performance appraisal: appraisal period, 227-228; behaviorally anchored rating scales, 211-213; characteristics of effective system 220-224; checklist method, 208-211; definition, 18, 203-204; essay method, 213-214; interviews, 224-225; management by objectives method, 214-215; methods of, 205-216; problems in, 217-220; ranking method, 206, 207; rating scales, 205-206, 207; responsibility for, 206-227; 360° method, 216; uses, 204-205' when to appraise, 228; work standard method, 213;

Performance-based stock plans. See Executive compensation

Perquisites. See Executive compensation

Phantom stock plans. See Executive compensation

Point of service plans, 166, 169

Policies, 245

POS. See Point of service plans

Position. See Job analysis

Position Analysis Schedule. See Job analysis, Position Analysis Schedule

PPO. See Preferred provider organization

Preferred Provider Organization, 166, 169

Pregnancy Discrimination Act of 1978, 28-29

Procedures, 245-246

Productivity, 9-10, 174

Profit sharing retirement plan, 185

Psychological compensation, 3, 48

Puerto Rico, 119

Purdue University, 69

Red circle rate. See Job pricing

Rehabilitation Act of 1973, 26-27, 31

Reliability. See Tests

Restricted stock plan. See Executive compensation

Retirement plans: ADEA regulation of, 26; defined benefit plans, 28; defined contribution plans, 28; responsibilities of fiduciaries, 28

ABOUT THE AUTHORS

Donald L. Caruth holds a doctorate degree in management and has consulted on human resource matters, particularly pay and other forms of compensation, for more than 30 years. He is also a professor of management at Amber University, author of numerous books and articles, and co-author of *Staffing the Contemporary Organization* (Quorum, 1997).

Gail D. Handlogten is a human resource management consultant. With an advanced degree in human resources and training, she is a certified mediator and arbitrator and author or coauthor of more than 30 articles and books, including *Staffing the Contemporary Organization* (Quorum, 1997).